# Sexual Inequalities
# and Social Justice

# Sexual Inequalities and Social Justice

Edited by
Niels Teunis and
Gilbert Herdt

*With a foreword by Richard Parker*

UNIVERSITY OF CALIFORNIA PRESS

*Berkeley / Los Angeles / London*

University of California Press, one of the most distinguished university presses in the United States, enriches lives around the world by advancing scholarship in the humanities, social sciences, and natural sciences. Its activities are supported by the UC Press Foundation and by philanthropic contributions from individuals and institutions. For more information, visit www.ucpress.edu.

University of California Press
Berkeley and Los Angeles, California

University of California Press, Ltd.
London, England

Library of Congress Cataloging-in-Publication Data

Sexual inequalities and social justice / edited by Niels Teunis and Gilbert Herdt, with a foreword by Richard Parker.
    p.     cm.
    Includes bibliographical references and index.
    ISBN-13: 978-0-520-24614-0 (cloth : alk. paper)
    ISBN-10: 0-520-24614-4 (cloth : alk. paper)
    ISBN-13: 978-0-520-24615-7 (pbk. : alk. paper)
    ISBN-10: 0-520-24615-2 (pbk. : alk. paper)
    1. Sex.   2. Equality.   3. Social justice.   4. Social action.
    5. Gender.   6. Ethnicity.   I. Teunis, Niels.   II. Herdt, Gilbert, 1949–
HQ1075.S495   2007
306.7086'94—dc22                        2006011270

Manufactured in the United States of America

15  14  13  12  11  10  09  08  07
10  9  8  7  6  5  4  3  2  1

This book is printed on New Leaf EcoBook 50, a 100% recycled fiber of which 50% is de-inked postconsumer waste, processed chlorine free. EcoBook 50 is acid free and meets the minimum requirements of ANSI/ASTM D5634–01 (*Permanence of Paper*).

*In remembrance of*
*Robert Tsosie*
*June 1963–December 2002*

# Contents

Foreword                                                               ix

Acknowledgments                                                        xv

Introduction: The Analysis of Sexual Inequality                         1
*Niels Teunis and Gilbert Herdt*

PART ONE: SEXUAL COERCION AND SEXUAL STIGMA                             31

1. Childhood Sexual Abuse and HIV among Latino Gay Men:
   The Price of Sexual Silence during the AIDS Epidemic                35
   *Sonya Grant Arreola*

2. In Our Own Backyard: HIV/AIDS Stigmatization
   in the Latino Gay Community                                         50
   *Rafael M. Díaz*

3. Knowing Girls: Gender and Learning in School-Based
   Sexuality Education                                                 66
   *Jessica Fields*

4. Sexual Enslavement and Reproductive Health: Narratives
   of *Han* among Korean Comfort Women Survivors                      86
   *Chunghee Sarah Soh*

PART TWO: SEEKING SEXUAL PLEASURE                                105

 5. Where Does Oppression End and Pleasure Begin?
    Confronting Sexual and Gender Inequality in HIV
    Prevention Work                                              109
    *Héctor Carrillo*

 6. Circuit Culture: Ethnographic Reflections on Inequality,
    Sexuality, and Life on the Gay Party Circuit                123
    *Christopher Carrington*

 7. *Confesiones de Mujer:* The Catholic Church and Sacred
    Morality in the Sex Lives of Mexican Immigrant Women        148
    *Gloria González-López*

 8. Disability and Sexuality: Toward a Constructionist Focus
    on Access and the Inclusion of Disabled People in the
    Sexual Rights Movement                                      174
    *Russell P. Shuttleworth*


PART THREE: SEXUAL INEQUALITY AND SOCIALITY                     209

 9. The Family-Friends of Older Gay Men and Lesbians            213
    *Brian de Vries and Patrick Hoctel*

10. Sexual Inequality, Youth Empowerment, and the GSA:
    A Community Study in California                              233
    *Gilbert Herdt, Stephen T. Russell, Jeffrey Sweat,
    and Michelle Marzullo*


    Contributors                                                253

    Index                                                       257

# Foreword

In recent years, the intersection between sexuality and social inequality has increasingly become a major focus of concern, both on the part of researchers seeking to understand intellectually the ways in which forms of inequality affect the constitution of diverse expressions of sexuality, and, perhaps even more powerfully, on the part of academics who hope to use their work in order to influence positive forms of social change.

This focus on the intersection of sexuality, social inequality, and the struggle for social change is still, of course, a very new phenomenon—and flies in the face of much of what has constituted the field of sexuality studies over the course of the past century. Indeed, it might easily be dismissed as little more than a slightly rebellious undercurrent in a much longer process of seeking professional respectability. After all, over the course of the twentieth century, perhaps the greatest challenge that was perceived in the study of sexuality was the need to achieve mainstream credibility and legitimacy—to transform the study of sex from a marginalized, eccentric, and vaguely suspect undertaking to a legitimate form of academic inquiry. Throughout this period, the most important way of achieving such legitimacy was in general to seek to emphasize the scientific credibility of sexuality research. The goal was what Paul Robinson aptly described as "the modernization of sex"—the progressive application of scientific methodological tools in order to wrest sexual behavior and experience from the realm of religion, superstition, or folklore, and to reconstitute it as part of the scientific record in relation to human life (see Robinson 1976).

In its first instance, then, the emphasis on the scientific study of human sexuality—whether in Havelock Ellis, Kinsey, Masters and Johnson, or others who followed in their footsteps—seemed to place primary emphasis less on social issues of such as inequality or social change than on the objective study of sexual behaviors, and psychology rather than sociology or anthropology tended to lead the way in defining the acceptable role of research practice. Yet over the course of the closing decades of the twentieth century, while many behavioral researchers continued to search for scientific legitimacy, much was in fact changing in society itself. The progressive emergence of multiple, yet often intersecting, movements for social change increasingly restructured the terrain on which studies of sexuality might be carried out. First in the overwhelming impact of feminism, and then successively in the emergence of gay and lesbian movements, in the response to HIV and AIDS, and in the broadening of some ethnic and anti- or postcolonial movements in countries and cultures around the world, the perceived certainties of the modern era began to give way—as much in relation to sexuality as in any other domain of human experience. As these changes took place—as everything solid seemed to melt into air—new concern with the social, cultural, and historical dimensions of sexuality increasingly came to the fore, and new approaches to the study (and practice) of sexuality/sexualities began to take shape.

Central to this changing field, as the chapters of this volume make clear, has been a fundamental concern with the mechanisms and processes of social inequality as they play across the construction of sexual life—and even the role of sexuality itself, at times, in the production and reproduction of inequality and difference. Attention has increasingly focused on what has been described as diverse forms of "structural violence" that shape and structure the possibilities of sexual expression: class, poverty, and economic exclusion, gender oppression, racism and ethnic discrimination, and, as illustrated in a number of the texts in this volume, even diverse forms of bodily exclusion have become key elements in our understanding of the working of sexual stigma, discrimination and oppression. Indeed, issues related to stigma and discrimination, once examined largely in relation to concerns such as racial or ethnic discrimination, have increasingly come to be a major focus of research attention in the study of sexuality and social inequality, and Erving Goffman's original notion of stigma as undesirable difference has helped to articulate new attention to the social processes through which stigma and discrimination are produced and reproduced—the socially constituted relations of devaluation in which sexual difference is transformed into social inequality (Goffman 1963).

At least since the publication of Kenneth Plummer's groundbreaking study *Sexual Stigma* (Plummer 1975), a focus on stigma and an understanding of the ways in which stigma is relational, historically constituted, and strategically deployed in the production and reproduction of social inequality have been central to this line of work. Increasingly, such understandings have been linked to a concern with power, and with conceptual tools such as Pierre Bourdieu's notion of "symbolic violence" or the Gramscian notion of "hegemony," in seeking to understand more fully the ways in which stigmatization functions in relation to what might be described as the axes of social inequality—class, gender, age, race or ethnicity, sexuality or sexual orientation. We have come to focus on the ways stigma is deployed by concrete social actors seeking to legitimize their own dominant status within existing structures of social inequality, and the ways in which social inequality is exercised in order to produce and reproduce forms of sexual legitimation and exclusion.

The various chapters in this volume offer multiple examples of such processes. In chapters such as Raphael M. Díaz's "In Our Own Backyard: HIV/AIDS Stigmatization in the Latino Gay Community," or Sonia Grant Arreola's "Childhood Sexual Abuse and HIV among Latino Gay Men: The Price of Sexual Silence during the AIDS Epidemic," for example, there is a focus on intersecting issues of poverty, racism, and homophobia (internal as well as external) as they play through the HIV and AIDS epidemic in the contemporary United States. In Gloria González-López's "*Confesiones de Mujer:* The Catholic Church and Sacred Morality in the Sex Lives of Mexican Immigrant Women," Chunghee Sarah Soh's "Sexual Enslavement and Reproductive Health: Narratives of *Han* among Korean Comfort Women Survivors," or Jessica Fields's "Knowing Girls: Gender and Learning in School-Based Sexuality Education," the focus turns to gender power as it affects heterosexual women and girls—and to the interactions between and both ethnic discrimination and social and economic exclusion. And in Brian de Vries and Patrick Hoctel's "The Family-Friends of Older Gay Men and Lesbians," and Russell P. Shuttleworth's "Disability and Sexuality: Toward a Constructionist Focus on Access and the Inclusion of Disabled People in the Sexual Rights Movement," to offer just two further examples, this focus shifts again to offer key insights into forms of age-based, physical, and bodily exclusion as they operate in the modern world. Throughout the volume as a whole, in these as well as in the other texts that the editors, Niels Teunis and Gilbert Herdt, have brought together, the multiple, intersecting axes of inequality become central not only to the social construction of sexuality, but also to the sexual construction of social life (Connell and Dowsett 1992).

Yet just as we recognize that this is the case, we must also confront what is at once a long-standing dilemma as well as a new challenge for a new form of engaged sexuality research: what is to be done? How can we transform theory into practice, and research into meaningful contributions to struggles for social change? The answers to such questions are by no means simple, nor can they be resolved in any single volume, no matter how exhaustive or complex. They clearly pass, among other things, through a fuller understanding of social movements—and, in particular, of the relationship between sexuality and social movements, and the transformation of identity and subjectivity that social movement organizing makes possible in the lives of those who are moved by them. And they no less clearly push us in the direction of a range of choices that we would not otherwise make if our concerns were not fundamentally with the struggles against inequality and in favor of greater social justice. They push us in the direction of new attention to the need for rights-based approaches aimed at increasing sexual citizenship, and at structural interventions aimed at transforming the conditions in which social and sexual actors might make choices aimed at reducing risk and vulnerability in their lives. They push us in the direction of what might be described as the enabling strategies that will be needed in order to confront the all too often disabling assumptions that structure and reproduce social and sexual inequalities in the contemporary world.

Perhaps more than anything else, the various studies that make up this volume focus new attention on the question of agency—on the role of sexual subjects as they seek to transform the conditions of their sexual worlds. Examples of this concern run through the essays, whether in the resistance of the Circuit party boys described in Christopher Carrington's "Circuit Culture: Ethnographic Reflections on Inequality, Sexuality, and Life on the Gay Party Circuit," in the struggles of lesbian, gay, bisexual, and transgender (LGBT) youth and the gay-straight alliances (GSAs) described by Gilbert Herdt and his colleagues in "Sexual Inequality, Youth Empowerment, and the GSA: A Community Study in California," or in the desiring bodies and the erotic sensibilities of the women and gay men in Mexico described in Héctor Carrillo's "Where Does Oppression End and Pleasure Begin? Confronting Sexual and Gender Inequality in HIV Prevention Work." It is the question of agency, of the possibilities not only of resistance but of constructing positive projects for social and sexual change (see Castells 1997) that lies at the heart of these studies—and, perhaps, at the heart of the greatest challenges faced by these authors themselves.

The authors whose work is represented in this volume clearly have a number of different responses to the complex question of how to transform research into meaningful social action rather than a single, unified perspective. Yet they all realize that making a commitment toward this goal—carrying out research that matters, that truly contributes to struggles for social justice—involves more than simply declaring one's own progressive ideology or stating that by virtue of being a progressive researcher one's research necessarily contributes to progressive goals. On the contrary, real engagement—and the role of research in contributing to progressive social change (especially in the anything but progressive political environment of the early twenty-first century)—involves far more complicated approximations and commitments, far less simple resolutions of the inherent contradictions that play across this field.

While the various texts collected in this volume do not resolve all of the complex questions that are involved in seeking to develop a truly engaged research practice capable of contributing to real, positive social change, they do nonetheless take a number of important steps down this road. Indeed, in nearly every chapter, the authors make an important advance by positioning their research (and their research fields) in a way that is far broader and more complex than the traditional anthropological and sociological dichotomy between "insider" and "outsider" perspectives. The "native's point of view" in these essays is simultaneously problematized and fundamental to the very possibility of an interpretive stance on the part of investigators whose own engagement in their fields of study is in many ways a condition of their research practice. These texts both recognize and theorize the existence of multiple, often intersecting—but also at times contradicting—identities. But they also recognize that researchers too must negotiate these same, multiple identities—identities that may coexist with greater or lesser ease depending on a range of extenuating circumstances. The voices that speak as authors within such texts speak not only as researchers and scholars, but also simultaneously as advocates and activists engaged in movements for social change and social justice—and this in turn has implications for their methodological choices and options, even though the methodological approaches represented here are themselves multiple and diverse.

Ultimately, just as sexual agency is perhaps the key question that drives the majority of these studies, it is also the central notion that seems to unite the work of these researchers. It lies at the heart of their various projects, suggesting agendas for social and sexual change, approaches to social and sexual justice, in the face of diverse and varied forms of structural violence and oppression. It offers hope that out of a greater understanding of the lived experience of both ourselves and others, we might be able not only to resist the forms of oppression that we confront, but to build meaningful lives—and loves—based on fundamental respect for difference and celebration of diversity.

Richard Parker

## References

Castells, M. 1997. *The power of identity.* Oxford: Blackwell.

Connell, R. W., and G. W. Dowsett. 1992. "The unclean motion of the generative parts": Frameworks in western thought on sexuality. In *Rethinking sex: Social theory and sexuality research,* ed. R. W. Connell and G. W. Dowsett. Philadelphia: Temple University Press.

Goffman, E. 1963. *Stigma: Notes on the management of a spoiled identity.* New York: Simon and Schuster.

Plummer, K. 1975. *Sexual stigma: An interactionist approach.* London: Routledge and Kegan Paul.

Robinson, P. 1976. *The modernization of sex.* New York: Harper and Row.

# Acknowledgments

The excitement from this book is the result of a collegial collaboration between all the contributors, who came together at various occasions. We all know one another and have shared over the years our interests, findings, ideas and theories, and in particular our commitment to investigate sexuality in the context of social inequalities. All the authors hope and try not only to add to their knowledge of the effects of social inequalities on people's sexual lives but also to help solve the question of how their work can promote social justice. Accurate knowledge of the mechanisms of social inequality is certainly a need and we pursue our work vigorously. In addition, we locate ourselves close to the different groups with whom we conduct our work, and it is this closeness that we highlight in our search for a meaningful involvement in social justice from our work.

Nine of the authors came together in a very successful panel at the American Anthropological Association meeting of 2001, titled "Sexuality and Social Inequality: New Approaches to Participatory Research and Ethnography," which was organized by Gilbert Herdt. The success of that panel and the distinct recognition of the participants that we shared a common question, pursued in various contexts, and also a common commitment to be part of the social movements that inform our questions encouraged us to bring together the presentations into one volume. We also decided to invite several new contributors. In April 2002, we conducted a one-day research seminar at which all of us presented our work. The common ground that binds our work together had previously been implicit, recognized at the AAA panel; at this meeting, we delighted in the explicit ways in which we shared our information and furthered one another's questions and pursuits. It was my distinct honor to bring together the various chapters in this volume.

The Ford Foundation has been an invaluable partner in the process of assembling this book. The foundation funds much of the research presented in this volume. Moreover, it has shown itself to be a supporter of sexuality research and outreach throughout the country and at San Francisco State University. As a result of the foundation's efforts, a critical mass of dedicated scholars is beginning to bring sexuality studies to the center of academic, social, and political interest, and this book proudly takes its place in that field.

The support staff at the National Sexuality Resource Center and of the César E. Chávez Institute (previously the Center for Community Research) helped with many of the practical details of the seminar and the book.

In the course of my research, I met Robert Tsosie, a Native American Two Spirit individual. Tsosie and I saw each other on several occasions, and I made a small contribution to a Harvest Feast that Tsosie organized for his community. As a result of Tsosie's activism, three organizations marched together in the San Francisco Gay Pride Day Parade: the Native American AIDS Project, the Gay American Indians, and the Bay Area American Indian Two Spirits. He built bridges because of his good heart, tremendous dignity, humor, and generosity. He passed away suddenly in an accident in December 2002.

I met Robert Tsosie on a few separate occasions, but he moved me personally very deeply as a committed, open-hearted individual, whose purpose was to create alliances, promote health for his community, and involve everybody in his activities. He was calm, loving, forthright, and enthusiastic, and had a unique capability to make you part of his world. I think of him every day. In a very short time, he had become as dear to me as a good friend. I remember the qualities he brought to his activism and draw inspiration from him, because I saw how effective he was in bringing people together, realizing that no one can stand alone in the struggle for social justice and happiness. Ultimately, he showed by his life not only that we have a common purpose but also that we genuinely stand together as we fight for our purpose. I think he would like this book and understand its value. I dedicate it to Robert Tsosie.

Niels Teunis

# Introduction

## The Analysis of Sexual Inequality

NIELS TEUNIS AND GILBERT HERDT

Sexual inequalities—the forms of indignity, social disadvantage, stigma, discrimination, and violence perpetuated by or based on sexual conduct, sexual identity, or perceived sexual orientation or membership in a sexual category or sexual culture—remain common in the United States. Social and legal protections against sexual injustice are minimal, and not surprisingly, knowledge of sexual health and sexual rights needed to advance social justice and sexual health policy are rather poorly developed in the United States. Study of these issues has been difficult—in some cases impossible— because of the historical barriers confronting sexuality research in the academy and the absence of community-based studies. Moreover, the role of the social scientist, including her sexual subjectivity and positionality, while critical to the methodological issues raised in this book and of growing concern to lesbian, gay, bisexual, and transgender (LGBT) studies, has largely been ignored in mainstream study. These social facts are constitutive of the reproduction of structural violence in its sexual forms in the United States and globally, and productive of a new approach to participatory research now emerging to help advance social justice.

The emergence of a new paradigm of social analysis that looks deeply at social oppression based on sexuality as the precursor or result of inequality is critical to social research in the twenty-first century. Some scholars see the sources of this transformation in the formative writings of Paulo Freire's (1970) seminal *Pedagogy of the Oppressed,* but it is noteworthy that Freire never discusses sexuality in his work. Sexual inequality has historically been sidelined in discussions of social oppression, with the exception of discussions of HIV/AIDS. Agency, power, subjectivity, social rights, and the social ethics of sexuality as conveyed via the positionality of the researcher in his or her community are part and parcel of a paradigm shift in epistemology and methodology. This change goes beyond the identity-based social movements and their insights that were so terribly disconnected from the academy in years past (Parker and Aggleton 2000). Thus the contributors to this book employ qualitative case studies and the ethnographic approach to reflect on the cultural logic and cultural emotions created through sexual inequality.

Although originally trained in the very different disciplines of anthropology, sociology, public health, and psychology, the contributors to this book are nevertheless committed to an analysis of "social inequality" as a lens for understanding the reproduction of sexual inequality, poor sexual health, and the lack of rights of women and of sexual minorities in civil society. All too often research has emphasized sexuality as an individual trait or state rather than as a social phenomenon; hence the epistemology of this work has favored individual, not social, difference theory (Herdt 1997a). The authors in this book emphasize instead the cultural meaning systems and social practices of actors in sexual cultures and social formations; in particular, we focus on the real-world processes of inequality, such as racism and homophobia, that disrupt civic participation, thwart the full achievement of social and sexual citizenship (Weeks and Holland 1996), and result in negative outcomes, especially in gender, sexual rights, and health—the most significant area of innovation and research of late (Krieger 2003; Parker, Barbosa, and Aggleton 2000). Thus this work is a contribution to the paradigm change now taking place—to intensive, multimethod, and contextual examination of how basic processes of social inequality constrict sexuality and rights in vulnerable communities. The focus on sociohistorical processes that create and reproduce inequality also reveal insights, arising from research on inequality, sociality, sexuality, and health, into the cultural production of knowledge in its conventional rhetoric as well as in its contradictions, as we shall show.

For those of us who live in Euro North American societies, it is dreadful but not surprising to observe that many people in the United States continue to face social oppression springing from multiple forms of structural violence: racism, heterosexism and homophobia, ageism, social class bias directed toward the poor and the homeless, xenophobia directed toward immigrants, and prejudice against disabled people. There are many instances in the media of dramatic oppression—the brutal murder of Matthew Shepard is one of them. But many others perpetrated against women and men and children go unnoticed or remain hidden. Inequality not only hurts; increasingly health and human rights studies reveal that discrimination harms health, as Krieger (1999: 295), Petchesky (2002), and Malluwa, Aggleton, and Parker (2002) have written. And such forms of structural violence persist not only in the United States but also are actively promoted globally in certain areas as an extension of U.S. policy (Farmer 1999; Girard 2004; Petchesky 2003; Setel 1999).

To analyze sexual inequality in myriad contexts requires an understanding of its relationship to other forms of structural violence. Paul Farmer (2003: 8) has defined structural poverty, racism, and inadequate health care as among the "host of offenses against human dignity." We would also include sexism, heterosexism and homophobia, social class bias, ableism, and xenophobia. In this book, however, we wish to emphasize the role of sexual inequality because we believe that its analysis has lagged behind the exposure of other forms of structural violence, especially in the United States.

Psychologists increasingly think of sexual inequality in the context of what Herek (2004) calls "sexual prejudice," negative attitudes based on sexual orientation criteria, typically directed toward those who engage in homosexual conduct and refer to themselves as gay, lesbian, bisexual, or transgender. Herek suggests that, like other forms of prejudice, sexuality creates attitudes or judgments that reductively target other social groups and their members. Generally, these are negative, involving hostility or even hatred (Herman 1997). Although too limiting for the range of sexual inequalities considered in this book, Herek's approach has the merit of focusing on attitudes and policies as these target and objectify sexual oppression, and of opening up both the historical (Van der Meer 2004) and psychosocial bases of sexual discrimination (Cohler and Galatzer-Levy 2000).

Sexual inequality is a form of structural violence rooted in sexual objectification by the oppressor and the concomitant sexual subjectivity of the dominated. These dual behavioral/subjective forms require an analysis of the changing contexts and impact of structural violence, such as how poverty may result in sexual injustice in particular communities and sexual cultures—both in the United States and internationally. For example, "survival sex" can only be understood in the South as a function of extreme poverty, lack of sexual rights among women and sexual minorities, and their vulnerability to men who carry the HIV virus (Preston-Whyte et al. 2000). As the essays in this book reveal, those who are victims of sexual coercion and sexual stigma are the most vulnerable to poor reproductive health (chapter 4), childhood sexual abuse (chapter 1), and shame, silence, and familial exclusion because of sexual orientation (chapter 2).

It was not academics but rather activists and advocates working outside the university who first challenged sexual inequality. We might trace their efforts back, for example, to the groundbreaking campaigns of Mary Calderone, the founder of SIECUS (Sex Information and Education Council of the United States), who in 1964 set about to "change the sexual culture" (Irvine 2002: 22). What distinguished her advocacy from the earlier work of Alfred Kinsey and his colleagues (Kinsey, Pomeroy, and Martin 1948) was the explicit aim of using science in the social marketplace to change attitudes and policies. Indeed Calderone's belief that speaking the truth about science "would set you free" (Irvine 2002: 29) is not unlike the strategy of second-wave feminists and gay and lesbian activists, especially those more inclined to academic study, who drew on science and research to support challenges to sexism and homophobia (Rubin 1997; Tolman 2002). By contrast, academics have been slow to follow (Gagnon and Parker 1995). The emergence of sexual rights out of a longer history of reproductive rights and claims provides further evidence of a tension, a divergence not only of rational goals or pedagogy and human rights advocacy (Miller 2000), but perhaps even more the "irreconcilable subjectivities" (Patton 1997: xvii) that have separated scholars from activists. Likewise, advocacy for sexual rights, academic feminism, and gay and lesbian studies was in many regards disconnected from sexual health and policy (Rubin 2002) until late.

In fact, science in general and social science (anthropology, sociology, and psychology) in particular have been silent or reluctant to address this gap (Herdt 2004) or to respond to the challenges of explicit or implicit government-sponsored sexual inequality, at least until the World Conference on Human Rights in Vienna in 1993 (Petchesky 2003). Note, for example, the very slow response of academics to the AIDS crisis in the United States, with psychology responding earlier than anthropology, after much death and suffering from the epidemic (reviewed in Herdt and Lindenbaum 1990; Brown 1997; and Parker, Khan, and Aggleton 1998).

The Vienna conference marked a turning point, as many commentators have noted: a new concern with sexuality as a human right surfaced in global and national discussions of sexual policy. The Vienna conference not only accomplished the recognition of "sexual violence" as a violation of human rights, but it also secured for the first time insertion of the term *sexuality* into the language of human rights (Petchesky 2003: 83). Major international conferences in Cairo (1994) and Beijing (1995) went much further, as we shall see. But again, there has been much greater attention to these sex and human rights politics in Western Europe and the Third World (the South) than in the United States. Indeed, the linkage between gender and sexuality and resistance and emancipation in the aftermath of the International Conference on Population and Development in Cairo in 1994 has resulted in some substantial international progress on sexual rights (Gruskin 2000; Parker, Barbosa, and Aggleton 2000). Much more discussion has been directed toward the South in this current of change, and only recently has American policy been studied as a global force (Girard 2004).

In the United States, the Surgeon General's Call to Action to Promote Sexual Health and Responsible Sexual Behavior (2001) may be seen as a watershed of change—an issue to which we shall return. It must be remembered, however, that the surgeon general's report was necessary because of the U.S. government's official policy on "abstinence-only" education, a policy largely bereft of scientific credibility (Kirby 2001). Moreover, the U.S. government opposed publication of the report and it was bitterly contested by right-wing anti–sex education organizations (Irvine 2002).

While a growing body of research has addressed disembodiment and social suffering in epidemiological study more broadly, much less attention has been directed toward sexual inequalities, particularly in qualitative research, and the mechanisms, either social or subjective, through which inequality is created and maintained. The subjectivities of sexual inequality have been especially ignored and are a focus of this book. The authors probe the concomitant effects of structural sexual inequality: how to understand the creation of barriers to agency and becoming empowered in response to struggles for sexual inequality and the effort to promote social justice and social change in the members of oppressed communities and sexual minorities.

Sexual inequality as a form of structural violence has thus had quite markedly worse effects in the United States than in other major industrialized countries. A comparison of Western European and U.S. epidemiological data on major areas of sexual health reveals the extent of this disconnect between research and policy in the greatly higher rates of unwanted pregnancy, higher rates of HIV infection, higher rates of complications from abortion, and much higher rates of sexual violence in the United States compared to Holland, France, and Germany. Americans remain largely undisturbed by the lack of equity in sexual rights and social justice. Indeed, we seem generally unmoved by the criminalization of sexual behavior, the brutal treatment of transgender people, the continued threat to lesbian rights in partner and maternal custody cases, the double stigma of being a person of color who is gay, and the humiliation and violence experienced by LGBTQ youths in high schools today (chapter 10). Until the 2003 Supreme Court case *Lawrence v. Texas*, sodomy laws criminalized same-sex relationships in many states.[1] As noted in the essays in this volume, each of these cultural forms of sexual inequality continues to disqualify and discredit the full personhood of individuals; that is, Americans and immigrants to America who fail to conform to the heteronormal standards of their communities experience compromised citizenship by virtue of their sexual inequality. Gloria González-López (chapter 7) studies the sexual experience of immigrants from Mexico to narrate and document this issue in a new way. On a global level, the treatment of survivors of sexual abuse and the sexual enslavement and threats to bodily integrity common in some regions of the world, no less than the Korean "comfort women" survivors (chapter 4), pose critical problems for academics and advocates today.

The epidemiology of social inequality in health that affects sexual inequalities has for several years been a subject of growing concern in the United States (Krieger 1999). HIV infection and AIDS, for example, seem firmly associated with structural violence, especially poverty, throughout the world and particularly in Africa, Asia, South America, and the Caribbean (UNAIDS 2002; Farmer 2003). Moreover, as Rafael M. Díaz suggests in chapter 2, the social force of poverty, racism, and homophobia have demonstrable effects on the most vulnerable individuals, such as Hispanic gay men living in the United States. Linking forms of social oppression to sexual health and health outcomes is of central concern in a variety of pursuits, such as medical anthropology. Paul Farmer (2003: 30) has framed the question thus: "By what mechanisms, precisely, do social forces ranging from poverty to racism become *embodied* as individual experience?"

We wish to reconsider subjectivity and agency as mechanisms of sexual inequality. Methodologically, we shall investigate how agency in general and the positionality of the anthropologist or social scientist in particular influence social change and policy when it comes to the sexual health and well-being of communities in the United States and internationally. The work of Parker, Barbosa, and Aggleton (2000) is most notable in this area, though it has focused primarily on the international side, profiling the enormous and critical impact of the AIDS epidemic.

In particular, the contributors in deep and probing ways analyze how the positionality of the researcher or social scientist has influenced the analysis of sexual inequality.[2] Increasingly, this has required that one must be a member of the community that is dominated. This volume discusses a spectrum of engagement between researchers and the communities in which they work.

Sexuality research typically ignored the researcher's own position in the past, largely owing to the empiricist/behavioralist conundrum that denied the engagement of the investigator in the phenomenon studied (Herdt and Stoller 1990; Herdt 2000). Consequently, the theoretical and methodological tools of social analysis required for this interrogation have eluded investigators—especially the dilemma of studying sexual cultures in the absence of understanding the double standards and contradictions of the researcher's own positionality in these sexual studies. Without an understanding of the social processes involved, or how they shape sexuality at a collective or personal level, we lack the insight and means to investigate how social suffering continues to be reproduced through sexuality.

## Sexual Inequality in the United States

American society, from the perspective of two anthropologists, one Dutch (Niels Teunis), the other American (Gilbert Herdt), is a very strange sexual culture: a disarming combination of raucous sexuality in film and on television, often intensely commercialized to sell products ranging from shaving cream to computers, and a continuing puritan ethic of shame and silence in the avoidance of open and frank discussion of sexuality within families and communities. Throughout the twentieth century, the invention of adolescent sexuality and the effort to curb sexual reform have plagued policy and sexuality education in American schools (Moran 2000). Powerful conservative lobbies continue to oppose comprehensive sexuality education, to advocate for regulation of sexual minorities, and to refuse to grant human rights to women, gays, lesbians, and bisexuals or protection against violence against women, gays, and transgender people in government policy (Irvine 2002). Consider one of the most famous and tragic cases of sexual violence in the United States—the brutal murder of a college student in Wyoming.

On October 7, 1998, twenty-one-year-old Matthew Shepard was found tied to a fence near Laramie. After having been savagely beaten by two young men, he was discovered eighteen hours later by a passerby who mistook his mutilated body for a scarecrow. He never regained consciousness and died five days later. Pictures of the young man were shown on television and appeared in newspapers around the world; the media reports revealed him to have been physically small (only five feet two inches and 105 pounds).

Matthew Shepard's torturers—Aaron McKinney and Russell Henderson—were arrested within days after their crime. What followed was, for the most part, a repeat of the sort of media theater that has taken place in myriad other incidents of antigay violence: blaming the victim for the crime (Van der Meer 2003). As Catharine MacKinnon (1987) has noted of rape cases as well, it is always the victims who are placed under scrutiny, not the rapists themselves. Moreover, such discourses, a characteristic of what David Halperin (1995: 32) has called this "genocidal era," are so pervasive and multiform that "they cannot be refuted by means of rational argument; they can only be resisted." The father of one of the assailants (McKinney) complained to the *New York Times* that his son did not stand a chance of a fair trial because he had already been "condemned" by public opinion. Were only the truth to be known, he said, Matthew Shepard "had made a pass at his son." He did not say it in so many words, but his message was clear: if Matthew Shepard had not deserved his fate because he had apparently "predated" one of his assailants, he at least had brought it on himself by the simple fact of being gay. According to this piece of cultural logic—the product, of course, not of common sense but of an ideology of sexual inequality that justifies sexual violence—McKinney acted in a way that any masculine man in his right mind would have done, given the same circumstances. As Michael Warner (1999: 30) has so astutely written of such flagrant moralism in another context, "Homos are immoral because they commit, or want to commit, criminal sex acts," thus justifying their lack of protection under the law: a perpetuation of structural violence in the United States.

Another familiar battleground of sexual inequality in the United States is the high school. It has become a constant stage on which has been played out social conflict surrounding sexual education and gender and sexual rights (Herdt and Boxer 1996; Irvine 2002; Moran 2000). As Jessica Fields shows in chapter 3, sexuality education discourse surrounding abstinence-only education opens up analysis of the hidden sociosexual oppression of communities played out in classrooms. Young people are its victims and perpetrators, but they act as proxies for the community and, in a larger sense, for the state. The controversy surrounding Surgeon General David Satcher's "Call to Action to Promote Sexual Health and Responsible Sexual Behavior" (2001) has signified the U.S. government's opposition to empowerment in the arena of sexual rights. Abstinence-only policies, officially endorsed by the government and paid for from public funds, continue to regard sexual freedom and agency as threats to citizenship and democracy. Moreover, the imagery surrounding these policies in the Welfare Reform Act of 1996 clearly racializes sexuality and stigmatizes poor women of color. Such policies affect sexual equality, including the right of young people and all cultural minorities to achieve the full potential of their sexual well-being or their ability to protect themselves from harm and disease.

We may take attitudes and policies regarding comprehensive sexuality education to be a general proxy for the reproduction of structural sexual violence and the promotion of a conservative economic agenda in the United States as supported by certain fundamentalist religious groups and traditional right-wing (what Janice Irvine [2002] calls "sexual conservatives" or the "New Right") activism. Public opinion polls conducted by a variety of organizations, including SIECUS and the Pew Trust, consistently demonstrate that Americans want "comprehensive" sexuality education (a concept typically taken to mean more than abstinence education, but including it with teaching about sexual disease prevention); however, these same polls suggest public confusion about how to achieve or implement this ideal. Public opinion is constantly manipulated through misinformation and fear by New Right organizations. Sexual conservatives have been continually successful in the creation of fear and the exaggeration of social differences through divisive sexual speech (Irvine 2002), typically in order to achieve a larger economic agenda. As Thomas Frank (2004: 5) has aptly put it, "Cultural anger is marshaled to achieve economic ends." As Duggin (2003: xvii) has argued, this major "economics/culture split" did not appear significantly until the 1980s.

Paradoxically, during this two-decade period, social studies as reviewed later in this introduction have shown how sexuality in the United States is at a unique turning point in history: ignorance of the most basic knowledge of human sexuality (even anatomy) continues to exist alongside explicit (and often inaccurate) television and Internet sexual content, as well as conservative criticism of multiculturalism and sexual rights, for example, the right to choose abortion, the right to bodily integrity, and the right to freedom from discrimination based on sexual orientation.

Nonetheless, there is a hopeful sign of late: the emergence of sex and sexuality as linked to positive sexual health in one form or another. The World Health Organization's (WHO) mid-1970s draft definition defines sexual health as a state of physical, emotional, mental, and social well-being related to sexuality; it is not merely the absence of disease, dysfunction, or infirmity. Sexual health requires a positive and respectful approach to sexuality and sexual relations, as well as the possibility of having pleasure and safe sexual experiences, free of coercion, discrimination, and violence. For sexual health to be attained and maintained, the sexual rights of all persons must be respected, protected, and fulfilled. This positive trend, including pleasure and prevention within the same frame, is the new "gold standard" of the Surgeon General's Report on Comprehensive Sexuality Education (2001)—and increasingly it is invoked to strengthen the relationships among sexual cultures, social policies, and the law.

## Reproduction of American Sexual Inequality

As the studies in this book underscore, American society is largely ambivalent about sexual health and is most uncomfortable or negative when it comes to dealing with "pleasure" in human sexuality. The historical underpinnings of contemporary resistance to sexual pleasure and the inclusion of sexual health and rights in a national policy agenda in the United States are the results of profound historical forces rooted in the deep and long history of racism and sexual essentialism in the United States (Cohen 1999; D'Emilio and Freedman 1988; Levine, Nardi, and Gagnon 1997). Sexuality, in this worldview, is regarded as innate, as individual, and as a moral rather than a health problem. Such a paradigm treats sexual pleasure and conduct as problems to be contained, or, as John Gagnon has often said, as a sore on the body of society to be scratched and bandaged, then hidden away.

Assertions of this sexual innatism continually reproduce sexual inequality: claims of racial inferiority and sexual promiscuity and hypersexuality regarding African Americans (McBride 2000); appeals to innate differences between the genders, such as the sex-drive ideology that objectifies women and treats their agency as nil (Tolman 2002); the stigmatization of homosexuality and the classification of all alternative sexualities as diseases; the treatment of transgender people as monsters or freaks to be feared and against whom to direct acts of violence; and the medical pathologization or treatment of categories of people, such as those with disabilities, as abnormal and biologically defective, and unfit for sexual relations.

As Lancaster (2003) has detailed for the United States, scientific ideologies, such as sociobiology, have enabled sexual orientation to be treated as a mode of essential or innate difference (see, for example, Bailey and Oberschneider 1997), with sexual inequality perpetuated in the academy, the law, and communities, and these scientific ideologies are fundamental to understanding how science and sexuality research took its historical shape in the twentieth century. Bias and prejudice in these areas was historically brought into sexuality, gender, and sexual health thinking, research, and education in myriad ways that continue to influence the national agenda in policy, the law, and health care writ large (Herek 2004; Irvine 2002). Even today, as Krieger (1999: 334–335) has noted, although race is no longer regarded as a scientifically valid category for the study of human variation, as confirmed by United Nations Educational, Scientific, and Cultural Organization (UNESCO) scientists and doctrine long ago, nonetheless many continue to perpetuate the category error and promote racist ideology, with deleterious effects on health.

The historical and cultural setting of normal science typically avoided advocacy, the application of science to implement change directly, and was in general suspicious of social research that too closely hovered over policy formation. Science was to remain aloof from these problems, it was believed, even though the social context of research and education folded society's cultural assumptions into scientific practice. The classic examples of efforts to bridge the pure versus applied science domains, such as the famous studies of the so-called culture of poverty (Lewis 1961) in Mexico, and the Moynihan Report in the United States (1965) on the African American family are now often pointed to as failed and even tragic attempts to challenge social oppression that actually produced the opposite effect—"new wine in old bottles" justifications for continued discrimination. Thus a generation of behavioral scientists was taught to avoid policy and to avoid sexuality as science (Escoffier 2004; Herdt 2004), resulting in a terrible hiatus when it came to the application of sexuality research to the improvement of social policy and prevention of disease, such as HIV/AIDS (Díaz and Ayala 2000; reviewed in Ehrhardt 2000; Epstein 1999). Of course, a variety of additional examples could be drawn on to show that such a dichotomy is antiquated, but nevertheless, the antipathy to applied social science, drummed into generations of social scientists, has not been easy to overturn (Gagnon and Parker 1995; Herdt 2004).

It is noticeable that little of gender got into this work, and nothing of sexuality. Moreover, social oppression and inequality were generally absent from the concerns of its proponents. This critique was mainly formulated by an anthropologist who took a Marxist position, highlighting the need for the study of political economy (Roseberry 1989). But with only a few exceptions, such as Adam (1978), the neo-Marxist writers of this period also ignored or were very shy about sexuality as a field of study (di Mauro, Herdt, and Parker 2003).

Social movements from the 1960s on, including the black power movement, second-wave feminism, and the gay liberation movement, were far removed from the academy and generally were far ahead of it in promoting a new dialogue on identity and rights-based social change. Social change in these movements, as Parker, Barbosa, and Aggleton (2000) have observed, typically preceded discursive study, and sometimes insight into social problems, in the academy. Thus we find feminists arguing for significant change in gender roles and norms, and their work leading to *Roe v. Wade* (1973) was iconic of the grassroots base of women's rights in the United States. The impact outside of the United States, in the aftermath of the International Conference on Population and Development (ICPD) in Cairo (1994) and the Fourth World Women's Conference in Beijing (1995), has been carefully examined by Petchesky (2002). She remarked on the notable gains achieved, but also on the ongoing problem that sexuality as a human right (like much of the human rights language) continues to be registered in negative terms—by harm done, by what is missing or absent from rights, and so on.

Early gay liberation movement actions, likewise, preceded any formation of significant discussion or change in the academy regarding homosexuality. For example, Altman's (1973) classic from this time contains more than a few diatribes against intellectuals and academy-based research and education. Notably, the same year (1973) as the *Roe v. Wade* decision witnessed the highly political decision of the American Psychiatric Association to "declassify" homosexuality as a disease. The long-term impact on sexual minorities and people of color has been considerable (Carrier 1995; Díaz 1998). Thirty years later, these remarkable transformations have ushered in major feminist, gay, lesbian, bisexual, queer, and transgender elements of the academy, from research and teaching to some work on social policy (Burrington 1998; Bem 2000; notable is Epstein 1999).

Public culture and the social and political position of the researcher in ethnography did not translate into what we are calling positionality. Notice that the intense attention to the public position of the ethnographer in this paradigm, deriving from such classic essays in period anthropology as "Notes on the Cock Fight," by Geertz (1973), although dealing with the participant-observer role and the conundrum of "thick description" as a highly observer-dependent enterprise, did not, ultimately, deal with positionality. By *positionality* we mean the social scientist's subjectivity in the context of the social, cultural, psychological, and political conditions of the times (Herdt and Stoller 1990). The 1970s interpretative paradigm largely precluded the subjectivities and agency of the ethnographer as we think of it now and seldom was informed by an "alliance" or participation directly by local people or collaborators in the communities under investigation. (Myriad discussions of ethics in recent years, notably the Yanomamö ethical debates, have renewed this domain in the anthropology of fieldwork.) Although Herdt and Stoller (1990) examined the identity and subjectivity issue in great detail, especially in the anthropology of sexuality, they did not make much of an inroad, especially in anthropology, much as Devereux's (1968) earlier plea for study of the counter-transference dynamics of the researcher was ignored.

It was the advent of social and political movements, such as the gay and lesbian movement of the 1960s and 1970s, and the women's health movement of the 1970s, that laid the groundwork for radical change in methodology and observer objectivity. The women's health movement, building on the feminism of the 1960s and 1970s, was quite pivotal to the next transformation of how social oppression and sexual inequality were treated by the academy (Rubin 1984). A sexualized rhetoric of objectification, the language and treatment of what Adrienne Rich referred to as "compulsory heterosexuality," arguably emerged from these identity-based movements. However, it was the new effort of women to reclaim, control, or take back control of their bodies from male doctors and to overcome the demeaning of the female body in general by medical hegemonic authorities that led to a new confederation of consciousness-raising groups across the United States (Tiefer 2000). The notions of women helping women, of women discovering the roots of their own medical knowledge, and of the embodiment of these meanings in grassroots social support and care were crucial to the times (Stimpson 1996). Indeed, this formation paved the way for the action of gay men regarding HIV in the subsequent decade (Levine, Nardi, and Gagnon 1997; Levine 1998).

The AIDS epidemic, as it became first a visible and then a high-profile national concern in the mid-1980s, especially following the deaths of media personalities such as Liberace and Rock Hudson, was a strong instigator of this change. Indeed, AIDS became a social movement in its own right (Brown 1997). Gay men, following the lead of lesbians and women who had created the women's health movement, began to wrest control from scientific and medical authorities, and were successful in influencing their medical treatment by what was perceived to be a hostile government and medical research establishment through the creation of community-based organizations (CBOs) such as the Gay Men's Health Crisis in New York. Here the ethical involvement of social scientists, spearheaded by psychologists and the American Psychological Association, indicated the need for advocacy and research. Clearly, policy could not be left in the hands of doctors. Like women who had resisted male doctors' directives about their bodies in the 1970s, which led to the challenge of a new women's health movement, and building on the declassification of homosexuality as a disease by the American Psychiatric Association in 1973, academics and advocates began to find themselves sometimes in alliance. For example, the study of gay and lesbian youths emerged as a way of empowering policy in this arena, and was the inevitable result of the rising political power of the gay and lesbian social movement (Herdt and Boxer 1993). The aftermath was the emergence of a new way of thinking about social analysis and its ends or purposes in the epidemic.

Michel Foucault's work *The History of Sexuality* (1980) became a standard tool of high social theory during this period, and its long-term effect on sexuality and gender studies and the articulation of critiques of sexual inequality cannot be overestimated. Notions of power and discourse, ideas of the historical emergence of repression and the critique of Freud and sexology, including innatism, surely were foundational to social constructionism in sexuality study (reviewed in Halperin 1995). To remember the fighting words of David Halperin (perhaps the foremost American scholar of Foucault): There can be no orgasm without ideology! Surely no phrase better captures the divide between preliberationist, preconstructionist writing, paving the way for the creation of the construct "heteronormativity," and the various forms of high theory that followed, than this quaint refrain.

By the 1990s, the contradictions between the needs of sexual health policy reform and academic theory were blatant. Postmodernism (and queer theory) were to emerge as distinctive epistemological projects—more about sexuality than had previously been allowed in the American academy—but the price was disembodiment: the presentation of sexuality in an elite, high language, cut off from the practicalities of lived experience or the problems of social policy. Writers in this genre attempted to challenge the conventions of doing and representing science in the academy. A change occurred in gay/lesbian studies, in which being "out" in the academy was of most importance, a focus on the self and its trappings in the text (gay autobiographies perhaps exemplify this genre best; see Robinson 1999), being queer, which rather emphasized the outing of a topic or field, its decentering and deheterosexing, was not merely a generational change located in boomers who came out in the 1970s, to Generation Xers who came out in the post-AIDS era (Herdt and de Vries 2004). It was also a profound attack on "normalcy" and the assertion of the normal = natural equation in many preconceptions of everyday life, such as the notion that one should bring up one's kids as gay (Bem 1996; Sedgwick 1991; Warner 1999). Here the romanticism of postmodern study triumphed in the academy. Like a generation earlier, when gay academics had attempted to radicalize their friends and advocates in the community without much success, queer theory and the queering of many intellectual venues was to leave largely untouched rampant sexual inequalities, such as the high rate of alienation, isolation, and victimization experienced by lesbian, gay, and bisexual youth, who are at high risk of suicide (Paul et al. 2002).

Meanwhile, sexuality research was unwittingly served by AIDS, as documented keenly in the work of Parker, Barbosa, and Aggleton (2000). The numerous studies of homosexuality as a variable contributing to HIV transmission began to take hold—especially in the academy, where previously the study of homosexuality was the kiss of death to a career (Escoffier 2004; Gagnon and Parker 1995). Bisexuality, prostitution, and homosexuality became fundable and necessary ways of addressing the epidemic. Academic researchers began to mainstream these efforts, with sexuality thus warranted, sub rosa, as an area of study. Overnight, a body of international research came into being regarding the knowledge, attitudes, and behavior leading to AIDS/HIV. Overnight, as well, new categories, such as partner, sex worker, and MSM (men who have sex with men) were exported from Centers for Disease Control (CDC) and WHO discourse into international studies of sexual health and behaviors (Parker, Carballo, and Herdt 1991).

However, change in the United States had been considerable but not as extensive in the areas of sexual health and sexuality education, and certainly not in the domain of sexual rights. Thus, this sociopolitical change is incomplete and has often been tempered with great political reluctance and personal resistance. As Janice Irvine (2002) has noted, sexual conservatives and their political organizations continue to employ and represent sexuality as a threat to public morality, and they use sexuality education as a rhetorical means to evoke fear in the public and thus control sexuality and sexual speech. Meanwhile, change continues to occur in social attitudes toward sexuality and the expression of tolerance in the public domain, as Laumann et al. (1994) have documented in their foundational survey study of the United States. The rise in public opinion poll support of homosexuality continues across time, in spite of discrimination against gays and lesbians in the military and the effort of late to impose new laws and even a constitutional amendment to ban gay and lesbian marriage. In spite of these politics, the change in American sexuality is impressive since the time of Kinsey, Pomeroy, and Martin (1948), as the role of social research has driven policy change in understanding the diversity of sexual behavior, intimate relations, and citizen participation in community development, and subsequently in the promotion of health and positive well-being.

However, in the face of this significant change, the positionality of the social scientist working in sexuality has not changed when it comes to sexuality; indeed, rather than being clarified, methodology has become more opaque. Social epidemiology has extolled quantitative surveys, for example, and still allowed only a small role for the subjectivity of the ethnographer in the qualitative study, as noted by Rafael M. Díaz (chapter 2). Moreover, the agency of the social scientist, in the sense of being a change agent, was not extolled, nor was there an understanding of how research drives policy. The lack of progress here is even more impressive when it is remembered that the concept of sexual culture as an explicit social and behavioral construct was given birth more than a decade ago, with a promise of change to come (Parker, Herdt, and Carballo 1991).

## Sexual Inequality and the Researcher's Positionality

The problems associated with the sexual subjectivity and positionality of the researcher are the missing link in the analysis of sexual inequality. The long historical barriers outlined earlier have had far-reaching consequences, planned and unplanned, in sexuality research and social policy. Even though by now precious few social scientists maintain that they strive toward a pure objectivity, the powerful hold of this central, hegemonic ideal on all who work in the academy has thwarted the investigation of sexual inequality. Why?

We maintain that in the critical areas of sexual inequality most in need of study, the researcher's positionality is not just a vital tool, but a necessary insight into what Paul Farmer (2003) called the mechanisms of structural violence.

To some extent it is true that social science has transformed from the objectivist pursuit of truth to more of an interpretive and dynamic instrument of social change (di Leonardo 1998). Certainly the credibility of science and its dedication to truth have been called into question over issues of sexuality, of which the AIDS epidemic is perhaps the most visible (Bancroft 2000; Gagnon 1989). The contribution of many gay and lesbian social scientists has been critical here; for example, how gay and lesbian subjectivities have positioned the work of anthropologists in the field is ground-breaking (Lewin and Leap 1996).

It is therefore necessary to formulate explicitly today what some sexuality researchers already know, namely, that positionality is not just a problem to overcome. In fact, positionality is the very basis of inspiration, innovation, and new insight in the field. We will not be able to analyze structural sexual violence without the meanings and understanding of the social practices that perpetuate it, and these depend mightily on the lived experience of community members. Positionality is what allows social scientists to do our work; therefore we need to be clear about what our own subjectivity does in supporting or opposing sexual inequality in real-life communities. Science in general seems to focus our attention on research without individuals, that is, a form of investigation that can be conducted by just about anyone who has training in the necessary skills. Taking positionality seriously means that we go beyond apologizing for a lack of objectivity and recognize explicitly that the subjective experiences of the researcher are precisely what make sexuality research possible and insightful. Translation of theory, method, and data will fail without this subjectivity. It is this sense of positionality that formulates so many of the relevant and critical questions, not because researchers investigate themselves but because they have a means of access to the research institutions to ask the very questions that matter to them.

The transformations in sexuality and society we have outlined thus far have to some extent ushered in a new era of self-examination and critical thinking in research methodology as applied to sexuality. Especially in gay and lesbian or queer studies, some writers have noted a true paradigm shift (Herdt 1997a; Rubin 2002; Weston 1993). Long before it became popular in the social sciences to talk about "agency" and "subjectivity," organic intellectuals were considering the role of conflict and awareness, and especially the tension between conflicted consciousness that arises out of power and obligation in grounded experience (Freire 1970). Indeed, it is useful to recall Freire's advice on this matter:

Some may think it inadvisable to include the people as investigators in the search for their own meaningful thematics: that their intrusive influence (n.b., the "intrusion" of those who are most interested—or ought to be—in their own education) will "adulterate" the findings and thereby sacrifice the objectivity of the investigation. This view mistakenly presupposes that these exist, in their original purity, as if these were *things*. . . . We must realize that the aspirations, the motives, and the objectives implicit in the meaningful thematics are human aspirations, motives, and objectives. They do not exist "out there," somewhere, as static entities; they are occurring. . . . Thematic investigation thus becomes a common striving towards awareness of reality and towards self-awareness, which makes this investigation a starting point for the educational process or for cultural action of a liberating character. (Freire 1970: 106–107)

In our view, this process of self-awareness and cultural action is inherent in the analysis of sexual inequality, but it requires more detailed study later in this introduction.

In recent decades, the development of action or applied health science, applied anthropology, and medical sociology as fields of study, the advance of participatory research in the realm of feminist methodology and gender studies, as well as the role of social and cultural study to examine neocolonial and postcolonial ideologies and practices in the aftermath of the Vietnam war (Appadurai 1996; di Leonardo 1998; Herdt 1997b) have all contributed to a reflexive trend. However, these changes writ large were not carried over into all disciplines or subfields at the same time or under the same conditions, and the health sciences until late tended to favor large-scale studies of social epidemiology rather than community-based examinations of qualitative case studies or ethnographies (Parker and Carballo 1990). When such studies have examined the effects of structural violence, they have demonstrated significant influences on health (Díaz 1998; Farmer 2003; Krieger 1999).

Cultural studies / queer theory formulations tended to collapse difference and romanticize relations of dominance. That is to say, a conflation of real-world social suffering and romantic versions of this suffering as sometimes depicted in autobiographical or biographical academic accounts tended to blur the face of domination occurring in communities and sexual cultures in the United States. This unfortunate trend therefore did not ultimately disrupt the historic tendency in the academy to ignore advocates and community needs, as argued forcefully by Héctor Carrillo (chapter 5).

Policy, in general, continues to be written entirely outside of the academy. The problem is that sexual policy formulations are then typically cut off from the necessary empirical research needed to respond to knowledge and methodology. This gap was a new form of silence in that it was thought that practitioners and advocates would not "understand" the terms of the research discourse or would push beyond science to advocacy. It is fascinating to read Urvashi Vaid's (1995) detailed and compelling account of the gay and lesbian movement in the United States, fraught with many political turns and the impact of the AIDS epidemic, only to notice the near total marginality of academic gay and lesbian voices in the history of this social change. The account suggests once again the void between academics and advocates that has stymied change and social policy based on sound empirical social science research.

The contributions in this book provide a more qualitative and policy advocacy–oriented academic response to these historical transformations — the result of studies by one key group of social science scholars, many of them working in communities of color or sexual minority communities, themselves members of these communities. Their research and policy are grounded in the significations of social oppression and grounded experience of conflict and conflicted consciousness in these sexual cultures. They reveal a new intellectual commitment to understanding and analyzing social oppression in the context of sexuality, gender, sexual health, and society.

The questions addressed by the essays in this volume include the following: How is sexuality structured in the context of social oppression? What are the factors of structural violence that condition sexual inequalities and the reaction to oppression in the United States? How do social policies and social representations of sexual inequality counter or reproduce social oppression? And what are the forms of sexual subjectivity and concomitant agency that emerge in sexual cultures marked by such persistent inequalities? These are some of the issues addressed by a new generation of multidisciplinary scholars living and working within diverse sexual cultures in the United States and abroad.

The contributors to this volume take these questions one step further — beyond scientific analysis. Each asks what her or his work contributes to positive social change, that is, to the decrease of social inequalities that underlie so much of the suffering documented in these chapters. What, in other words, is the contribution of each of us as a social scientist to social change? This is far from an easy question, because none of the contributors believe any longer that providing analysis of inequalities is sufficient to make a positive contribution. Far too much valuable and urgent research by committed social scientists is tucked away in unanalyzed data storage facilities (especially true of AIDS and sexually transmitted disease — STD — projects of the 1990s) and libraries where only the most privileged students or most dedicated colleagues access these contributions. It is not enough to advocate in writing that our work is *intended* to contribute to positive social change; we must ask ourselves *how* our work can make such a contribution.

This question has been made harder to pose, ironically, by very serious and critical social thinkers, who have deconstructed so carefully the very basis on which one can take a position in a social struggle. Gender is performative, race is a biological nonentity, and sexual orientation has become so queer that a firm declaration of preference for one or the other gender marks one as an essentialist dinosaur. In other words, the subject has become so decentered that no position of struggle against social oppression can be maintained. Therefore, rather than maintaining a fully decentered subject, the authors of this volume all investigate the intersection of multiple identities that all individuals engage in, including the authors themselves. We move beyond the tired dichotomy of insider/outsider. That debate has been well hashed out and positions are firmly entrenched.

However, the researchers themselves negotiate multiple identities, not only those of the insider or outsider researcher. These researchers are a diverse lot; the majority of them are nonnative speakers of English, for instance. They choose their research topics and communities carefully, and often engaged them in various ways, precisely to make sure that their work interrogates questions of sexual rights and oppression in the context of social inequality. The contributors investigate in various ways exactly how they are involved in the questions or social problems they research and the communities with which they work, no longer engaging in a simple dichotomy, insider/outsider. Rather, by reflecting on the various ways in which their work as researchers is conducted and represented (to which they are all fully committed), each researcher reconsiders the influence of her or his relationship with the individuals and communities on the analysis of social and sexual oppression.

What role do academic discipline and particularly disciplinary perspectives play in the process of sexual inequality analysis? Studies conducted within the strict confines of any one discipline tend, first and foremost, to ask questions that matter for that discipline. But whether those questions actually speak to lived experiences in situations of social oppression is not at all certain. This is a central insight that emerged from discussion at the 2000 Rio de Janeiro conference on sexuality and social change convened by Richard Parker (funded by the Ford Foundation), at which we were present. Moreover, it accords with the lessons learned by the Social Science Research Council Program in Sexuality Research

Fellowships (di Mauro, Herdt, and Parker 2003). These authors are fully vested in their respective disciplinary backgrounds, but at the same time they are completely engaged in multidisciplinary collaboration at every step of the research process. In fact, most authors here recognize that they must engage with colleagues from other disciplines in order to solve the problems that face the individuals and communities with which they work. Thus, these case studies ask pertinent questions with regard to the nature of social oppression and the meaning of their work for new directions in the field.

## Challenging the Culture of Sexual Inequality

The social scientists' position in sexuality research today needs rethinking as a mechanism of social change. The framework opted for here is closer to the feminist methodologies that have advocated for change in heterosexism and homophobia (Tolman 2002), with feminist methodology producing a means of researchers enabling individuals to become more agentic and thus agents of change. This model accepts that human beings are complex and have multiple identities, corresponding to their multiple roles or positions, in society. Multiple social rights and human rights entail a different set of social ethics for research in the twenty-first century. Although social scientists have long understood such complexity or multivocality, less often has it been translated into sexuality research, certainly not of the subalterns whose cultural worlds have remained silent or hidden. The use of informant voices as a proxy or stand-in for the voice of the social scientist is one such stratagem. Using the tools of sociocultural analysis to lay bare the power dynamics and reproduction of oppression of particular communities, including their stigma, is relevant (Herdt 2001; Parker, Barbosa, and Aggleton 2000; Teunis 2001).

Culture and the power dynamics underlying sexual inequality, in this view, are closer to how Antonio Gramsci understood the cultural realities of subalterns in terms of class and domination (Crehan 2002). The anthropological concept of culture is a means of understanding how social class is lived as an embedded set of beliefs, assumptions, and social practices related to life, sex, gender, family, and community. What Geertz and his followers have typified as "moral worlds" (Shweder 1996) are actually historically constructed ways of perceiving and, in turn, acting on these perceptions of equality and social oppression—but without a complete understanding of what Crehan (2002: 205) calls "subaltern culture," the inability to grasp "the larger landscapes of oppression in which they are located." Such a view reminds us of Freire's (1970) constant concern with encompassing both the oppressor and the oppressed in a common framework that is necessary if oppression is to be removed.

Culture in this frame is power as practiced and gradually built into a seamless image of person, selfhood, gender, sexuality, and sociality, and it ultimately is the political basis for how sexuality and gender enter into definitions of sexual rights and citizenship (Hostetler and Herdt 1998; Petchesky 2002). The surrender of the self to such a sexual culture—as observed in many of the case studies to follow—occurs through this mode of accommodating the expectations of others in intimate, love- and passion-filled relationships and being (Herdt 1994, 1999). Being a member of such a culture and understanding its sexual mores enables one to do an analysis of its equality and inequalities, but the task is not without contradictions (Lewin and Leap 1996); indeed, a whole discipline may be able to overlook contradictions of power and heteronormativity for generations (see, for example, Herdt 1991, 2003). However, such a form of research, or participatory research, with people who are members of the community carries with it special demands for describing the positionality of the researchers in the same setting and community (Herdt 2000; Patton 1997).

When speaking of subjectivity, we distinguish in this volume between the subjectivity of the research subject and that of the researcher. Both influence one another in the research process and they must ultimately be regarded in their mutual interaction. First of all, and we repeat ourselves, we state the obvious: When the search for objectivity has been recognized as the attempt of an interested party to maintain hegemony over the academy against the inroads made by, for instance, feminist scholars, scholars of color, and lesbian, gay, bisexual, and transgender scholars, then we must firmly go in the opposite direction. Then we recognize and even celebrate subjectivity not as a hindrance to sound scholarship, but as the creative inspiration behind it, as the impulse that urges us to work not just to advance theory, though we do that quite well, but also to think seriously about the ways in which our work can advance social justice. Rather than being shy about our positionality, we propose to highlight the choices that we make, the specific contributions that our vantage points makes possible, and yes, we also recognize that we have blind spots, biases, and shortcomings in certain areas. We focus, however, on the positive contribution the subjective input of each individual researcher tries to make in fights against inequities.

Several contributors make specific references to their choice of methodologies, which result precisely from their motivation to fight for social justice. Even though most contributors think alike when it comes to motivation for their research, that does not mean that they make similar choices, with respect to their methods for instance. Rafael M. Díaz (chapter 2), on the one hand, quite explicitly combines qualitative methods, which brings out voices of individuals, with quantitative measurements to show the prevalence of the subjective experiences he heard. Christopher Carrington (chapter 6) chooses, on the other hand, though not in disagreement with Rafael Díaz, to conduct a full-fledged ethnography in order to delve as deeply as possible into the subjective experiences of the Circuit boys who are so often and so easily disparaged, even by many in gay communities around the world. Héctor Carrillo (chapter 5) makes a similar choice to show how even the most well-intentioned health education messages can run counter to the subjective experience of sexual pleasure, and in fact can even end up being oppressive of sexual excitement.

Subjective experience of our interlocutors completes the understanding of individuals' circumstances that we would otherwise not gain. In the cases that Carrington and Carrillo present, we see that health education efforts, including HIV prevention, must understand the subjective experience of sexual pleasure and sexual identity. Health educators are in peril of having their message fall on deaf ears, in the best-case scenario, or alienate their target audience. Sonya Grant Arreola (chapter 1) explains how the subjective experience of sexual experience before the age of sixteen must be taken into account if we are to understand why such sexual experience leads to higher risk for infection with HIV for some and not for others. So-called objective measures simply do not do justice to the complexity of these issues and can in the end only aggravate the problems for those who are at greatest risk for infection with HIV because not only are their experiences not recognized, but without attention to subjective experiences, these individuals will actually be blamed for the predicament they find themselves in.

The authors of this volume suggest that it is not enough simply to assume that the individuals and communities they work with have agency. We recognize, on the contrary, that the struggle for agency is exactly at the heart of the problem, and perhaps is an area where we can make a contribution. In this volume, Russell P. Shuttleworth (chapter 8) explains that the struggle for agency of men with cerebral palsy faces tremendous prejudice in American society, which by and large holds that disabled individuals, like children, have no sexuality. In this respect, these men face obstacles very similar to those faced by older gays and lesbians, who also have to assert their sexuality as a continually essential part of their lives (chapter 9). Korean women who were abducted by the Japanese military during World War II today strive for recognition of their survival in the face of severe trauma, exactly because public recognition will support their struggle for greater autonomy and dignity in Korean life (chapter 4). Agency is in all these examples precisely what oppressed groups fight for, and it is that struggle that these contributors seek to support.

That is not to deny the remarkable agency that many claim despite great odds. Young people today form groups in high schools, gay-straight alliances, that support gay and lesbian students in their struggle for decent and love-filled lives (chapter 10). Not so long ago, these kids had to find their spaces well outside of the view of their peers in high school and well outside of the reach of their parents, to prevent predictable harassment and other dangers (Herdt and Boxer 1993). Forming these alliances in schools today is nothing but heroic and came about entirely without prediction by any social scientist. In another contribution, Gloria González-López (chapter 7) shows how the age-old and tired stereotypes of Mexican women, who are supposed to live either as Madonnas or as whores, have prevented us from seeing the rich sexual experiences that these women claim for themselves, while fully engaging with, for instance, discourses of their church that deny them these experiences. To miss these remarkable achievements is to miss the possibility for social change entirely. For even though the authors in this book seek to support the fight for social justice of the communities they work in, nobody here patronizes these groups by thinking that we can come up with a way to struggle not previously conceived by precisely those we are writing about.

To highlight agency, then, is in part to oppose the silences that surround many of the experiences that we describe here, because those silences are such a strong part of the problem—the silent assumptions, for instance, that surround young African American students in North Carolina, which maintain the notion that their sexuality is not under control and is costly for society (chapter 3). These are stories and narratives that connect the researcher's positionality to social oppression and the production of sexual inequalities in such communities.

The case studies in this book thus build on prior decades of social change and intellectual progress, but not without a variety of barriers and social and political obstacles that have entangled the study of sexuality. In the years to come, we expect a new alignment or perhaps even a partnership between academics and advocates, who will work together to produce research and policy briefs necessary to foment change in the law and social life to ameliorate these conditions of social oppression. Science, again, is part of society, and the reduction of sexuality to innate things, alluded to at the opening of this introduction, has not gone away and will not disappear from the rhetoric of the United States. However, social change as implemented by rights advocates and intellectuals such as the scholars represented in this volume marks a significant watershed in the long struggle to create progress out of the work of scholarship in social oppression and sexual inequality.

## Notes

1. Until 1998, nineteen states in the United States continued to perpetuate violence against LGBT people through the so-called sodomy laws, one of the chief means of regulating access to public space in the United States (Burrington 1998: 108).

2. By *positionality* is meant the particular social position and subjectivity of the researcher in this position that has shaped the project and how it is experienced in thought and action, including the writing up and representation.

## References

Adam, B. 1978. *The survival of domination.* New York: Elsevier.

Altman, D. 1973. *Homosexual: Liberation or oppression?* New York: Penguin.

Appadurai, A. 1996. *Modernity at large.* Minneapolis: University of Minnesota Press.

Bailey, J. M., and M. Oberschneider. 1997. Sexual orientation: Professional dance. *Archives of Sexual Behavior* 26: 433–444.

Bancroft, J., ed. 2000. *The role of theory in sex research.* Bloomington: Indiana University Press.

Bem, D. 1996. Exotic becomes erotic: A developmental theory of sexual orientation. *Psychological Review,* 103: 320–335.

———. 2000. The exotic-becomes-erotic theory of sexual orientation. In *The role of theory in sex research,* ed. J. Bancroft. Bloomington: Indiana University Press.

Brown, M. P. 1997. *Replacing citizenship: AIDS and radical democracy.* New York: Guilford Press.

Burrington, D. 1998. The public square and citizen queer. *Polity* 31: 107–131.

Carrier, J. 1995. *De los otros: Intimacy and homosexuality among Mexican men.* New York: Columbia University Press.

Cohen, C. 1999. *Boundaries of blackness: AIDS and the breakdown of black politics.* Chicago: University of Chicago Press.

Cohler, B., and R. M. Galatzer-Levy. 2000. *The course of gay and lesbian lives: Social and psychoanalytic perspectives*. Chicago: University of Chicago Press.

Crehan, K. 2002. *Gramsci, culture, and anthropology*. Berkeley and Los Angeles: University of California Press.

D'Emilio, J. D., and E. B. Freedman. 1988. *Intimate matters: A history of sexuality in America*. New York: Harper and Row.

Devereux, G. 1968. *From anxiety to method in the behavioral sciences*. The Hague: Mouton.

Díaz, R. 1998. *Latino gay men and HIV: Culture, sexuality and risk*. New York: Routledge.

Díaz, R., and G. Ayala. 2000. *The impact of social discrimination on health outcomes: The case of Latino gay men and HIV*. New York: National Gay and Lesbian Task Force.

di Leonardo, M. 1998. *Exotics at home*. Chicago: University of Chicago Press.

di Mauro, D., G. Herdt, and R. Parker, eds., 2003. *Training initiatives in sexuality research*. New York: Social Science Research Council.

Duggin, L. 2003. *The twilight of equality*. Boston: Beacon Press.

Ehrhardt, A. A. 2000. Gender, sexuality, and human development. In *The role of theory in sex research,* ed. J. Bancroft. Bloomington: University of Indiana Press.

Epstein, S. 1999. Gay and lesbian movements in the United States: Dilemmas of identity, diversity and political strategy. In *The global emergence of gay and lesbian politics,* by B. D. Adam, J. W. Duyvendak, and A. Krouwel. Philadelphia: Temple University Press.

Escoffier, J. 2004. Preface. In *An interpretation of desire,* by J. Gagnon. Chicago: University of Chicago Press.

Farmer, Paul. 1999. *Infections and inequalities: The modern plagues*. Berkeley and Los Angeles: University of California Press.

———. 2003. *Pathologies of power*. Berkeley and Los Angeles: University of California Press.

Foucault, M. 1980. *The history of sexuality*. Trans. R. Hurley. New York: Viking.

Frank, T. 2004. *What's the matter with Kansas?* New York: Metropolitan Books.

Freire, P. 1970. *Pedagogy of the oppressed*. New York: Continuum.

Gagnon, J. H. 1989. Sexual conduct and the life course. In *AIDS, sexual behavior and IV drug use,* ed. C. F. Turner et al. Washington, D.C.: National Academy Press.

Gagnon, J. H., and R. Parker. 1995. Introduction. In *Conceiving sexuality*. New York: Routledge.

Geertz, C. 1973. *The interpretation of cultures*. New York: Basic Books.

Girard, F. 2004. Global implications of US domestic and international policies on sexuality. International Working Group Paper #1, Columbia University.

Gruskin, S. 2000. The conceptual and practical implications of reproductive and sexual rights: How far have we come? *Health and Human Rights* 4 (2): 1–6.

Halperin, D. 1995 *Saint Foucault*. New York: Oxford University Press.

Herdt, G. 1991. Representations of homosexuality in traditional societies: An essay on cultural ontology and historical comparison. *Journal of the History of Sexuality* 1: 481–504.

——, ed. 1994. *Third sex, third gender: Beyond sexual dimorphism in culture and history.* New York: Zone Books.

——. 1997a. *Same sex, different cultures: Perspectives on gay and lesbian lives.* New York: Westview Press.

——. 1997b. Sexual cultures and population movement: Implications for HIV/STDs. In *Sexual cultures and migration in the era of AIDS: Anthropological and demographic perspectives,* ed. G. Herdt. New York: Oxford University Press.

——. 1999. *Sambia sexual culture: Essays from the field.* Chicago: University of Chicago Press.

——. 2000. Clinical ethnography and sexual study. *Annual Review of Sex Research* 10: 100–119.

——. 2001. Stigma and the ethnographic study of HIV: Problems and prospects. *AIDS and Behavior* 52: 141–149.

——. 2003. *Secrecy and cultural reality.* Ann Arbor: University of Michigan Press.

——. 2004. Sexual development, social oppression, and local culture. *Sexuality Research and Social Policy* 1: 1–24.

Herdt, G., and A. Boxer. 1993. *Children of horizons: How gay and lesbian youth are forging a new way out of the closet.* Boston: Beacon Press.

——. 1996. Afterword. In paperback edition of *Children of horizons.* Boston: Beacon Press.

——. 2003. *Gay and lesbian aging.* New York: Springer.

Herdt, G. H., and B. de Vries, eds. 2004. *Gay and lesbian aging: Research and future directions.* New York: Springer.

Herdt, G. H., and S. Lindenbaum, eds. 1992. *The time of AIDS: Social analysis, theory, and method.* Newbury Park, Calif.: Sage Publications.

Herdt, G., and R. J. Stoller. 1990. *Intimate communications: Erotics and the study of culture.* New York: Columbia University Press.

Herek, G. M. 2004. Beyond homophobia: Thinking and sexual prejudice and stigma in the twenty-first century. *Sexuality Research and Social Policy* 1: 6–24.

Herman, D. 1997. *The anti-gay agenda: Orthodox vision and the Christian right.* Chicago: University of Chicago Press.

Hostetler, A., and G. Herdt. 1998. Culture, sexual lifeways, and developmental subjectivities: Rethinking sexual taxonomies. *Journal of Social Research* 65: 249–290.

Irvine, J. 2002. *Talk about sex.* Berkeley and Los Angeles: University of California Press.

Kinsey, A., B. Pomeroy, and C. E. Martin. 1948. *Sexual behavior and the human male.* Philadelphia: W. B. Saunders.

Kirby, D. 2001. Emerging answers: Research findings on programs to reduce teen pregnancy. *SIECUS Reports.*

Krieger, N. 1999. Embodying inequality: A review of concepts, measures, and methods for studying health consequences of discrimination. *International Journal of Health Services* 292: 295–352.

———. 2003. Genders, sexes, and health: what are the connections and why does it matter? *International Journal of Epidemiology* 32: 652–657.

Lancaster, R. N. 2003. *The trouble with nature: Sex in science and popular culture.* Berkeley and Los Angeles: University of California Press.

Laumann, E. O., J. H. Gagnon, R. T. Michael, and S. Michaels. 1994. *The social organization of sexuality: Sexual practices in the United States.* Chicago: University of Chicago Press.

Levine, M. 1998. *Gay macho: Life and death of the homosexual clone.* New York: NYU Press.

Levine, M., P. M. Nardi, and J. H. Gagnon, eds. 1997. *In changing times: Gay men and lesbians encounter HIV/AIDS.* Chicago: University of Chicago Press.

Lewin, E., and W. Leap, eds. 1996. *Out in the field.* Urbana: University of Illinois Press.

Lewis, O. 1961. *The children of Sánchez, autobiography of a Mexican family.* New York: Random House.

MacKinnon, C. A. 1987. *Feminism unmodified: Discourses on life and law.* Cambridge, Mass.: Harvard University Press.

Malluwa, M., P. Aggleton, and R. Parker. 2002. HIV and AIDS-related stigma, discrimination and human rights: A critical overview. *Health and Human Rights* 6: 1–18.

McBride, Dwight A. 2000. Can the queen speak? Racial essentialism, sexuality and the problem of authority. In *The greatest taboo: Homosexuality in black communities,* ed. D. C. Simms. Los Angeles: Alyson Books.

Miller, A. 2000. Sexual but not reproductive: Exploring the junction and disjunction of sexual and reproductive rights. *Health and Human Rights* 4: 68–109.

Moran, J. P. 2000. *Teaching sex: The shaping of adolescence in the twentieth century.* Cambridge, Mass.: Harvard University Press.

Parker, R. 1991. *Bodies, pleasures, and passions.* Boston: Beacon.

———. 1999. *Beneath the equator: Cultures of desire, male homosexuality, and emerging gay communities in Brazil.* New York: Routledge.

Parker, R. G., and P. Aggleton. 1999. *Culture, society and sexuality: A reader.* London: UCL Press.

Parker, R. G., R. M. Barbosa, and P. Aggleton. 2000. *Framing the sexual subject: The politics of gender, sexuality, and power.* Berkeley and Los Angeles: University of California Press.

Parker, R. G. and M. Carballo. 1990. Qualitative research on homosexual and bisexual behavior relevant to HIV/AIDS. *Journal of Sex Research* 27: 497–525.

Parker, R., M. Carballo, and G. Herdt. 1991. Sexual culture, HIV transmission, and AIDS research. *Journal of Sex Research* 28: 75–96.

Parker, R., and S. Correa. 2004. Sexuality, human rights, and demographic thinking: Connections and disjunctions in a changing world. *Sexuality Research and Social Policy* 1: 15–38.

Parker, R., G. Herdt, and M. Carballo. 1991. Sexual culture, HIV transmission, and AIDS research. *Journal of Sex Research* 281: 75–96.

Parker, R., S. Khan, and P. Aggleton. 1998. Conspicuous by their absence? Men who have sex with men (msm) in developing countries: Implications for HIV prevention. *Critical Public Health* 8 (4): 329–346.

Patton, C. 1997. Preface. In *Replacing citizenship: AIDS and radical democracy,* by M. P. Brown. New York: Guilford Press.

Paul, J., J. Catania, L. Pollack, J. Moskowitz, J. Canchola, T. Mills, D. Binson, and R. Stall. 2002. Suicide attempts among gay and bisexual men: Lifetime prevalence and antecedents. *American Journal of Public Health* 92: 1338–1345.

Petchesky, R. 2002. Sexual rights: Inventing a concept, mapping international practice. In *Framing the sexual subject,* ed. R. Parker, R. Barbosa, and P. Aggleton. Berkeley and Los Angeles: University of California Press.

———. 2003. *Global prescriptions: Gendering health and human rights.* London: Zed Books.

Preston-Whyte, E., C. Varga, H. Oosthuizen, R. Roberts, and F. Blose. 2000. Survival sex and HIV/AIDS in an African city. In *Framing the sexual subject: The politics of gender, sexuality, and power,* ed. R. G. Parker, R. M. Barbosa, and P. Aggleton. Berkeley and Los Angeles: University of California Press.

Robinson, P. A. 1999. *Gay lives: Homosexual autobiography from John Addington Symonds to Paul Monette.* Chicago: University of Chicago Press.

Rose, T. 1994. *Black noise.* Middletown, Conn.: Wesleyan University Press.

Roseberry, W. 1989. *Anthropologies and histories: Essays in culture, history, and political economy.* New Brunswick, N.J.: Rutgers University Press.

Rubin, G. 1984. Thinking sex: Notes for a radical theory of the politics of sexuality. In *Pleasure and danger: Exploring female sexuality,* ed. C. S. Vance. New York: Routledge and Kegan Paul.

———. 1997. Elegy for the valley of kings: AIDS and the leather community in San Francisco, 1981–1996. In *In changing times: : Gay men and lesbians encounter HIV/AIDS,* ed. M. Levine, P. Nardi, and J. Gagnon. Chicago: University of Chicago Press.

———. 2002. Studying sexual subcultures: Excavating the ethnography of gay communities in urban North America. In *Out in theory,* ed. E. Lewin and W. Leap. Urbana: University of Illinois Press.

Sedgwick, E. K. 1991. How to bring your kids up gay: The war on effeminate boys. *Social Context* 2: 19–27.

Setel, P. 1999. *A plague of paradoxes.* Chicago: University of Chicago Press.

Shweder, R. 1996. True ethnography: The lore, the law, and the lure. In *Ethnography and human development: Context and meaning,* ed. R. Jessor, A. Colby, and R. Shweder. Chicago: University of Chicago Press.

Stimpson, C. R. 1996. Women's studies and its discontents. *Dissent* 43: 67–75.

Surgeon General's Call to Action to Promote Sexual Health and Responsible Sexual Behavior. 2001. A Letter from the Surgeon General, U.S. Department of Health and Human Services. Office of the United States Surgeon General, July 9.

Teunis, N. 2001. Same-sex sexuality in Africa: A case study from Senegal. *AIDS and Behavior* 52: 173–182.

Tiefer, L. 2000. Discussion paper: Let's look at contexts. In *The role of theory in sex research,* ed. J. Bancroft. Bloomington: Indiana University Press.

Tolman, D. 2002. *Dilemmas of desire: Teenage girls talk about sexuality.* Cambridge, Mass.: Harvard University Press.

UNAIDS. 2002. Report on the global HIV/AIDS epidemic, July 2002. Barcelona report.

Vaid, U. 1995. *Virtual equality.* New York: Anchor Books.

Van der Meer, T. 2003. Dutch gay bashers. *Culture Sexuality and Health* 5 (2): 153–165.

———. 2004. Premodern origins of modern homosexuality and masculinity. *Sexuality Research and Social Policy* 12: 99–90.

Warner, M. 1999. *The trouble with normal.* New York: Free Press

Weeks, J., and J. Holland, eds. 1996. *Sexual cultures: communities, values, and intimacy.* New York: St. Martin's Press.

Weston, K. 1993. Lesbian/gay studies in the house of anthropology. *Annual Review of Anthropology* 22: 339–367.

# PART ONE

# Sexual Coercion
# and Sexual Stigma

It is remarkable that the topics of the essays in this part deal with forms of sexual oppression that can victimize everybody. Children from all racial and ethnic backgrounds and all social and economic classes suffer sexual abuse by family members or close family friends. Stigma is attached to HIV infection in many parts of the world and to individuals from all strata of society. Those who were forced into sexual slavery carry a burden of shame for the rest of their lives. Most individuals who enter a sexually charged environment are being sexually objectified.

This being the case, however, it becomes immediately apparent after reading these contributions that membership in an oppressed population, first, increases the chance that these types of violence will occur and, second, causes these forms of violence to carry greater consequences for their victims. Women, not men, carry the burden of *han* in Korean society after they were targeted for sexual abuse by Japanese occupiers. Men of color are not sexually objectified simply because of the way they look but because the color of their skin already puts them in an underprivileged position in society. And these men have a harder time balancing sexual objectification with a recognized agency in a hegemonically white community. Likewise, although many children suffer from childhood sexual abuse, Mexican gay men appear to suffer at much greater rates than their age mates do. Having suffered abuse, these men are then at great risk for HIV infection, given the oppressed position in society they occupy, a position that enabled the abuse in the first place. And once Latino gay men are HIV positive, they find that they are stigmatized and shunned by those of their own community. Their community members themselves experience so little control over the threat of infection with HIV that the only recourse they have is to create distance between themselves and those they know who are HIV positive.

The essays in this part explore these interfaces among sexual trauma, coercion, and sexual stigma, highlighting how lesser privilege increases the risk and enlarges the harmful consequences for those who suffer.

33

# CHAPTER I

# Childhood Sexual Abuse and HIV among Latino Gay Men

## The Price of Sexual Silence during the AIDS Epidemic

SONYA GRANT ARREOLA

In the mid-1980s, I worked as the director of an AIDS-prevention program in Long Beach, California. This program provided education and counseling to gay men who were struggling to avoid HIV infection or coping with being infected with HIV. The program evolved to include workshops for Spanish-speaking gay men, and I quickly learned that simply translating into Spanish the workshops designed for English-speaking gay men was woefully insufficient. Although the gay men who attended the clinic had much in common, it became clear that the differences between Latino gay men and non-Latino gay men went beyond the complexities of managing issues of discrimination, immigration, and language. Being Latino in a culture that did not value what they loved most about themselves led to feelings of invisibility. Over the years I was there, these men repeatedly tried to reveal themselves to me, hoping, and sometimes explicitly stating their wish, that I be able to capture their experiences and somehow give them voice.

Many years later, I still think of these young men fighting to be heard and wanting to make a difference for future generations. Among many of the stories they would share, their accounts of sexual initiation were particularly salient and seemed to be inextricably linked to their adult sexual experiences. Many related experiences of forced sex in childhood that sounded more severe, longer in duration, and more buried in secrecy than those I would hear from the men in the English-speaking groups. At that time, I was unable to make sense of what I was witnessing. Since then, I have learned of the dramatic influence childhood sexual abuse has on later risky sexual behaviors that are related to risk for HIV infection, and I have begun a research agenda that asks why and how it is that early childhood sexual experiences (especially abusive ones) have such a strong effect on later sexual risk-taking behaviors among Latino gay men. Most important, I recognized the central role of the subjective experiences of those whose lives we intend to interpret.

In the summer of 2001, after researching what little was known about childhood sexual abuse among Latino gay men, I had the privilege of interviewing Latino gay men who were eager to influence the discourse about the sexuality of Latino gay men generally, and childhood sexual abuse specifically. In this essay I will present some of what I have learned about Latino gay men, childhood sexual abuse, and HIV, drawing from the existing literature, my own quantitative research, and the voices of Latino gay men themselves. I will begin by presenting some of the epidemiology of HIV infection among Latino gay men, as it is precisely the disproportionate representation of Latino gay men among those infected with HIV in the United States that has, among other issues, motivated me to focus on this vulnerable population.

## Risk for HIV among Latino Gay Men in the United States

Latino gay men comprise one of the most vulnerable groups in the United States for transmission of HIV. Latino gay men have higher prevalence and incidence rates of HIV and are twice as likely to be infected with HIV as white gay men (Valleroy et al. 2000; Centers for Disease Control and Prevention 2001a). Further, Latino men who have sex with men have accounted for an increasing proportion of AIDS cases and have had smaller proportionate declines in AIDS incidence and deaths (Valleroy et al. 2000; Centers for Disease Control and Prevention 2001a). Even as high as these estimates are, the reported prevalence and incidence of HIV infection and AIDS among Latino gay/bisexual men probably underestimate the actual prevalence and incidence, owing to low rates of testing among ethnic minorities who engage in high-risk behaviors. Thirty-five percent of Latinos with perceived HIV risk or reported HIV risk behavior report never having been tested for HIV infection (Centers for Disease Control and Prevention 2001b). Nonetheless, the high rate of infection is consistent with the finding that Latino men report the highest rates of unprotected anal intercourse, compared to men from other ethnic minority groups (Díaz 1998).

More than 50 percent of Latino gay men report having had unprotected anal sex within a year of being asked, in spite of substantial knowledge about HIV, accurate perceptions of personal risk, and strong intentions to practice safer sex (Díaz 1998). These findings indicate that knowledge and the intention to practice safer sex may not be sufficient causes for the actual practice of safer sex. As a result of the qualitative interviews I conducted with Latino gay men, I would suggest that a history of childhood sexual abuse alters boys' cognitive and emotional orientation to the world, thereby inhibiting their ability to integrate their intentions to practice safer sex with their actual behavior. In particular, I believe the silence around sex generally, and around sexual desire for men and childhood sexual abuse specifically, all contribute to impeding integration of intention with actual behavior. In the following sections, I will present quantitative and qualitative findings that illustrate the enormous cost of silence concerning sex, especially childhood sexual abuse, to the well-being of Latino gay men. First I will explain why this question is so important: because of overwhelming evidence of a link between childhood sexual abuse and risk for HIV infection.

## Childhood Sexual Abuse and Risk for HIV Infection

There is compelling evidence that a history of childhood sexual abuse increases the likelihood of both psychological (e.g., depression, post-traumatic stress disorder) and biomedical (e.g., sexually transmitted infections) outcomes. One of the most robust findings is the link between childhood sexual abuse and HIV infection (Jinich et al. 1998; Paul et al. 2001). One explanation for this link is that men who have histories of childhood sexual abuse are more likely to engage in unprotected anal intercourse and to be infected with HIV (Jinich et al. 1998; Paul et al. 2001).

Compared to non–gay/bisexual men, the prevalence of childhood sexual abuse is higher among gay/bisexual men based on research comparing homosexual to heterosexual samples, as well as comparing sexual orientation in abused and nonabused samples (Cameron et al. 1986; Cunningham et al. 1994; Johnson and Shrier 1985). As high as the prevalence is among gay/bisexual men, it is even higher among Latino gay/bisexual men. Latino gay/bisexual men are twice as likely to have experienced childhood sexual abuse as non-Latino gay/bisexual men (Jinich et al. 1998; Arreola et al. In press). Not only is there a higher prevalence of childhood sexual abuse among Latino gay/bisexual men compared to non-Latino gay/bisexual men, the abuse is generally more severe among Latino boys: compared to African American boys, Latino boys are more likely to have been sexually abused by an extended family member such as a cousin or uncle, to have experienced more genital fondling, to have been exposed to more sexually abusive behaviors, and to have experienced more anal abuse (Moisan, Sanders-Phillips, and Moisan 1997; Lindholm and Willey 1986).

What struck me most about these findings is how they highlight some of the measurable costs of childhood sexual abuse (HIV infection, in this case) and make clear that Latino gay men are particularly vulnerable. However, they fail to explain how childhood sexual abuse may contribute to an increased likelihood of engaging in behaviors that lead to risk for HIV infection. Additionally, as I tried to understand these issues, I realized that researchers' assumptions varied regarding what constitutes childhood sexual abuse, and in some cases, researchers based their criteria for childhood sexual abuse on personal or political agendas.

## Definitions of Childhood Sexual Abuse

Although researchers attempting to define childhood sexual abuse all struggle with the cut-off age that distinguishes childhood from adulthood, generally ranging from thirteen to eighteen, definitions tend to fall into three conceptual categories. The first category emphasizes age differences between the child and the perpetrator of the abuse, usually of five or more years, noting that this age difference creates a power differential that presumably constitutes an abusive relationship. The second category focuses primarily on the subjective experience or self-report of a coercive or forced sexual episode. This may include specific descriptions of the actions of the perpetrator that would constitute pressure or force. Finally, the third and most restrictive category combines both the age differential and the subjective report of the respondent. For example, an individual would be considered to have experienced childhood sexual abuse if he or she reported having had sex, which he or she considered to be forced, before age sixteen, with someone five or more years older.

As a result of varying definitions or operationalizations of childhood sexual abuse in the literature, research findings attempting to document the effects of childhood sexual abuse in childhood also vary in their ability to capture the outcomes under investigation. Nevertheless, the finding that childhood sexual abuse increases risk for HIV-related outcomes is consistent regardless of how childhood sexual abuse is defined, though strongest when the most restricted definition is applied. My own research suggests that it is important to take into account the subjective experience of sexual encounters as well as age differential if we are to understand the mechanisms that explain the link between childhood sexual abuse and risk for HIV infection.

## Childhood Sexual Abuse and Risky Sexual Situations

When I performed preliminary quantitative analyses of a large representative sample of self-identified Latino gay men along a series of sexual-risk outcomes, I found no differences between Latino gay men who reported no sex before age sixteen and those who reported sex that was *not* against their will before age sixteen with someone five or more years older. These findings indicate how important it is to understand the subjective experiences of those whose lives we intend to interpret. It has been assumed that sex in childhood or adolescence with someone older is necessarily abusive, based on the implied power differential between the younger and older person. However, these data show that men's interpretation of early sexual experiences as voluntary predict outcomes that are similar to the outcomes for those who do not initiate sex until much later. In other words, those who initiate sex voluntarily before age sixteen, even if the partner is much older, are at no greater risk for HIV infection than those who do not initiate sex until much later.

I did, however, find significant differences between those reporting having had sex before age sixteen with someone five or more years older when it *was* against their will and those who had either no or voluntary sex before age sixteen. Specifically, compared to those who had no sex before age sixteen and those who had voluntary sex before age sixteen, those who reported nonvoluntary sex before age sixteen were significantly more likely to report sexual situations involving: (1) drug and or alcohol use, (2) an escape from loneliness or depression, (3) a nonmonogamous partner, and (4) difficulty maintaining an erection. Notably, there is a strong relationship between these risky sexual situations and actual sexual risk-taking behavior such as unprotected penetrative anal sex with someone whose HIV serostatus is unknown.

The findings that (1) sexual risk outcomes among Latino gay men who had voluntary sex before age sixteen are indistinguishable from those who had no sex before age sixteen, but (2) those who had nonvoluntary sex before age sixteen had riskier sexual profiles than the first two groups have political implications that go beyond the health implications mentioned earlier. They indicate that careful attention must be paid to the definition of childhood sexual abuse if we are to: (1) avoid betraying children abused in childhood by ignoring the abusive behavior and its effects, as well as (2) refrain from blindly labeling all juvenile sex as abusive and potentially providing ammunition for discrimination based on sexual orientation or ethnicity. I would argue that definitions of childhood sexual abuse must be specific and restrictive to include criteria based on actual subjective and objective empirical data.[1]

The link between nonvoluntary or forced sex before age sixteen and later sexual risk profiles also led me to wonder what it was about these early childhood sexual abuse experiences that led to risk for HIV infection. The data are important, as they point to some of the situational risks that help explain the link between childhood sexual abuse and risk for HIV infection. However, they did not capture the subjective experiences of the men whose lives I wanted to understand.

## The Latino Gay Men's Sexuality Study

After learning as much as I could from the existing literature and conducting some of my own preliminary analyses, I realized that I knew only other researchers' theories regarding the link between childhood sexual abuse and HIV, and that in my own investigations I asked questions using these same assumptions. I did not have any sense of how Latino gay men experienced childhood sexual abuse or how and whether they felt it was related to their current sexual lives. In the summer of 2001, I had the privilege of interviewing thirty self-identified Latino gay men living in the San Francisco Bay Area in two-hour-long individual in-depth interviews. The men were invited to participate in a study on Latino men's sexuality, and they were recruited from gay venues such as clubs, bars, social gatherings, and groups in the San Francisco Bay Area. I had thought that I would have to oversample for childhood sexual abuse in order to get a sufficient number of interviews with men who had experienced childhood sexual abuse. However, I accepted the first thirty men who met the criteria for the study, including: (1) age between twenty and forty, (2) self-identified as nonheterosexual, and (3) Latino or Hispanic. I was surprised to find that these first thirty men fell into three categories in thirds: Those who had had no sex before age sixteen; those who had had sex before age sixteen that they described as having been volitional; and those who had had sex before age sixteen that was forced. Their stories were consistent with the quantitative findings reported earlier, in that the first two groups described similar narratives regarding their adult sexuality, whereas the third group (those who reported forced sex before age sixteen) reported the most difficulty negotiating their adult sexual lives. I was struck by how often the men explained that they rarely or never talked about some aspect of their sexual development or the concerns they had about it with anyone. I was intrigued by their theories of how this silence influenced their adult sexual lives.

## SEXUAL SILENCE

All the men described some degree of silence about sex generally when growing up, and about gay sex particularly. Some men were able to articulate how this affected the way they approached sex as adults. For example, Juan, who had never been forced to have sex, explained that the silence around what it meant to love or have sex with another man led to his initiating sex with a young man his age (twelve years old) with the conviction that it was dirty and bad. He contrasted this with how proud he thought his father would have been if he had initiated sex with a girl. Juan tried to explain how this affected his adult sexual life: "The idea of keeping it a secret and feelings of guilt and shame around it are still really present when I start having sex as an adult." Juan went on to describe how he "never talked to anybody about it [sex] and it's something that I did in secret." This resulted in his sexuality becoming "kind of separate from my—my sexuality with men was separate from how—my individuality. It was like another persona."

Juan, like many of the men, tried to elucidate how attached his erotic life was to feelings of shame and guilt, and how, by extension, this made it difficult to integrate his feelings of desire for men with his sense of who he is as an individual presently. I believe it was adaptive for Juan to keep his feelings of attraction to men separate in the context of a family and environment that would denigrate him for having these feelings. However, the inability of his family and social environment to facilitate his making sense of and assimilating his developing sense of desire for men with loving and warm feelings resulted in his need to keep his sexual feelings separate (or silent, even to himself) from the rest of his developing sense of self. It is no wonder, then, that as an adult it would be difficult for him to integrate messages of safe sex into sexual situations and contexts that are already laden with feelings of guilt and disgrace. Or as Juan would say, "There was a whole separate secret identity around sex and I knew how to hide that and how to live with that, so it was easy to take living— it is easy to take that—keeping my sexuality a secret." The men would look to adulthood for a way to cope with these hidden desires.

Pablo, another interviewee, characterized the effect of growing up be-lieving sex with men was evil as "confusing." He described reaching adult-hood and seducing men as a way of feeling in charge. When I asked how he felt about it, he said: "Successful. I felt like a spider and they were like flies on my [web] in my trap. I got it. I'm going to get some [sex] tonight. I would feel like I got laid and it was just like an accomplishment, like I did it." Afterward, however, he "would feel like a tramp. At the same time I felt like a slut; I felt like a tramp; I felt cheap; I felt sleazy." Pablo was not unusual in his attempts to use sex as a way to feel better about himself, or in his apparent feeling of success during the encounter followed by a let-down and a need to cope with the ensuing self-condemnation. Pablo noted that it was in the context of telling me about these encounters that he could recall these feelings, since usually he tried to "not think too much" about them or about sex. I believe that the silence the men felt they needed to maintain regarding sexual feelings and behaviors in order to be in the world was critical for managing the dissonance between their feelings of love and desire for other men and the internalized sense of shame and guilt.

Another way the men looked to ease the tension they experienced when negotiating silenced internal desires that conflicted with societal and fa-milial norms was by abandoning their homes for a place where they might feel more accepted. In the interviews, the men generally began by dis-cussing how they had immigrated to the San Francisco Bay Area, or "gay Mecca," and what it meant to them to leave their homes in Latin Amer-ica, the Caribbean, or other parts of the United States. They came seek-ing refuge from environments in which they felt they had to be silent about their sexual identities, and they believed that in the Castro district (the gay neighborhood in San Francisco), they would discover the acceptance and freedom they had longed to find. Many did not find what they were seeking. Juan explains: "I think the Castro is really a complex situation because I think it is kind of politically designed to kind of—I think ex-clude people who are not white and gay. I don't feel like it is an inclusive society. Often when I've gone there I've always felt like an outsider." In-stead, they described finding themselves accepted as fetishized objects ("For the white guys it is just something different to be with a Latino guy," said Federico), who were appreciated for their exotic otherness in sexual encounters but ostracized from the rest of the cultural, economic, and intellectual life of San Francisco, unless, according to Alberto, "You look like the jeans guy." In spite of this objectification, some of the men said that they enjoyed and even played up their Latinoness, finding temporary distraction and pleasure in sexual encounters, but left these episodes feeling empty and lonely, and longing for intimacy and affection in their everyday lives. It was clear from the interviews that the manner in which Latino gay men are accepted into gay life reinforces their experience of separation of their sexual identities from the rest of the way they see themselves.

### SEXUAL INITIATION

Consistent with the quantitative data presented earlier, the men who described voluntary sexual initiation before age sixteen described as varied experiences as those who initiated voluntary sex after age sixteen, independent of the age difference between the partners. Although some men who initiated sex before age sixteen did so with partners their own age, many did so with much older partners. Carlos tells of his first love and sexual encounter at age thirteen with "a much older man":

One summer I would spend at my cousin—my other aunt's house in the beach area—I went to see my other cousin play soccer. I was biking and I just saw this very handsome man and we started talking. Next day I said oh my God, I'm in love I think. The next day I went to see him again and he was not playing. He had hurt himself and—it was so obvious that when I saw him, I got a hard-on and he noticed. It was so, so awkward that he noticed and he knows what was up. So the next day he invites me to bike around. He took me to this outdoor area and we had the great sex. It was first time I was penetrated. I know he was much older. I don't know how much. He was an adult.

Carlos also gives voice to the possibility of experiencing mutually respectful sex with someone much older:

And he was very careful and he probably was my first time. I didn't feel much pain. Anal sex can be painful. He was very tender and careful. It was great. It was very great and the next day there I was happy to see him again, and I went to visit his girlfriend. That was the end of it. But I still remember him with a lot of tenderness. I still remember him really well, the way he looked.

Finally, Carlos links his initial sexual experience with his adult views of his own sexuality: "How he treated me, which I think probably influenced the way I had sex from there on. I think it was a good experience, therefore, I see sex positive."

Carlos's story is testament to the importance of considering the subjective experience of sexuality when trying to understand childhood sexual abuse. Under some definitions, his experience would be construed as childhood sexual abuse, even though his narrative is full of fondness for the older man and their experience. Indeed, he attributes his positive sexual attitudes to this very encounter. To define Carlos' experience as childhood sexual abuse undermines the constructive power of his tender initiation, as well as the destructive and wounding effects of early coercive sexual experiences. One has only to read Ramon's story to fully grasp the difference between the two experiences.

## CHILDHOOD SEXUAL ABUSE

Ramón was eight years old the first time his uncle forced Ramón to have sex with him. Ramón captures the horror of a sexually abusive encounter when describing his memories of this abuse:

He would put his leg over me, or sometimes he would just put his arm and leg over me just to kind of hug me like an uncle. Like something that is nurturing me, but at the same time I would feel—I guess this woke me up. I would feel his erection and then I would feel his penis pulsate. You know how it pulsates. Then that woke me up and I guess he was horny and then he was just moving too much. Then he got my hand and he unzipped his pants and he pulled it out. He pulled out his dick and then he got my hand and he placed my hand on his dick. That completely woke me up and then I went into tremors and I started shaking. I remember I was shaking so much. I was so scared. I was petrified; I was nervous. I had never gone into like, you know, a nervous state like that before. I was just so nervous and I'm like oh my God. I was so scared. Then he would, without words, he would just grab my hand and he would go like this, like stroking. I want you to stroke my dick. And then he would say *volteate,* like turn around, and then he would turn me around. Then he pulled down my pants. I have shaking; I was nervous. Then he would pull down my underwear and he would spit on his hand and then lubricate me back there. Then he would lubricate his own and he would do me. All that happened in one night. So he, he penetrated me all the way. No protection.

Ramón's account reveals his initial confusion between the nurturing he expected from his uncle and the actuality of his uncle's blatant sexual objectification of young Ramón. When Ramón is finally "completely" awake, he is consumed with fear and anxiety. Ramón goes on to explain his disorientation: "Then I was just so nervous. I didn't know what was going on. What is he doing? I didn't sleep that night. I was just like wow, what happened? I was really scared like what happened. I didn't know what to think?" How could Ramón know what to think?

Ramón explains the importance of secrecy in maintaining his uncle's prospect for continued abuse:

I felt like something had happened that wasn't supposed to happen. That's how I felt. Something happened that wasn't supposed to happen. I just felt weird; I felt awkward, especially being around him. Then there was a moment the next day in the afternoon. He caught me by myself and then he grabbed me. He just kind of pulled me towards him and he's like—he spanked my ass and he's like this is my ass and this is our little secret. Don't tell anybody that we're doing this. Don't tell your mom; don't tell your brothers and sisters. This is our little secret. You are mine.

When asked whether he ever did tell anyone about this when he was a kid, Ramón exclaimed: "No, never. How can you talk about sex in a [Latino] family, in the traditional [Latino] family? How often do you talk about gay sex for that matter? How often do you talk about rape? Did I know what to do at that age? I kept it a secret." Ramón exemplifies what has long been documented in the literature about secrecy surrounding childhood sexual abuse.

Of the men who were abused sexually in childhood, about half stated that they had never talked about it with anyone else, and all said they had not talked about it with anyone else during childhood. This need to keep their experiences of childhood sexual abuse silent did not surprise me. I was, however, astonished by the deep levels of silence within themselves. In the stories of childhood sexual abuse, I was struck by the ability of the men to distance themselves from their experiences so dramatically as to be able to narrate these incidents as if they had happened to other people. This ability to dissociate themselves from the experience may have been an adaptive strategy for dealing with conflicting impulses in childhood. However, I believe that maintaining this split in adulthood contributes to some men's inability to integrate intended behaviors, such as safer sex, with actual practice. Keeping secret (especially from themselves) these early traumatic experiences makes the sense of humiliation and shame associated with sex that these men have internalized unavailable to consciousness. To the extent that the unwanted thoughts and feelings from the past are mingled with sexual desire in the present, sexual impulses are acted on without the benefit of creative mindful choosing.

Many of the men explained that the initially traumatic childhood sexual encounters were soon confused with the experience of pleasure. Of note, the men who reported being forced to have sex in childhood were forced into unwanted sexual activities over periods of time ranging from one summer to several years. None of the men reported an isolated incident of childhood sexual abuse. This is consistent with the finding that childhood sexual abuse is more severe among Latino gay men than among non-Latino gay men (Moisan, Sanders-Phillips, and Moisan 1997; Lindholm and Willey 1986). It made sense to me that they would want to keep silent about their experiences when they explained the rationale that perhaps they had deserved to be forced into having sex at such young ages, given that they would eventually get pleasure from it. However, when asked directly whether they believed they deserved it, they all said no.

Matched by social norms to maintain silence regarding childhood sexual abuse, it is no wonder that these men find no space in which to openly explore what they survived. Roberto tried to make clear how he thinks silence about sexuality affects his sexual behaviors: "Ah, well, I think it might lead to me having sex when I have said that I'm not going to, or changing some decisions, personal decisions I have made because I'm trying to please other people or kind of fit expectations or something." Roberto learned to put the wishes of others above his own. He goes on to give an explicit theory about the link with HIV: "my working theory about HIV being spread is that people don't really have a love for themselves or don't at the very heart of it think that they are worth protecting—so I'm not sure. I'm not sure to what degree that is true but that is the only thing I've been able to come up with as far as HIV spreading so quickly within communities of color."

## Conclusion

Roberto's theory regarding the importance of self-worth and self-love to HIV prevention was echoed throughout the interviews. Is it any wonder that Latino gay men would find loving themselves difficult, given a long history of repeated subtle and explicit messages signifying the worthlessness of gay men? These messages—communicated through lifelong statements disparaging men loving men in sexual ways; silence regarding those who are brave enough to do so; implicit suggestions that they are acceptable only as fetishized Latino sexual objects in the gay world; unacknowledged acts of violence against young effeminate or gay boys; and, in many instances, the unwitting or willful complicity of families, societies, and the legal, health-care, and scientific communities in these crimes—are powerful obstacles to Latino gay men's attempts to love themselves. It is easy to imagine Latino gay men who have grown up with these cumulative insults vacillating between feeling outraged and fighting against these insidious messages, and simply accepting them as truth, even if unconsciously. I believe that these implicit beliefs, fueled and maintained by harmful sociocultural norms, impede Latino gay men's intentions to protect themselves. These norms are all the more detrimental to the extent that they are conveyed silently or without recognition. It is harmful enough that some of these Latino gay men's sexual initiations were violent and abusive. It is truly reprehensible that their experiences were then silenced, leaving them to grow up attributing fault to themselves, thereby confirming to them that the feelings they had for other boys or men were inherently wrong. The commingling of shame and guilt with sexual desire makes open, caring, mindful sexual relationships very problematical.

The results of my research to date suggest several things. First, they highlight the critical roles of both qualitative and quantitative research in building a theory to explain complex human behaviors such as sex. Although my early quantitative data provided some grounding for the importance of the question, I could not have imagined the depth of the impact of childhood sexual abuse on the men's adult lives without having heard their stories. More important, their voices are what breathed life into my beginning understanding of the mechanisms that shape this process.

Second, the results direct the next steps in a research agenda that asks why and how it is that early childhood sexual experiences have such a strong effect on later sexual risk-taking behaviors among Latino gay men. Although childhood sexual abuse is only one of the issues of disempowerment that contribute to risk (see chapter 2), it is clearly one that deserves further research. It is important now to discover whether the themes I heard from Latino gay men between the ages of twenty and forty hold up among an older cohort of Latino gay men. Once the major themes are captured, coupled with theoretical implications from research in other areas, it will be beneficial to build and test a model that reflects these hypothesized mechanisms among a large representative sample of Latino gay men. Armed with data that show the contributing factors, including the sociocultural factors, that maintain this process, I think it will become more difficult to blame individuals for unsafe behavior and make it easier to point to the responsibility we all share for supporting individuals' intentions toward health. To the degree that sociocultural, -economic, and -political will contribute to accepting and supportive environments, individuals will be better able to comply with their stated intentions. Or, as Roberto implied, they will come to believe that they are worth protecting and loving.

Finally, these preliminary findings already point to the need for interventions targeting the sociocultural norms that support these devastating negative attitudes about gayness and preserve the silence that allows childhood sexual abuse to continue. It is unconscionable to place the burden of change exclusively on already-vulnerable individuals who are struggling with repeated powerful messages of worthlessness. Although I can understand the pressures, growing out of personal or cultural values, to remain silent , I think it is essential that we begin to challenge them if we want our Latino gay brothers, sons, cousins, and friends to live long, satisfying, and loving lives.

## Note

1. I thank the reviewers of this manuscript for highlighting the political implications of childhood sexual abuse definitions.

## References

Arreola, S. G., T. B. Neilands, L. M. Pollack, J. P. Paul, and J. A. Catania. 2005. Higher prevalence of childhood sexual abuse among Latino men who have sex with men than non-Latino men who have sex with men: Data from the Urban Men's Health Study. *Child Abuse and Neglect* 29: 285–290.

Cameron, P., K. Proctor, W. Coburn, and N. Forde. 1986. Child molestation and homosexuality. *Psychological Reports* 58 (1): 327–337.

Centers for Disease Control and Prevention. 2001a. HIV incidence among young men who have sex with men: Seven U.S. cities, 1994–2000. *Morbidity Mortality Weekly Reports* 50: 440–444.

———. 2001b. HIV testing among racial/ethnic minorities: United States, 1999. *U.S. Morbidity Mortality Weekly Reports* 50: 1054–1058.

Cunningham, R. M., A. R. Stiffman, P. Dore, and F. Earls. 1994. The association of physical and sexual abuse with HIV risk behaviors in adolescence and young adulthood: Implications for public health. *Child Abuse and Neglect* 18 (3): 233–245.

Díaz, R. M. 1998. *Latino gay men and HIV: Culture, sexuality, and risk behavior.* New York: Routledge.

Jinich, S., J. P. Paul, R. Stall, M. Acree, S. M. Kegeles, C. Hoff, and T. J. Coates. 1998. Childhood sexual abuse and HIV risk-taking behavior among gay and bisexual men. *AIDS and Behavior* 2 (1): 41–51.

Johnson, R. L., and D. K. Shrier. 1985. Sexual victimization of boys: Experience at an adolescent medicine clinic. *Journal of Adolescent Health Care* 6 (5): 372–376.

Lindholm, K. J., and R. Willey. 1986. Ethnic differences in child abuse and sexual abuse. *Hispanic Journal of Behavioral Sciences* 8 (2): 111–125.

Moisan, P. A., K. Sanders-Phillips, and P. M. Moisan. 1997. Ethnic differences in circumstances of abuse and symptoms of depression and anger among sexually abused black and Latino boys. *Child Abuse and Neglect* 21 (5): 473–488.

Paul, J. P., J. Catania, L. Pollack, and R. Stall. 2001. Understanding childhood sexual abuse as a predictor of sexual risk-taking among men who have sex with men: The Urban Men's Health Study. *Child Abuse and Neglect* 25 (4): 557–584.

Valleroy, L. A., D. A. MacKellar, J. M. Karon, D. H. Rosen, W. McFarland, D. A. Shehan, S. R. Stoyanoff, M. LaLota, D. D. Celentano, B. A. Koblin, H. Thiede, M. H. Katz, L. V. Torian, and R. S. Janssen. 2000. HIV prevalence and associated risks in young men who have sex with men: Young Men's Survey Study Group. *Journal of the American Medical Association* 284 (2): 198–204.

# CHAPTER 2

# In Our Own Backyard

*HIV/AIDS Stigmatization
in the Latino Gay Community*

RAFAEL M. DÍAZ

---

> "People who are [HIV] positive are hiding it from their
> families, hiding it from their co-workers, and hiding it from
> their friends. They do not want to be judged."
>
> Dr. Robert Scott, African American physician,
> quoted in the *San Francisco Chronicle,* July 24, 2002

I began this chapter just a few days after the closing ceremonies of the Fourteenth International AIDS Conference in Barcelona. The conference news was mostly bad, highlighted by the plight of the poor who die preventable deaths in Africa, Asia, and Latin America, with millions of orphans left behind. In the United States, facing our own—though perhaps less overwhelming—battles with the epidemic, HIV workers and researchers were shaken by grim statistics about the spread of HIV among young gay men. An alarming and surprising finding reported by the Centers for Disease Control and Prevention (CDC) rippled through the media, namely, that the majority (70 percent) of young (ages fifteen to twenty-nine) gay and bisexual men in the United States who are infected with HIV do not know their own serostatus. The findings came along with the all too familiar racial/ethnic disparity: 90 percent of young African American, 70 percent of young Latino, and 60 percent of young white gay men who are HIV positive do not know their HIV status. The scientific validity of the finding is supported by a carefully drawn probability sample of 5,719 men in six U.S. cities, involving both self-report and biomedical measures. Because knowledge and disclosure of one's HIV status is a crucial ingredient in negotiated safer sex practices, the news forecasts imminent disaster. The finding constitutes a real and upsetting challenge for HIV prevention practices, given the fact that gay/bisexual men in the United States are perhaps one of the most educated groups in the world regarding HIV, including the benefits of HIV testing.

The CDC data reported in Barcelona added yet another layer of disheartening complexity to recent studies that document significant increases in sexual risk behavior (Ekstrand et al. 1999) and unacceptably high HIV prevalence and incidence rates among young gay men, particularly young gay men of color (Valleroy et al. 2000). Recent increases in sexual risk behavior and the consequent rise in new HIV infections among gay men during the last few years have been attributed mostly to the impact of new HIV medications, that is, to a lessening of fear or caring about infection, as HIV/AIDS moves from a fatal to a manageable chronic disease. The proposed explanation is that young gay men in the United States—notably unfamiliar with the horrors of sickness, death, and dying witnessed by older generations of gay men prior to the use of protease inhibitors, and frequently exposed to live and printed images of healthy, muscular, and attractive HIV-positive men—do not fear the disease strongly enough to comply with the demands of safer sex practices. Thus, it is not surprising that the same interpretation has been given to the CDC's recent finding regarding young men's lack of serostatus awareness, namely, that it is just another indication of their lack of caring and concern, less pejoratively referred to as "HIV optimism."

Without discounting the possible impact of new HIV treatments on safer sex practices, I do believe that other interpretations of the CDC findings are possible, particularly if we examine the phenomena beyond the perspective of medical or health cost/benefits analyses. Although it is clear that there are multiple medical benefits of knowing your HIV status, it is time that we ask: What are the social costs? My hypothesis is that the presence of severe HIV/AIDS stigmatization within the gay community—experienced mostly in the context of romantic partnering and potential sexual situations—might be the main detractor for young gay men, particularly young gay men of color, from finding out their own HIV status. The social costs of stigmatizing rejection and alienation in response to an HIV-positive disclosure might far outweigh the medical benefits of knowing your status for the purpose of subjectively less pressing issues such as viral load monitoring and early treatment.

In an editorial published in the *American Journal of Public Health,* Valdiserri (2002) reviews the latest findings regarding HIV/AIDS stigma in the United States. Based mostly on Herek et al.'s (1993, 2002) data from population-based samples in the United States, Valdiserri reports both positive and negative news on the prevalence of HIV/AIDS stigma in the country, warning the reader about its role as an impediment in the fight against AIDS. Indeed, Herek et al. (2002) show that while there was a well-documented decrease of HIV/AIDS stigmatization in the U.S. population during the 1990s, in 1999, 20 percent of Americans still "feared" persons with AIDS (PWAs), 25 percent believe that PWAs "have gotten what they deserve," and 48 percent feel that "most people with AIDS are responsible for their illness." Valdiserri takes the editorial one step further, suggesting an implicit link to the avoidance of HIV testing:

The CDC estimates that as many as 300,000 persons living with HIV infection in America are unaware of their infection status. A broad range of studies has shown that, for some of these individuals, fear of receiving a positive test result remains a potent disincentive to seeking HIV testing. To what degree is this fear related to an understandable reluctance to learn that one has a life-threatening illness? How much of it can be ascribed to feelings of shame or concern about the potential for others to discover one's HIV infection? (Valdiserri 2002: 341)

Because there is general agreement that HIV/AIDS is perceived less and less as a life-threatening illness, particularly among young gay men (recall the "optimism" argument mentioned earlier), a more likely explanation is that the reluctance to become aware of one's HIV status is strongly connected to the fear of stigmatizing attitudes. Valdiserri's questions are in fact partly answered by his colleagues at the CDC, in the same issue of the *American Journal of Public Health,* in which Fortenberry et al. (2002) show a strong relationship between sexually transmitted disease–related stigma and not testing for either HIV or gonorrhea in the last year, even when statistically controlling for individual differences in age, gender, and health service utilization.

Most of our knowledge to date on HIV/AIDS stigma in the United States comes from studies conducted in the general population, and to my knowledge, there seem to be no equivalent studies of HIV/AIDS stigma among self-identified gay/bisexual men or among men who have sex with men, regardless of self-identification. Professor Herek confirmed this observation in a recent personal communication. However, a lack of studies of HIV/AIDS stigma among gay/bisexual men is not surprising, given the fact that stigmatizing attitudes toward PWAs correlates highly with antigay attitudes or prejudice against sexual minorities. Thus, most of the research on the issue has focused on correlating decreases of

HIV/AIDS stigma with decreases in sexual prejudice in the general population. Apparently, there is a hidden assumption that HIV/AIDS stigma is much lower to nonexistent among openly self-identified gay men.

## HIV Stigma as Internalized Oppression

For the past ten years, I have focused my research activities on documenting the impact of triple oppression—experiences of homophobia, racism, and poverty—on the psychological, social, and sexual lives of Latino gay men, in an attempt to understand their increased vulnerability to HIV infection. This research agenda is and has been of great personal importance to me, a Latino gay man living in San Francisco who has witnessed the devastation of the AIDS epidemic first-hand among lovers, friends, and brothers, particularly in communities of color. The research is motivated not only by the fact that HIV transmission among Latino gay men is disproportionately high, but also because sexual risk behavior (e.g., unprotected anal intercourse with nonmonogamous sexual partners) exists paradoxically in the presence of high levels of information, motivation, and skills to prevent HIV infection. As a research psychologist, I have been both troubled and intrigued by a set of puzzling research findings indicating that strong personal intentions to practice safer sex coexist with high rates of sexual risk behavior. Serious study and careful explanations were needed to make sense of this intention-behavior incongruence, beyond individual-based self-regulatory models of sexuality. If individual intentions do not predict what Latino gay men do sexually, then what, other than personal behavioral intentions, regulates and organizes their sexuality?

I started the work by investigating the day-to-day sexual lives—both social contexts and subjective experiences—of Latino gay men as they struggled to live and express their sexuality within a homophobic, heterosexist society, within a racially segregated gay community, and in the midst of a devastating sexually transmitted epidemic. The findings of this ten-year-old research agenda have been clear and consistent: HIV risk behavior occurs within particular contexts and situations—such as sexual activity aimed to alleviate exhaustion and depression, or sexual activity within relationships of unequal power—where it is extremely difficult, if not impossible, to act according to intentions for personal health and safety. Such high-risk sexual situations, my research shows, are strongly connected to individual and group histories of social (racial, economic, and sexual) discrimination and to the negative impact of such discrimination on men's social connectedness and self-worth (see, e.g., Díaz 1998; Díaz and Ayala 2001; Díaz, Ayala, and Bein 2004). It is obvious that the HIV epidemic among Latino gay men—as well as in many other communities of color—is shaped not by deficits in individuals' information, motivation, or skills, but rather by forces of social oppression, where poverty, racism, and homophobia organize sexual lives, creating contexts of sexual risk that compete with personal safer sex intentions.

Perhaps the most important and moving lesson from my research is the observation that social oppression seems to have its most devastating effects when it is internalized, that is, when men begin seeing themselves and one another with the eyes of the oppressor. The problem is not so much that men have been told time and again—through multiple channels and at different stages of development—that their homosexuality is shameful and dishonorable to their families. The problem is that such homophobic statements are now experienced as deeply felt shame and guilt in response to same-sex desire, and experienced as an internal sense of "dirtiness" that sometimes can be alleviated only by using psychoactive substances during homosexual encounters. The problem is not so much that many other gay men treat them as racially marked—dark and exotic—objects of sexual pleasure, but the fact that their sense of personal worth is highly dependent on their attributes as pleasurable and pleasing sexual objects. In other words, the data have pushed me to examine oppression not as events "out there," as what other people do to us, but rather as what we do now to ourselves, as well as to one another.

This essay is thus an attempt to examine one aspect of internalized oppression or discrimination as it happens "in our own backyard," in the form of HIV stigmatization within the Latino gay community. By *HIV stigmatization*, I refer to the expression of a cognitive and affective worldview—expressed as attitudes, beliefs, and behavior—in which HIV-positive men are seen and treated in discriminatory and morally demeaning ways. HIV stigmatization can be seen in the fact that HIV-positive men are often blamed for their own infection and are seen as morally deficient in ways that make them responsible for their own infection and the spread of HIV. This essay documents these stigmatizing beliefs and behavior on the part of HIV-negative men, and also explores the consequences of such stigmatization on the well-being of HIV-positive men. The essay ends with an attempt to explain the processes of HIV stigmatization as a sign of internalized oppression, as HIV-negative men—oppressed men themselves—try to cope in socially disruptive ways

with a sense of great vulnerability vis-à-vis HIV infection. My hope is that this essay will not be seen as another opportunity to blame the stigmatizers, who are victims themselves, but rather as a documentation of how internalized oppression makes social oppression even more deeply destructive to individuals and communities.

More specifically, this essay documents, qualitatively and quantitatively, the nature and prevalence of HIV/AIDS stigma among self-identified Latino gay/bisexual men in the United States. It also documents, descriptively as well as correlationally, the impact that such stigmatization has on HIV-positive men, in particular, its effects on their mental health and well-being. The data come from two studies—one qualitative (focus groups), the other quantitative (survey)—jointly titled "Nuestras Voces" (Our Voices). Nuestras Voces was a four-year (1996–1999) study designed to document the impact of social discrimination—homophobia, racism, and poverty—on the social and sexual lives of Latino gay men in the United States, focusing on the impact of social oppression on three health-related outcomes: sexual risk behavior, substance use/abuse, and psychological symptoms of anxiety and depression. As we began qualitative data collection for the study, we became painfully aware of heavily stigmatizing attitudes toward people infected with HIV, and thus included in our later quantitative survey a series of items that assessed stigmatizing attitudes in those who reported an HIV-negative status, and another set of items that assessed the impact of stigmatization on those who reported an HIV-positive status.

## Nuestras Voces: Findings from the Focus Group Study

Between December 1996 and March 1997, a total of 397 men were recruited in twenty-four Latino-identified gay bars in the cities of New York, Los Angeles, and Miami. Guided by a brief screening questionnaire, administered at the bar, men were invited to participate in the study only if they identified as Latino/Hispanic and as other than heterosexual. As required by the study design, approximately half of the men recruited were under the age of thirty ("younger" men) and the other half were thirty or older ("older" men); also, because half of the focus groups were conducted in Spanish, half of the sample had to indicate both dominance and preference in the Spanish language, as assessed by the screening instrument.

Men recruited at the bars were invited to participate in a two-hour focus group discussion for Latino gay/bisexual men about issues related to

HIV. Based on answers to screening questions, men were assigned and scheduled to participate in the appropriate age (younger vs. older) and language (English vs. Spanish) groups. Focus group interviews, ranging from four to fifteen participants, took place in marketing research facilities that were easily accessible to men in each city. The focus group interviews were audiotaped and later transcribed for qualitative analysis. Focus group questions centered on experiences of discrimination on account of being Latino and gay, issues of gay life as a man of color in the respective cities, sexuality, social and family networks, general well-being, the impact of AIDS, and reasons for Latinos to engage in unprotected sex in their respective cities. Immediately following the focus group discussion, participants were asked to fill out a short (four-page), individual, self-administered questionnaire, including items on demographic information, which took about fifteen minutes to complete. After the short survey, participants were thanked and given fifty dollars each as compensation for their participation.

As the following quotations suggest, we found a substantial number of negative attitudes expressed toward those who are infected with HIV, as well as accounts of how difficult it is for HIV-positive men to deal with such stigmatizing attitudes. HIV-positive men were often referred to as more promiscuous, interested only in sex, less caring about themselves or the welfare of others, ultimately responsible for getting infected, and, paradoxically, responsible for infecting others. There was general agreement that in many of the social circles that these men frequented, HIV status was a matter of "gossip," and that when the word is out about someone being HIV positive, that person is subjected to considerable rejection:

There's probably a bunch of guys in their circle that's positive that are really silent and not talking about it, because they're afraid of the gossip or people treating them bad, or nobody wanting to have sex with them anymore. Because I've seen this happen, you go into a club and I'll say to a friend of mine, "Oh that boy's cute." . . . "Positive!" It's like immediately they'll label that person and no one will want to either relate to them or have anything to do with them.

It was clear that many men in these social circles do not want to have sex with HIV-positive persons because it is perceived as a dangerous event, even when condoms are available or the sexual practice is objectively low-risk. In fact, there is a sense that *all* sexual activity with an HIV-positive man, even in the absence of semen or blood exchange, is dangerous. Consequently, there was a shared belief that HIV-negative men would not want to be boyfriends or partners with those who are HIV positive. "He wanted me to be his boyfriend. And I said, well, let's get to know each other better. . . . One of his best friends told me he was HIV-positive. And I talked to him and I go: I can be your friend but I cannot be your boyfriend, I cannot risk my life. And he went away from me, didn't want my friendship." It was clear that for that HIV-negative participant, becoming romantically involved with an HIV-positive man was seen as risky behavior ("I cannot risk my life"). Immediately after, another participant added: "Well you are better off without him because of the fact that he hid it from you to begin with; he should have been straight up."

The brief exchange quoted here illustrates one of the most challenging situations experienced by HIV-positive men in the context of romantic sexual interactions, namely, when is the best time to disclose serostatus to a potential boyfriend/lover? If you tell at the very beginning, some HIV-positive men remarked, the potential lover only sees you through that "HIV lens" or from that perspective. That is, the potential boyfriend will see only the HIV status, will impose all kinds of negative attributes and judgments, and ultimately will not take the opportunity to know the person beyond the HIV infection. On the other hand, if an HIV-positive person does not immediately disclose, with the hope of communicating and sharing about himself through lenses other than HIV, then he is typically blamed for not telling soon enough. If some sexual activity happens to occur before disclosure, even if the event was protected and carries no discernible risk of HIV transmission, the HIV-positive person is likely to be blamed for the lack of disclosure. This is the very real dilemma for an HIV-positive person who falls in love with an HIV-negative person: Delay HIV disclosure so the HIV-negative partner gets to know you first, but then get blamed for lack of early disclosure *versus* disclose as early as possible, but quickly get rejected without him knowing who you truly are. As someone in the sample suggested, it is a "lose-lose" situation.

Within this climate of discrimination, it was no surprise that many HIV-negative men expressed the fear that HIV-positive men will not typically disclose their status, or will even lie about their status. This was particularly poignant for those who suggested that many HIV-positive men, on account of the new HIV medications, appear healthy and muscular, and thus find it easy to "pass" as HIV negative. This situation, of potentially being lied to and unknowingly having sex with an HIV-positive man, led to some harsh and punitive attitudes: "I would have this system where you would have to go . . . it would be required by the law for you to get tested once every six months. Kind of like your car registration. If you came up positive, they would have a tattoo." In summary, we found multiple expressions of harsh attitudes, beliefs, and behaviors that revealed the presence of HIV/AIDS stigmatization in the Latino gay community, particularly among the younger men. Typically, HIV/AIDS stigma was expressed in terms of negative and morally demeaning descriptions of HIV-infected individuals, as well as by a resistance to relating—sexually or romantically—to them. The descriptions revealed processes of cognitive and interpersonal distancing, an "othering," that underlie prejudice and discriminatory behavior toward stigmatized populations (Lott 2002). Focus group participants expressed these stigmatizing attitudes and beliefs assuming that other members of the group were also HIV-negative and that HIV-positive men are those "other" people who were not present in the room. The stigmatizing comments in fact silenced the (undisclosed) HIV-positive participants, who never contested the allegations. Our exit interview data showed that many of these groups did include men who are HIV positive, and who disclosed their status privately and anonymously only in the self-administered exit interview given at the end of each focus group. Disclosure of an HIV-positive status in the context of the focus group discussion happened infrequently, and only in the context of the groups of older men. In the majority of cases, when it happened, HIV disclosure had the effect of tempering or virtually stopping the stigmatizing statements in the group discussion.

## Nuestras Voces: Findings from the Quantitative Survey

Based on the qualitative findings, we created survey items that assessed HIV/AIDS stigmatizing attitudes in order to estimate their prevalence as well as their impact on the health and well-being of HIV-positive men in a larger representative sample. Our research team converted the focus group narratives into a survey instrument that would reliably measure, among other constructs, HIV-negative men's stigmatizing attitudes toward HIV-positive men and, conversely, the impact of those stigmatizing attitudes on HIV-positive men. For example, we asked HIV-negative men questions such as:

Are HIV-positive people to blame for the spread of AIDS?

Are you willing to have an HIV-positive boyfriend or girlfriend?

If condoms are available, are you willing to have sex with someone who is HIV positive?

Do you believe that HIV-positive people are more sexually promiscuous?

The HIV-positive men, on the other hand, were asked questions about the impact of stigmatization, such as:

Has being HIV-positive made it more difficult to find sex?

Has being HIV-positive made it more difficult to find lover relationships?

Do you think that sexual partners would reject you if they knew you were HIV-positive?

Do you believe that you have to hide your HIV status to find acceptance from your family and friends?

How often have you been treated unfairly because you are HIV positive?

A quantitative survey in a probability sample of Latino gay men was extremely important for the following reason: Although the qualitative focus group data informed us with richness and depth about men's stigmatizing attitudes and behavior, only the quantitative data could give us the true dimensions of the problem, namely, how many men did actually share those stigmatizing beliefs? In addition, the quantitative data from HIV-positive men on their experiences of HIV discrimination could be used to assess correlationally the impact of such discrimination on their mental health and well-being.

Between October 1998 and March 1999, a time-location probability sample of 912 men was drawn from men entering social venues (bars, clubs, and weeknight events) identified as Latino and gay in the cities of New York, Miami, and Los Angeles. Details of the venue-based probability sampling procedures can be found in Díaz et al. (2001) and also in Díaz and Ayala (2001). We were able to approach a total of 5,097 men in the three cities. Of those, 3,086 (or 61 percent) agreed to be screened at the venue at the time of recruitment. Of those whom we screened at the venues, 1,546 (or 50 percent) met qualifying criteria for inclusion in the study. Of those who qualified, 1,324 (or 86 percent) gave contact information to be interviewed.

Appointments for individual interviews were made either at the time of recruitment or through the contact information. Interviews were conducted individually, and participants responded verbally to an interviewer in a face-to-face format. Interviews were administered in either English or Spanish according to the participant's stated language preference. Interviews occurred in different accessible locations (typically interviewing rooms of marketing research companies) in the three different cities. Interviewing stopped when we reached (actually, slightly exceeded) our goal, with an N = 912; n = 309 in New York; n = 302 in Miami; and n = 301 in Los Angeles. A discussion of results by different cities is beyond the scope of the present essay; thus, all data and analyses will be reported for the combined three-city sample. It should be noted, however, that all statistical analyses were conducted controlling for the effects of city, age, and degree of acculturation as measured by language use with friends.

## PREVALENCE OF HIV/AIDS STIGMA AMONG HIV-NEGATIVE MEN

Analysis of the data for HIV-negative men revealed a high prevalence of stigmatizing attitudes toward people infected with HIV. More than half of the sample (57 percent) believed that HIV-positive individuals are responsible for getting infected, and close to half (46 percent) of the sample believed that HIV-positive persons are to be blamed for the spread of AIDS. In addition, 52 percent of the sample saw HIV-positive men as more sexually promiscuous, and 18 percent believed that they are people who cannot be trusted. In the realm of sexual interactions and romantic relationships, the overwhelming majority (82 percent) of HIV-negative men felt that sex with HIV-positive men is dangerous, with 57 percent saying that they were not willing to have sex with an HIV-positive person even if condoms were available. Close to two-thirds (57 percent) of HIV-negative men reported that they were not willing to have an HIV-positive person as a boyfriend or girlfriend.

## IMPACT OF HIV/AIDS STIGMA ON HIV-POSITIVE MEN

A large proportion of HIV-positive men in the sample reported that being HIV positive has negatively affected their social and sexual lives, beyond the physical/medical challenges posed by their HIV infection. For example, about half of the sample (46 percent) felt that HIV had made it more difficult for them to find sex and an even lager proportion (58 percent) felt that HIV made it more difficult to find lover relationships. Two-thirds (66 percent) of the sample reported that HIV has made it harder for them to enjoy sex. On items closely related to the presence of HIV/AIDS stigma, nearly half (46 percent) of all HIV-positive participants reported having been treated unfairly because of their serostatus and

45 percent believed that they had to hide their status to find acceptance from their families and friends. The overwhelming majority (82 percent) of HIV-positive men thought sexual partners might reject them if they knew their HIV serostatus, a finding that is not surprising and exactly mirrors the fact (reported earlier) that 82 percent of HIV-negative men believe that sex with an HIV-positive man is a dangerous event.

## CONSEQUENCES OF HIV/AIDS STIGMA FOR THE WELL-BEING OF HIV-POSITIVE MEN

Based on data from the Nuestras Voces survey, we have reported elsewhere the impact of triple oppression—homophobia, racism, and poverty—on the mental health of Latino gay/bisexual men, based on an analysis that combined both HIV-negative and HIV-positive men (Díaz et al. 2001). Using a series of multiple linear regression equations, we were able to show that triple oppression affects mental health (operationalized as the presence of psychological symptoms), and that this impact is mediated through levels of social isolation and low self-esteem. In other words, triple oppression affects mental health by producing higher levels of social isolation and lower levels of self-esteem, which in turn are related to a higher prevalence of psychological symptoms of anxiety and depression, including suicidal ideation. We also showed that measures of resiliency (including assessments of family acceptance, satisfaction with social and sexual networks, community involvement, and having gay role models in childhood) positively affected the mediators by improving self-esteem and diminishing social isolation. The whole multivariate mediational model (see Díaz et al. 2001 for details) predicted 38 percent of the variance ($R^2 = .38$) in psychological symptoms for the whole sample.

In order to test the impact of HIV/AIDS stigma on the well-being of HIV-positive men, for the purpose of this essay, we repeated the multivariate model only with HIV-positive men, using the following analytic procedures. First, we predicted social isolation and low self-esteem as outcomes in an equation that included experiences of the three oppressors—homophobia, poverty, and racism—and resiliency factors (labeled the "basic" model). We then repeated the analysis, adding to the basic model a fourth measure of oppression, namely, the impact of HIV stigmatization described earlier (labeled the "enhanced" model). We then tested the impact of HIV stigmatization by comparing the increases in the variance explained ($\Delta R^2$) from the basic to the enhanced model. Following these procedures, we found a large increase in the proportion of variance explained for social isolation with $R^2$ = .30 for the basic model and $R^2$ = .48 for the enhanced model ($\Delta R^2$ = .18, p < .0001) by the addition of the HIV/AIDS stigma variable. For the outcome of low self-esteem, we found a modest though statistically significant increase in the proportion of variance explained, with $R^2$ = .28 for the basic model and $R^2$ = .31 for the enhanced model ($\Delta R^2$ = .03, p < .05). Finally, we repeated the "basic-enhanced" model comparison to predict psychological symptoms, this time including social isolation and low self-esteem as additional predictors in the model. For this outcome of psychological symptoms, we found a high and significant increase in the proportion of variance explained with $R^2$ = .24 for the basic model and $R^2$ = .35 for the enhanced model ($\Delta R^2$ = .11, p < .01), indicating again the negative and powerful impact of HIV/AIDS stigmatization on the mental health and psychological well-being of HIV-positive Latino gay men.

## Discussion

In this essay, we have defined HIV stigmatization as the expression of a cognitive and affective worldview—expressed as attitudes, beliefs, and behavior—in which HIV-positive individuals are seen and treated in discriminatory and morally demeaning ways. HIV stigmatization is evident when HIV-positive individuals are blamed for their own infection and are perceived as both dangerous and morally deficient in ways that make them responsible for both their own infection and the spread of HIV to innocent others. The two—qualitative and quantitative—studies we reported here show that HIV/AIDS–related stigmatization is highly prevalent in the Latino gay community.

Specifically, HIV/AIDS stigmatization was expressed as a set of beliefs that portray HIV-positive men as sexually promiscuous and uncaring, as ultimately responsible (paradoxically) both for their own infections and for infecting others. Stigmatization was particularly evident in the context of sexual and romantic relations, with many HIV-negative men stating that they would not have sex with an HIV-positive person even if condoms were available, and would not have an HIV-positive person as a boyfriend, girlfriend, or lover. The prevalence rates of stigmatizing beliefs among this group of self-identified gay and bisexual men is comparable to and even higher than those reported by Herek et al. (2002) for the general U.S. population. For example, 48 percent of the U.S. population endorsed an item stating that HIV-infected individuals are responsible for their own infection; a comparable item was endorsed by an even higher proportion (57 percent) of the Latino gay men sampled.

Thus, the most important question at hand is: What explains such high rates of HIV/AIDS stigmatization among self-identified gay/bisexual men, who are relatively highly educated and who possess substantial knowledge about HIV/AIDS? I offer three possible hypotheses.

First, given the difficult demands of condom use 100 percent of the time and the negative attitudes about condoms shared by this population, many men are trying to achieve protection in sexual encounters by establishing seroconcordance with sexual partners. That is, sexual safety vis-à-vis HIV infection is established not by condom use but by finding a partner who shares the same HIV status. Establishing seroconcordance is part of negotiated safer sex practices, a popular practice adopted by many gay men and endorsed by many public health officials. It is possible that what we have measured as HIV stigmatization (e.g., not willing to have sex with an HIV-positive partner) is partly an expression of such attempts at negotiated safety. Other stigmatizing beliefs and attitudes could be seen as "secondary effects" of negotiated safety, as men attempt to sort out partners around HIV-status. Making stereotypical statements about the character, personality, and behavior of HIV-positive could be seen as attempts to sort out potential partners with markers other than direct disclosure, particularly when asking or telling directly is seen as conflictual or confrontational in the context of sexual and romantic relationships. In other words, if HIV-positive men are uncaring and promiscuous, and this particular person is not, then he cannot be HIV positive; so the (largely subconscious) logic would go.

A second hypothesis is that HIV stigmatization is used as a way to regulate the sense of HIV vulnerability among a group that is objectively highly vulnerable to HIV infection, given the relative high rates of unprotected intercourse and the high prevalence of HIV infection among their sexual partners. Stigmatization, among other things, is an expression of deeper processes of "distancing" and "othering," in which the stigmatized person or group is clearly established as different—morally and behaviorally—from the self or the self-referent group. Thus, functionally, the stigmatization process affirms the cognition that "I am not like that" and, therefore, not likely to be infected. It is clear to many of us that vicious homophobic attacks (verbal or physical) can be carried out by men who are insecure about their manhood or who fear their own homosexual impulses; in this case, the stigmatizing attitudes and behavior reaffirm the difference between self and homosexuals. A similar process may take place with respect to HIV status for those men who feel highly vulnerable and afraid of infection; in this case, HIV-related stigmatization assuages their fear by creating an "other" personality or person (different from the self) to whom HIV happens.

A third hypothesis, closely related to the second, is that HIV stigmatization is a reflection of unresolved internalized homophobia, where, within the gay community, HIV-positive men become the target of internalized negative attitudes toward homosexuality. In our focus group transcripts, attributes of promiscuity and uncaring hypersexuality—typically found in homophobic discourses—seemed to be rerouted and redefined as attributes of HIV-positive men. At times, it seemed as if men were making a distinction between "good gays" and "bad gays," where the latter—those truly deserving of homophobic accusations—are the ones that get HIV. This process of "displaced abjection" (Stallybrass and White 1996) is perhaps the most profound and destructive effect of oppression, and it is not surprising to find it among highly victimized and oppressed groups.

Regardless of the reasons that may explain the high levels of HIV stigmatization among Latino gay men, our data are clear about the negative impact that such stigmatization has on HIV-positive men. We found substantive evidence that HIV stigmatization constitutes an independent predictor of social isolation, low self-esteem, and psychological symptoms among HIV-positive men. Empirically, HIV stigmatization functions as yet another oppressor, adding a fourth layer of negative influence to men already oppressed by poverty, racism, and homophobia. Taking into account these findings from the Nuestras Voces study, I am not surprised that the CDC reported such high levels of unknown HIV status among young gay men. I am convinced more than ever that this lack of HIV awareness is not a reflection of "HIV optimism," as many public health discourses affirm, but rather is a reflection of the high social costs an HIV-positive diagnosis entails. Prevention efforts among gay men in the United States cannot proceed without careful attention to the prevalence and effects of HIV stigmatization, which is seemingly rampant within the gay community.

## References

Díaz, R M. 1998. *Latino gay men and HIV: Culture, sexuality and risk behavior.* New York: Routledge.

Díaz R. M., and G. Ayala. 2001. Social discrimination and health: The case of Latino gay men and HIV risk. Policy Institute of the National Gay and Lesbian Task Force.

Díaz, R. M., G. Ayala, and E. Bein. 2004. Sexual risk as an outcome of social oppression: Data from a probability sample of Latino gay men in three US cities. *Cultural Diversity and Ethnic Minority Psychology* 10: 255–267.

Díaz, R. M., G. Ayala, E. Bein, J. Henne, and B. V. Marin. 2001. The impact of homophobia, poverty, and racism on the mental health of gay and bisexual men: Findings from 3 US cities. *American Journal of Public Health* 91: 927–932.

Ekstrand, M. L., R. D. Stall, J. P. Paul, D. H. Osmond, and T. J. Coates. 1999. Gay men report high rates of unprotected anal sex with partners of unknown or discordant HIV status. *AIDS* 13: 1525–1533.

Fortenberry, J. D., M. Mcfarlane, A. Bleakley, S. Bull, M. Fishbein, D. M. Grimley, C. K. Malotte, and B. P. Stoner. 2002. Relationships of stigma and shame to gonorrhea and HIV screening. *American Journal of Public Health* 92: 378–381.

Herek, G. M., and J. P. Capitanio. 1993. Public reactions to AIDS in the United States: A second decade of stigma. *American Journal of Public Health* 83: 574–577.

Herek G. M., J. P. Capitanio, and K. F. Widaman. 2002. HIV-related stigma and knowledge in the United States: Prevalence and trends, 1991–1999. *American Journal of Public Health* 92: 371–377.

Lott, B. 2002. Cognitive and behavioral distancing from the poor. *American Psychologist.* 57: 100–110.

Stallybrass, P., and A. White. 1996. *The politics and poetics of transgression.* Ithaca, N.Y.: Cornell University Press.

Valdiserri, R. O. 2002. "HIV/AIDS stigma: An impediment to public health." *American Journal of Public Health* 92: 341–342.

Valleroy, L. A., D. A. MacKellar, J. M. Karon, D. H. Rosen, W. McFarland, D. A. Shehan, S. R. Stoyanoff, M. LaLota, D. D. Celentano, B. A. Koblin, H. Thiede, M. H. Katz, L. V. Torian, and R. S. Janssen. 2000. HIV prevalence and associated risks in young men who have sex with men. *Journal of the American Medical Association* 284: 198–204.

# CHAPTER 3

# Knowing Girls

*Gender and Learning in
School-Based Sexuality Education*

JESSICA FIELDS

In spring 1996, I took a graduate course on feminist theory. The instructor and other students were all women. One afternoon, at the beginning of class, another graduate student told us that she had been surprised to learn the night before that her son's eighth-grade sexuality education class included lessons on clitoral and vaginal orgasms. Many of us in the room were similarly surprised and troubled. We wondered aloud if eighth-graders needed such intimate information about women's and girls' bodies. What would they do with the information? One woman eventually interrupted and asked what we found threatening about young people's access to this information. What place did we think girls' pleasure should have in young people's sexuality education? When did we want young people to learn about clitorises and orgasms?

That same semester, North Carolina's state newspapers featured stories on a new state law requiring schools to teach students "the risks of premarital sexual intercourse" (North Carolina State Board of Education/Department of Public Instruction 1996). According to "Teach Abstinence until Marriage" (TAUM), as the legislation was known, school-based instruction was to focus on what the legislature called "medically accurate" information about sexual danger and risk, including risks of pregnancy, contraceptive failure rates, and the risks of HIV and other sexually transmitted infections (STI) (North Carolina General Assembly 1995).[1] Local debates emphasized girls' vulnerability to pregnancy and exploitation (Fields forthcoming). I decided to explore further the issue of young people gaining sexual knowledge—the implications for adults and young people of students learning through schools about sexuality. I was especially concerned with the lessons about girls' and women's bodies, pleasure, and desire that North Carolina's public schools would provide under TAUM. The lessons available at the local liberal private school about girls' and women's sexual pleasure may have initially struck my colleagues and me as risqué. However, the early responses to TAUM in the state's public schools indicated that students would receive lessons that were troubling for different reasons. These lessons, typical of contemporary school-based sexuality education, would cast girls as consistently at risk of pregnancy, disease, victimization, and moral compromise (Fine 1988; Kempner 2004). Along with my colleagues in the graduate seminar, I had been surprised and initially unsettled to learn that a middle-school curriculum would cast female sexuality as a site of pleasure: the information seemed itself to compromise young women's and girls' safety. However, when I confronted North Carolina's legislated alternative of learning about girls' and women's sexuality solely as a site of danger, I was more deeply concerned. Discussions of the possibilities for pleasure and danger in women's and girls' sexual lives have long been troubling to many audiences—conservatives and feminists included (see, for example, Fine 1988; Vance 1984). The continuing debate over abstinence-only education in U.S. schools indicates that these discussions continue to trouble.

This essay explores the competing understandings of sexual knowledge and female sexuality that advocates, educators, and students brought to sexuality education classrooms and community debates; I focus in particular on sexuality education in a public North Carolina middle school. After discussing the setting and methods of my research, I sketch teacher and student experiences of sexuality education: the significance they attached to knowing, not knowing, and being curious about girls' and women's sexuality. The public school teacher strove to present sexual knowledge as rational and separable from sexual attitudes and behaviors. However, students' classroom interactions suggest, first, that knowledge and behavior were relentlessly intertwined, gendered, and sexualized practices and, second, that knowledge about girls as well as girls' knowledge were especially treacherous. Next I discuss the understandings of sexual knowledge that adult educators, researchers, and community activists brought to their discussions of school-based sexuality education. I find that even those who disagreed about curricular issues shared an epistemological assumption that sexuality educators' responsibilities included maintaining an asexual classroom. Educators asked students to arrive in their classrooms either (1) innocent of sexual knowledge or experience, or (2) willing to redefine their previous sexual understandings and experiences as misunderstandings and missteps. In both abstinence-only and abstinence-plus models, students were to be receptive to the official knowledge that would allow them to adopt healthy sexual behaviors. In the concluding pages, I explore the inadequacy of these assumptions and consider how educators and policy makers might respond differently, acknowledging the many ways in which, for young people, sexual knowledge is rife with questions of sexual identity, desires, and practices.

## Research Setting: Southern County, North Carolina

In 1995, North Carolina's General Assembly passed Teach Abstinence until Marriage, legislation that required public schools to provide sexuality education that emphasized "the positive benefits of abstaining from sex outside of marriage and the risks of premarital sex." The legislation's liberal opponents managed to include in its final version a stipulation that permitted local districts to teach students about, for example, contraception or abortion if they adopted such abstinence-plus curricula after first debating them in public school board meetings. After a period of community review in which parents were invited to examine proposed materials and curricular objectives, school boards would convene for public comment and then vote on their county's sexuality education program.

I attended and studied these public meetings in Southern County, North Carolina.[2] As part of a Bible Belt state, Southern is subject to conservative state laws that, for example, do not allow insurance carriers to cover the cost of contraceptives; deny state funding for abortions except in the case of rape, incest, or when women's lives are in danger; and require parental consent for minors and a waiting period before performing abortions. Teach Abstinence until Marriage requires that public schools provide information on pregnancy and disease prevention, including HIV/AIDS; however, that information rests in a conservative curriculum that officially emphasizes that those who engage in sexual behavior outside of heterosexual marriage risk broad psychological, physical, and social harm.

Southern County is part of Metropolitan Region, a three-county region of North Carolina with a population of almost one million that includes Southern, Gardner, and Jefferson counties. In comparison with the rest of North Carolina, Metropolitan Region is characterized by prosperity, liberal politics, and sexual progressivism. Metropolitan's affluence is not, however, evenly distributed. One-third to one-half of Metropolitan Region renters' housing costs are beyond their means (North Carolina Low Income Housing Coalition 2004); and while Metropolitan Region is as a whole more prosperous than the rest of North Carolina, white residents are the primary beneficiaries of Metropolitan's affluence. In Southern County, African American residents constitute 40 percent of the county's population and 57 percent of those in poverty. Similarly, Southern's political and sexual progressivism is contested: the county is home not only to a lesbian, gay, bisexual, and transgender youth organization and community center, but also to a chapter of the Christian Coalition, members of which were active in the Southern County sexuality education debate.

In Southern County's community forums on abstinence-only education, educators and parents advanced visions of how schools can help girls and boys weather what most participating adults perceived to be a crisis of adolescent promiscuity, pregnancy, and disease. I was interested in the process and outcomes of these debates: who would attend these meetings, what positions they would advance, and what visions would prevail. I recognized, however, that administrative and legislative decisions were only moments in an ongoing process of curricular negotiation (Schaafsma 1998). Administrators may adopt instructional programs—in this case, abstinence-only or abstinence-plus sexuality education programs—and teachers may faithfully implement those priorities. Alternatively, teachers may adapt administration priorities to meet their own instructional aims as well as the challenges they anticipate in the classroom. Once inside the classroom, the negotiations continue as students receive, resist, and revise their teachers' lessons. Thus, in addition to participant observation in school board meetings, I attended middle-school sexuality education classrooms to study the informal negotiations that would help determine what the state's abstinence legislation would mean for North Carolina's communities, schools, and students.

Southern County public schools served more than twenty-five thousand students, the majority of whom (60 percent) were African American; almost half (45 percent) were eligible for free or subsidized school lunches in 1998–1999. Robeson Middle School was one of Southern's eight middle schools housing grades six to eight. Robeson students were generally eleven to fourteen years old, though a few of them were younger or older because they had skipped or repeated grades. The school offered a six- to nine-week health education course to coeducational classes of twenty to thirty students; about two weeks of this course were spent on an abstinence-plus curriculum.

Rose Gianni was Robeson's health and sexuality education teacher. Ms. Gianni, as her students called her, was an Italian American woman in her midtwenties who had moved recently from the northeastern United States to North Carolina. Ms. Gianni was trained as a health educator, but she had been hired as a science teacher at Robeson Middle School. After one year at Robeson, she successfully lobbied the principal to create a separate health curriculum that would be part of Robeson's physical education department. Ms. Gianni worked in a former home economics classroom, complete with ovens, refrigerators, countertops, and adjacent laundry facilities. This setting confirmed that Ms. Gianni's course was an afterthought in Robeson's curriculum. Undeterred, Ms. Gianni hung health education posters and student work around the room and transformed the classroom into "the health room." Students sat at desks grouped in clusters of four or five, facing the chalkboard and projection screen at the front of the room.

## Research Methods and Practices

From July 1996 to March 1998, I conducted approximately three hundred hours of participant observation in school board and administrative meetings and middle-school sexuality education classrooms.[3] At Robeson, I observed the whole of the school's six- to nine-week coeducational health class, two weeks of which focused on sexuality issues. After each participant observation session, I recorded near-verbatim fieldnotes, noting what I observed in the setting and my reactions to my observations. I also interviewed administrators, educators, and students. Interviews lasted from thirty minutes to three hours. I interviewed people in their homes, offices, restaurants, and coffeehouses. I tape recorded and, with the help of paid transcribers, transcribed all of the interviews. Throughout my fieldwork, I wrote "notes-on-notes" soon after fieldwork or an interview in order to develop early analysis (Kleinman and Copp 1993; Lofland and Lofland [1971] 1995). After completing data collection, I identified themes that ran across my fieldnotes, interviews, and notes-on-notes. I then sorted the data and analytical notes thematically; the patterns I explore in this essay emerged during that interpretive process.

Like other feminist researchers (see, for example, Bordo 1990; Haraway 1988; Reinharz 1992; Smith 1987), I recognize and even insist that my fieldwork and analysis reflect my social position, biography, and commitments. Russell Shuttleworth argues that researchers who participate in the "lifeworld of informants" write the most incisive ethnographic analyses (see chapter 8). According to Shuttleworth, one becomes a participatory ethnographer through either a shared identity or "a prolonged intimate association with the researched group or research issue." My research indicates that those associations take multiple forms. Some of the ways I associated with respondents were not of my choosing, many were neither prolonged nor intimate, but all were in some way participatory and instructive.

First, age characterized my associations with students. Fieldwork in the classroom with young people poses particular challenges (Fine and Sandstrom 1988). Chief among those is how not to appear like most adults in the children's worlds—that is, like an authority figure. Though I entered the classroom through adult gatekeepers (in each school, my first contact was with a teacher), I did not want to be associated exclusively with them. I tried to position myself, as much as possible, as a "friend" (Fine and Sandstrom 1988: 17–18; Thorne 1995). I sat with students, not teachers, during classes, and I did not "tell on" students if they misbehaved. I usually refused when students asked me to intervene as a teacher might, claiming ignorance about school policy or that I did not have the proper authority; I stepped in only if no other adult was in the room and someone was in danger of being hurt. I do not mean to suggest that I was able to shed my adult authority. Few students refused my request for an interview. Though I assured them that the interviews were entirely voluntary, I routinely suspected that they were participating because adults and teachers had encouraged them to do so. However, though the students readily consented to interviews, many were reluctant to talk with me about their sexuality education and offered only perfunctory answers to my questions once the interview began. They found ways to resist and, in doing so, suggested that students negotiate—and do not simply accept—adult authority. My interviews with students necessarily reflect those negotiations as students offered their descriptions of sexuality education to an interviewer who may have seemed friendlike but remained an adult.

If my status as an adult complicated my fieldwork, so too did my lesbian sexuality (Lewin and Leap 1996; Newton 2000). Interviews with conservative Christians were especially challenging: they would explain to me that homosexuality was a sin and unnatural. In turn, I nodded, took notes, and left those interviews exhausted and scared. During participant observation in classrooms, the silence about gay, lesbian, and bisexuality itself felt deafening. When people did address GLB sexuality, their language was often painful to hear. I sat through lessons in which teachers explained that homosexuality was illegal in North Carolina. I listened to students call one another "fag" and "lezzie."

I was consciously closeted about my sexuality—that is, I passed as straight—in interviews with abstinence-only advocates. I realized near the end of my time in Robeson Middle School how closeted I had been with students and teachers. I became particularly friendly with Jimmy, an African American sixth grader at Robeson Middle School. Jimmy's assigned seat was near mine, and we often chatted before and after class. Most days I wore slacks and a blouse to Robeson. Toward the end of my fieldwork, I became more relaxed and wore more casual pants to school one day; as I left the house, I noted that I felt more like myself than I had in weeks of fieldwork. As Jimmy left class that afternoon, he said, "No offense, but you look like a tomboy today." Jimmy's comment marked for me how I had managed my sexuality not only by not disclosing it verbally but also by adopting a conventionally feminine mode of self-presentation. I had been aware of dressing conservatively when I interviewed Christian activists; now I understood that I was also making a concerted— if unconscious—effort to mask my lesbianism while visiting schools.

Race and gender were also fundamental to my analytical position in this study and to my relationships with respondents. Most African American women were cautious approaching me—a white, apparently middle-class woman who was trying to understand sexuality education in a predominantly African American and low-income school system. Some African American respondents seemed never to speak to me frankly. On the other hand, white women were often surprisingly quick to trust me and to assume that, even if I disagreed with their views on youth, sexuality, or education, I would represent their interests fairly in any publications and presentations that resulted from my research. Though some were more reticent than others, all of the women—regardless of race— honored my request for an interview. Two men refused my requests, and during interviews all men seemed impatient for the conversation to end. Rather than celebrate white people's openness or consider the reticence of African Americans, men, and young people something to overcome in order to achieve full disclosure, I "recognize the performative qualities of social life and talk" (Atkinson and Coffey 2001: 802) and consider the respondents' openness and caution instructive. Both point to rules governing talk about sexuality in Southern County and Robeson Middle School.

My critical feminism informed my work in ways over which I had more control. I am concerned with power and justice in sexuality education, and I have a long-standing commitment to challenging oppressive ideologies and material conditions that compromise all women's and girls' sexual freedom. These theoretical and political commitments informed my data collection and analysis practice. For example, I shared with abstinence-plus advocates readings and other resources that supported their defeat of abstinence-only instruction. My analysis of knowledge of and about girls' bodies in sexuality education has roots also in symbolic interactionism (Blumer 1969). That is, I examine the meanings that people ascribe to girls' bodies as they discuss female sexuality and what those meanings imply for girls' and women's experiences of themselves. I approach the discourse about sexuality education, knowledge, and female bodies as "language that constitutes rather than reflects reality" (Miller 2000: 317). Thus, I consider the debates and classroom instruction in Southern County moments in which educators, young people, parents, and policy makers negotiated, taught, and learned the social meanings of sexuality, knowledge, and female bodies.

## Knowing Behavior: Sexual Knowledge in the Classroom

Ms. Gianni was popular with her students, who, in interviews with me, said they liked her sense of humor, youth, and no-nonsense classroom style. On her classroom door, Ms. Gianni had posted a hand-drawn sign that read "Ms. Gianni's K.A.B. Company" and pictured a yellow taxicab. Inside the room was a poster, also hand-drawn, that read as follows.

KNOWLEDGE

+

ATTITUDE

+

BEHAVIOR

=

HEALTH

This poster hung in Ms. Gianni's classroom throughout the school year, but it was of particular importance at the beginning of the health unit. On her first day with each new group of students, Ms. Gianni stood before the poster and explained what she called "the health equation": their health, sexual and otherwise, depended on all parts of the K.A.B.—what they knew, the attitudes they adopted, and how they behaved. As their teacher—"the K.A.B. driver"—she would provide them with the knowledge necessary to making healthy decisions about how to behave. Students' attitudes and behaviors were their responsibilities—concerns about which they would decide on their own, after leaving her classroom.

The implicit and explicit logic of Ms. Gianni's health equation characterizes many researchers' and educators' understandings of knowledge and sexuality. School-based sexuality education rests in large part on the "instrumental" assumption of a causal relationship among discrete items: knowledge, attitudes, behavior, and sexual health (Moran 2000). As Ms. Gianni's poster and explanation demonstrate, all pieces of the "health equation" contribute to a person's sexual well-being. However, the pieces are not of equal weight or concern in the sexuality education classroom. Knowledge and attitudes foster particular behaviors; as Ms. Gianni presented it to her students, the causal link begins there. Knowledge is the schools' responsibility, while individuals must tend independently to their attitudes and decide on behaviors.

This division was not an easy one to maintain. Students flirt, harass, menstruate, get erections, date, break up, and have crushes at school; and sexuality education addresses many of these concerns more directly than any other middle-school class. (See Table 3.1 for Ms. Gianni's curriculum.) The trainers and administrators who prepared Ms. Gianni and her colleagues to implement the county's sexuality education curriculum directed the teachers to desexualize students' concerns and to approach bodily issues with the detachment of medicine or science (fieldnotes). Knowledge was to take precedence over attitudes and behaviors.

Ms. Gianni embraced these desexualizing strategies; as she recounted to me after the close of the school year, "I discussed the parts and the functions the same way I did the brain and the spinal cord." At the beginning of her sexuality education unit, Ms. Gianni established ground rules, one of which was that no one should speak directly from her or his own experience or ask about another person's experiences. Instead, she asked students to refer to unnamed "friends" or to pose entirely hypothetical questions. Ms. Gianni also stripped sexuality education of most of its sexual and social significance. The clitoris, for example, was "erectile tissue" in Ms. Gianni's classroom—she did not describe the clitoris as a site of sexual pleasure or as a body part that is often obscured in a society that routinely denies women's sexual agency and desires. "Puberty" was a series of "primary and secondary sex characteristics." Ms. Gianni offered students a question box in which they could anonymously drop slips of pa-

TABLE 3.1. Sexuality Education Curriculum, Robeson Middle School

| Grade | Lesson Topics |
| --- | --- |
| 6 | Definitions of health; conflict resolution; "I" statements; guidelines for discussion; reproductive system—definitions, functions, processes; puberty and associated changes (video); sexuality in song lyrics; hygiene; unwanted touch and sexual assault; dating; test; adolescents in families |
| 7 | Definitions of health; conflict resolution; guidelines for discussion; pretest; basic sexuality; changes during adolescence; reproductive system—definitions, functions, processes; pregnancy and fetal development; pregnancy prevention; HIV/AIDS prevention; STDs and STD prevention; breast and testicular self-examination; abstinence; test |
| 8 | Definitions of health; life goals; guidelines for discussion; pretest; reproductive system—definitions, functions, processes; media messages about sexuality; HIV/AIDS prevention; STDs and STD prevention; sexual assault; sexual harassment; date rape (guest speakers); pregnancy prevention; test |

per with questions about sexuality—questions they were reluctant to ask out loud. The students asked questions about girls experiencing pain during sex, heterosexual anal intercourse, and girls masturbating. Ms. Gianni reported that she found answering these questions to be challenging and that her strategy was "to be very technical and get through it quickly" (interview). Ms. Gianni and most other teachers I observed were adamant: sexual knowledge was decidedly neither sexual nor personal (Fields 2001). Gender was similarly uncomplicated: composed of femaleness and maleness, both of which Ms. Gianni traced easily to bodies with clearly different parts and functions. Gender ambiguity and transgender experiences were absent from all discussions, as was any attention to the social significance of gender.

Despite her efforts, the "A" and "B" of Ms. Gianni's K.A.B. formula were ever-present as attitudes about sexual knowledge found expression in students' behavior. Throughout my fieldwork, I watched middle-school girls and boys retch, groan, laugh, and avert their eyes when their teachers played sexuality education videos detailing the physical changes associated with puberty, explained menstruation, or discussed the mechanics of vaginal-penile intercourse. Both girls and boys participated in this degradation ritual, but to different ends. Images of penises and discussions of boys' and men's erections, wet dreams, and sperm and semen seemed to titillate students, eliciting laughter and shrieks. Female bodies and bodily functions, on the other hand, elicited contempt, and this scorn for women's bodies encouraged girls to publicly degrade their own bodies through the moans, laughter, and aversion they shared with their classmates.

The girls I interviewed feared that their classmates associated their bodies with those depicted in classroom videos, textbooks, discussions, and flip charts. This association was consistently sexualized and potentially humiliating. For example, Kamii Stewart, an African American girl in the sixth grade, described for me her greatest concern about Ms. Gianni's sexuality education class:

> *Kamii:* The boys would see the picture of one of the girls with nothing on them.
>
> *Jessica:* What did that make you feel like?
>
> *Kamii:* Weird. . . . That maybe they could be picturing you, and they might pick on you about some stuff that you have and they do not. (Interview)

Kamii's concerns were not unique. Girls regularly spoke in interviews about their embarrassment when the subject turned to female bodies.

Boys, on the other hand, sometimes expressed similar embarrassment about having to talk with girls about sex and puberty, but they did not worry either that their peers would confuse their bodies with the bodies they discussed in class or that the information their peers gained would become fodder for teasing. When I asked Charles, an African American sixth grader in Kamii's class, how he felt about having sexuality education with girls, he, like many other boys, said that he sometimes wished they were not in the room. However, in words that also echoed the sentiments of other boys, Charles added, "It is kind of neat, though, that they were there because now they know what happens to males also" (interview). The meaning of knowing was differently gendered for girls and boys in Ms. Gianni's sixth-grade sexuality education classroom. While both might experience some embarrassment, girls, more than boys, found that with knowledge came vulnerability.

Ms. Gianni's health equation suggested that attitudes would come later in her students' lives. However, students' classroom interactions indicate that attitudes already informed their experiences of learning and knowing. Knowledge of female bodies seemed synonymous with knowing the specific female bodies now occupying the classroom. Despite Ms. Gianni's efforts to offer sexual knowledge as rational and disembodied, many students behaved as if knowledge of female sexuality was comparable with sexual intimacy. Students told me that the classroom was an always-sexual space for them. Curiosity in the sexuality education classroom was sexual; knowledge was sexual; so too was ignorance. According to many of their peers, what students knew and did not know reflected directly on their sexual experience. Girls complained in interviews that if they answered one of Ms. Gianni's questions incorrectly, they would be signaling to classmates that they were sexually inexperienced. Bethany was a seventh-grade white girl. As her story makes clear, the alternative was no less appealing: if girls knew too much, their classmates might believe they were sexually promiscuous.

> *Bethany:*  Like I told you, that one time I did not get an answer right [in class], and somebody walked up to me in the hallway [afterward] and asked me if I was a virgin because I did not know the answer.
>
> *Jessica:*  Do you remember what the question was?
>
> *Bethany:*  I think it was on the male reproductive system. So, they think if you do not know the stuff, then you're a virgin and do not do nothing. But if you know it, then you are not a virgin and you do a lot of stuff.

The double-edged sword that characterizes standards of girls' sexual behavior (Risman and Schwartz 2002) extended into the classroom and their pursuit of knowledge. Girls could neither know nor not know about sexuality; either way they were vulnerable—as the tired story goes, either prudes or sluts.

## The Public Debate: Knowing in Abstinence-Plus and Abstinence-Only Sexuality Education

Southern County's public debate over sexuality education was in large part a struggle over knowledge—both the curricular issues of what and when students should know *and* epistemological questions about what it means for young people to know about sexual behaviors, desires, and identities. Citizens disagreed over which curriculum would be best for Southern County schools—abstinence-only or abstinence-plus (Fields 2001). However, like Ms. Gianni, all embraced instrumentalist aims and "supported sexuality education for the behavioral and social changes it promised to deliver" (Moran 2000: 35). Within this instrumentalist view, sexual knowledge promotes or discourages particular sexual behaviors, and sexuality educators provide students with the information about puberty and sexuality that they believe will advantageously influence their later behavior and health. Information about contraceptives might, for example, help a student avert pregnancy or sexually transmitted infection

(STI), or information on the failure rates of condoms might help convince students that there is no possibility of safe sexual behavior. In either case, to promote sexual knowledge and understanding was to encourage particular behaviors in their sexual lives. Sexuality educators' task was to postpone initiation of students' sexual lives until outside the classroom, in their adulthoods, after they were married. Sexuality education did not recognize the sexual worlds students always and already inhabited as young people, regardless of whether they had sexual partners.

### THE COMFORT OF NOT KNOWING

Though Southern's curriculum offered little guidance in how to address young people's everyday sexual concerns, ironically, the struggles of girls like Kamii and Bethany helped to propel Southern County's sexuality education debate. A small but vocal group of conservative Christians led those adults who were fighting for abstinence-only curricula in Southern County school board meetings, wrote letters to the editor, and held workshops advocating abstinence-only education in the county's schools. These homemakers, conservative activists, real estate agents, physicians, accountants, educators, and computer consultants argued for instruction that established a single standard for adolescent sexual activity: that there be none. If girls were to be safe inside the classroom and out, abstinence-only advocates argued, their sexuality should remain inactive, unspoken of, and virginal.

Eleanor Taylor was a white homemaker in her forties, a conservative Christian, a wife, and the mother of three school-age children. I interviewed her in her large home in a wealthy residential neighborhood of Southern County. Taylor explained that if girls were appropriately pure, they would find mixed-gender conversation about female sexuality not simply embarrassing but actually unbearable:

I have a little ten-year-old girl, and she would just die if she had to sit in a mixed classroom like that. And I don't think there's anything wrong with that. I think that's perfectly OK. . . . I would think there was something wrong if she wasn't embarrassed to sit there and talk about how to put in a tampon and everything else with guys sitting all around her. I would think that was strange. (Interview)

Taylor expected her daughter to find coeducational conversations about menstruation and sexuality mortifying and would have thought it "strange" to learn that her daughter was comfortable talking with boys about her own and their bodies.

Tammy Reynolds echoed Taylor's comments. Reynolds was a married, Christian, white woman in her forties; she worked outside the home. Reynolds spoke at school board meetings and wrote letters to the editor of state newspapers throughout the Southern County debate, motivated by the series of indignities that she believed her daughter had suffered in Southern public schools. Reynolds argued that sexuality education equipped boys to express sexual aggression and to harass their female classmates. She described one of these events: "One little boy said to Rebecca, 'Tomorrow I'm going to learn about your vagina.' As a fifth grader, that just totally—I mean, it just threw her. She came home crying. She didn't know what to wear to school the next day. She wanted to wear something from [her neck] down to her ankles" (Interview). Reynolds and other conservatives feared that knowledge of female bodies equipped boys to harass girls. Sexuality education debased Rebecca's sexuality—indeed, her vagina—and exposed her to ridicule.

If school-based sexuality education compromised girls' modesty in the classroom, abstinence-only proponents argued, their modesty outside of school would be similarly threatened. Throughout the Southern County debates, abstinence-only advocates promoted a conventional vision of heterosexuality in which women appeal to men in part because they are inscrutable and exotic. Lee Ann Finch, a married, Christian, white woman in her fifties, directed a pregnancy support services agency. She explained, "You need to separate the boys and the girls anyhow, because you are breaking down all of those inhibitions. You know, there's nothing left that's mysterious, and you want that [mystery]. Romance is built on a little bit of not knowing everything" (interview). Echoing conventional and conservative cultural scripts of female sexuality, Finch worried that sexuality education, and in particular coeducational sexuality education, compromised the mystery and romance that lent value to women's bodies.

The response of Reynolds and other abstinence-only proponents to the real threat of sexual harassment was to shut down discussions of sexuality. They did not confront the boy's sexism or defuse the threat of the boy's knowledge by exploring with him what it means to know about vaginas and working to decouple sexual knowledge, vulnerability, and aggression. In this conservative understanding of sexuality education, boys could not learn about female bodies without also leaving girls vulnerable to harassment. When the subject was sex, boys' curiosity, which was a usually laudable characteristic in students, signaled for abstinence-only advocates prurient and predatory interests.

## THE PROTECTION OF KNOWING

A coalition of schoolteachers, health care providers, and health educators from local reproductive rights and HIV/AIDS service organizations opposed the abstinence-only curriculum that Reynolds, Finch, and Taylor advocated. The opposition advocated instead that Southern County adopt an abstinence-plus sexuality education curriculum. Such programs address topics many consider controversial (for example, masturbation, abortion, and gay and lesbian sexuality) and offer practical skills for disease and pregnancy prevention. In community debates and letters to the editor, proponents of abstinence-plus education routinely cast sexuality as a contentious terrain for which educators had to prepare girls and boys with necessary information and understanding.

Those advocating abstinence-plus sexuality education routinely articulated a fundamental trust in the exchange of information. Cobi Lewis was a twenty-something white lesbian who directed a leadership program for lesbian, gay, bisexual, and transgender (LGBT) youths in Southern County. Lewis linked dialogue and education to queer liberation: "Any discussion around sexuality helps us. It is opening doors for people to talk about their sexual lives, which we need to do desperately, [and] not just about queer stuff" (interview). Similarly, Gina Beale, an African American woman in her early thirties, advocated abstinence-plus sexuality education in her work as a public health educator, teacher trainer, and citizen advisor to Southern's school board. Like other supporters of abstinence-plus sexuality education curricula, Beale argued, "I just do not believe education harms anything" (interview). Beale argued that any sexuality education that successfully promoted sexual health would have to include frank discussions of female bodies: "I think we fail kids when we do not give them as much knowledge as they need to know about their bodies. . . . We [need to] know what our physical bodies look like. We need to understand—girls especially, we need to know how we got to where we are physically" (interview). Lewis, like Beale, embraced education and knowing as means to sexual well-being. In doing so, they failed to address the challenges girls faced in sexuality education classes when the subject was female sexuality. As Kamii's and Bethany's accounts of Ms. Gianni's classroom indicate, not all discussions were helpful, and classroom education was sometimes harmful.

Abstinence-plus educators did recognize, however, that girls, as girls, confront sexual dangers, but they located those dangers *outside* the classroom. Like Ms. Gianni, they posited the classroom as a place in which students learn to prepare for later sexual behaviors. For example, Elaine

Adams, an African American school board member and community leader in her late forties, was unwavering in her support for abstinence-plus sexuality education in Southern County schools. Sitting in Adams's office at one of North Carolina's strongest historically black public universities, I asked her what she considered important about providing Southern's students with abstinence-plus sexuality education. Adams's response typifies the call for schools to provide students with a comprehensive store of protective knowledge: "You must give individuals the arsenal, and the ability, and the ammunition to deal with any encounters. . . . You need to make a decision [about whether to be sexually active]. If that decision is, 'No, I'm not gonna do this'—great. But what if you decide that you are? . . . You do not prepare a person for war without giving them some weapons." Like other abstinence-plus advocates, Adams looked to school-based sexuality education to offer young people the understanding necessary to navigate a fearsome sexual world characterized by violence and loss. The sexual terrain for which Adams and other abstinence-plus advocates aimed to prepare young people was external to the classroom and not, as the students experienced it, integral to the classroom environment.

## Conclusions

This essay opened with my initial discomfort with eighth graders learning about women's orgasms and clitorises. When I began this project, the prospect of a boy understanding female sexual pleasure left my feminist colleagues and me feeling vulnerable; the knowledge felt dangerous. My research suggests that lessons about female sexual pleasure and bodies violate a widely held tenet that female sexuality is most valuable and least vulnerable when unknown and unknowable.

Ironically, my feminist classmates and I shared with conservative Christians in Southern County a strategy for protecting our sexual selves from this victimization. The conservative women with whom I spoke thought that as sexuality education made female sexuality knowable, it compromised girls' chastity and made girls vulnerable to male aggression. They wanted to halt conversations about sexuality in the school to prevent the debasement of girls and women. Those administrators and sexuality educators who promoted abstinence-plus sexuality education also recognized dangers in female sexuality. Rather than seek protection in conventional femininity and marriage, as abstinence-only proponents did, abstinence-plus advocates sought refuge in desexualized, abstracted representations of female sexuality. Schoolteachers' stance of objectivity allowed them to retreat from the social and political complexities of sexuality. Female sexual desires, pleasures, and danger became biological concerns—definable, knowable, and manageable.

Barbara Smith ([1983] 1998) notes that "more than a little courage is required" to challenge sexism and heterosexism in the classroom (p. 114). Educators and researchers need a critique of sexism in sexuality education—a critique that allows for an association between the sex organs depicted in student worksheets and the bodies students and teachers inhabit in the classroom and that confronts the systemic oppression that makes that association so treacherous. The patterns of gender and sexual inequality characterizing our society make lessons against sexism critical to girls' and women's healthy sexual lives. Critical feminist sexuality education might aim to create classroom environments in which students and teachers learn and know out of a commitment to recognizing and contending with sexual desires, power, and inequality. My interviews with students suggest that they are ready to participate in such an effort. When I asked Lyonne Murphy, an African American / Native American seventh grader at Robeson Middle School, what she wanted from her school-based sexuality education, she answered, "I think we need a social time. You need to socialize; that's a part of your life, too. . . . They're not teaching us that in regular school. I think they should make a time for socializing, just 30 or 15 minutes. Then we learn other people's problems, and they can learn ours, and we could just see how we could work it out" (interview). Lyonne's response anticipates new conversations among students—beyond those in which students refuse to become sexually active, discern the risks posed by their partners' sexual histories, or insist on contraceptives. Lyonne's "social time" is more than a chance to hang out with one's friends. It is a "social education" (Lees 1986: 149–150) that recognizes young people's contribution to, curiosity about, and knowledge of sexual identities, desires, and possibilities.

For most of the middle-school girls I observed, sexual knowledge was not about fighting off abstract enemies—STI, pregnancy, and an aggressive boy that might characterize abstinence-plus educators' war. Nor did sexual knowledge mark their initiation into a sexual world, as abstinence-only advocates feared. Instead, sexual knowledge was part of the girls' lives right now. As symbolic interactionists and feminists argue, the institutional and ideological conditions of sexuality and knowledge are products of human interaction and social conditions, and people can subvert these conditions. We can remake the ways we talk, learn, and know about sexuality and strive for an antisexist sexuality education that would address what it means to know and learn about girls' bodies and sexuality. In such a sexuality education, we would engage critically with oppressive attitudes about sexuality, gender, and girls' and women's bodies. We would explore the ways that knowledge, ideas, and behaviors are inextricably linked, and, indeed, come to understand and appreciate the pleasure and significance of knowing about clitoral and vaginal orgasms.

## Notes

For insightful comments and critiques, I thank Sherryl Kleinman, Gilbert Herdt, Kate Holum, Jamie Small, Niels Teunis, the members of my University of North Carolina and San Francisco State University writing groups, and the other contributors to *Sexual Inequalities*. A Sexuality Research Fellowship from the Social Science Research Council, with funds from the Ford Foundation, supported this research. I received additional support from a University of North Carolina (UNC) Royster Society of Fellows Dissertation Completion Fellowship, Jessie Ball duPont Fellowship for Studies in Early Adolescence, UNC Off-Campus Dissertation Research Fellowship, Woodrow Wilson–Johnson & Johnson Dissertation Grant in Women's Health, and Society for the Psychological Study of Social Issues Grant-in-Aid. Finally, I want to recognize the support I received from the San Francisco State University Human Sexuality Studies Program and the National Sexuality Resource Center through an award from the Ford Foundation Grant on Practitioner Training and Education (Gilbert Herdt, director).

1. Many sexuality researchers and educators now use the term *sexually transmitted infections* (STI) instead of *sexually transmitted diseases* (STD). *Infection* is the broader term. *STD* most accurately refers only to those infections that are causing symptoms.

2. I have changed the names of respondents, counties, and schools. I refer to North Carolina and its Teach Abstinence until Marriage legislation by their actual names.

3. I focused on middle schools because North Carolina's formal school-based sexuality education begins there and because early adolescence is generally understood to be a time of profound physical, social, and other sexual changes for girls and boys.

## References

Atkinson, P., and A. Coffey. 2001. Revisiting the relationship between participant observation and interviewing. In *Handbook of interview research: Context and method,* ed. J. F. Gubrium and J. A. Holstein. Thousand Oaks, Calif.: Sage Publications.

Blumer, H. 1969. *Symbolic interactionism: Perspective and method.* Berkeley and Los Angeles: University of California Press.

Bordo, S. 1990. Feminism, postmodernism, and gender-skepticism. In *Feminism/postmodernism,* ed. L. Nicholson. New York: Routledge.

Fields, J. 2001. Risky lessons: Sexuality and inequality in school-based sex education. Ph.D. diss., University of North Carolina at Chapel Hill.

———. Forthcoming. Children-having-children: Race, innocence, and sexuality education. *Social Problems.*

Fine, G. A., and K. L. Sandstrom. 1988. *Knowing children: Issues of participant observation with minors.* Beverly Hills, Calif.: Sage Publications.

Fine, M. 1988. Sexuality, schooling, and adolescent females: The missing discourse of desire. *Harvard Educational Review* 58: 29–53.

Haraway, D. 1988. Situated knowledges: The science question in feminism and the privilege of partial experience. *Feminist Studies* 14 (3): 575–600.

Kempner, M. E. 2004. More than just say no: What some abstinence-only-until-marriage curricula teach young people about gender. *SIECUS Report* 32 (3).

Kleinman, S., and M. A. Copp. 1993. *Emotions and fieldwork.* Newbury Park, Calif.: Sage Publications.

Lees, S. 1986. *Losing out: Sexuality and adolescent girls.* London: Hutchinson.

Lewin, E., and W. L. Leap, eds. 1996. *Out in the field: Reflections of lesbian and gay anthropologists.* Champaign: University of Illinois Press.

Lofland, J., and L. H. Lofland. [1971] 1995. *Analyzing social settings: A guide to qualitative observation and analysis.* Belmont, Calif.: Wadsworth.

Miller, L. J. 2000. The poverty of truth-seeking: Postmodernism, discourse analysis, and critical feminism. *Theory and Psychology* 10 (3): 313–352.

Moran, J. P. 2000. *Teaching sex: The shaping of adolescence in the twentieth century.* Cambridge, Mass.: Harvard University Press.

Newton, E. 2000. *Margaret Mead made me gay: Personal essays, public ideas.* Durham, N.C.: Duke University Press.

North Carolina General Assembly. 1995. Ratified House Bill 834. Teach Abstinence until Marriage (short title).

North Carolina Low Income Housing Coalition. 2004. County statistics. Retrieved July 22, 2004, from www.nclihc.org/stats/countyindex.shtml.

North Carolina State Board of Education/Department of Public Instruction. 1996. Healthful living curriculum: Grade 7. Retrieved April 25, 2001, from www.dpi .state.nc.us/curriculum/health/grade_7.htm.

Reinharz, S. 1992. *Feminist methods in social research.* New York: Oxford University Press.

Risman, B., and P. Schwartz. 2002. After the sexual revolution: Gender politics in teen dating. *Contexts* 1 (1): 16–24.

Schaafsma, D. 1998. Performing the self: Constructing written and curricular fictions. In *Foucault's challenge: Discourse, knowledge, and power in education,* ed. T. S. Popkewitz and M. Brennan. New York: Teachers College Press.

Smith, B. [1983] 1998. Homophobia: Why bring it up? In *The truth that never hurts: Writings on race, gender, and freedom.* New Brunswick, N.J.: Rutgers University Press.

Smith, D. E. 1987. *The everyday world as problematic: A feminist sociology.* Toronto: University of Toronto Press.

Thorne, B. 1995. *Gender play: Girls and boys in school.* New Brunswick, N.J.: Rutgers University Press.

Vance, C. S., ed. 1984. *Pleasure and danger: Towards a politics of sexuality.* New York: Routledge and Kegan Paul.

# CHAPTER 4

# Sexual Enslavement
# and Reproductive Health

*Narratives of* Han *among*
*Korean Comfort Women Survivors*

CHUNGHEE SARAH SOH

My deepest *han* is that I became infertile as a result of my life
as a comfort woman.

Yi Sun-ok (b. 1921)

The term *comfort women* refers to numerous young girls and women in
Asia, including Japanese and Dutch, who were pressed into prostitution
and sexual slavery for Japanese troops during the Asia Pacific War (1931–
1945). Estimates of their number range between fifty thousand and two
hundred thousand (see Yoshimi 1995: 79–80). It is believed that most came
from colonial Korea (1910–1945). However, there is no documentary evidence to determine either how many young girls and women were used,
or how many of them were forced into the role, except for the Dutch case,
in which at least sixty-five among the two to three hundred women of
European descent were "forced into prostitution" according to the report
of the Dutch Government (1993–1994).

This essay is concerned with the effect of sexual enslavement on the
reproductive health of comfort women survivors by analyzing their life-
historical testimonial stories with a focus on the Korean cases. I explore
the social psychological and physiological impact of sexual enslavement on
the patterns of postwar lives of Korean comfort women survivors by reading closely their testimonials, which I refer to as "narratives of *han*." *Han,*
a Korean ethno-psychological term (which will be discussed in detail be-
low), refers to a complex of emotions and sentiments such as sadness, regret, anger, remorse, and resignation.[1] In the Korean ethno-psychological

imagination, *han* takes the form of an invisible painful knot in the heart. Not surprisingly, one of the most frequently expressed emotions in survivors' testimonials is *han,* which was especially salient among the unmarried or married but infertile ones. In their postwar lives, many chose to remain single because they thought that their "shameful" history of having been comfort women disqualified them from being wives. Among the 165 survivors about whom the information was available, less than 50 percent (seventy-nine) of them married after the end of the war. The proportion of childbirth among the married was a little over one-third.[2] For both single and married infertile survivors, the fundamental source of their personal *han* is rooted in their childlessness, and they blame it, implicitly or explicitly, on the physical abuse and sexual overwork their bodies had to sustain during their time at military brothels called "comfort stations" (*ianjo* in Japanese).

From a macrolevel structural perspective, the factors of class and ethnic discrimination under colonialism were the fundamental variables that precipitated their recruitment into military prostitution and sexual slavery in the first place. From a microlevel sexual and social psychological perspective, in contrast, there are intragroup differences that further complicate the causal factors for social inequality and personal suffering of former comfort women. My analysis of their *han* narratives posits that, aside from individual differences in physical constitution, it is the cumulative number of incidents (as well as the degree of roughness) of forced sexual intercourse an individual woman had to endure that appears to have affected her reproductive capacity in her postwar marital life. Since information on neither the frequency nor the quality of such sexual intercourse is available, in this essay I substitute the *length* of sexual enslavement as the primary operational variable. Additionally, I identify important intervening factors (such as physical beauty and pleasant personality) that caused some individual comfort women to receive exceptionally privileged treatment, resulting in a significantly lighter sexual workload and better working conditions from having to serve only a small number of officers or sometimes only the highest-ranking officer. Such "special treatment" that some sexually attractive individuals received at comfort stations, I suggest, undoubtedly contributed to the maintenance of the relative health of their reproductive organs, even when they were subjected to multiple years of sexual enslavement.

The data for this essay are drawn from larger, long-term, multisited ethnographic research on the comfort women issue conducted in Korea, Japan, the United States, and the Netherlands since 1995. In discussing the *han* narratives, I speak from my location as a Korean-born naturalized American anthropologist. Despite the undeniable differences of educational and social class backgrounds as well as historical and political circumstances of our lives, I share with my research subjects some of the fundamental personal and social suffering that derives from pervasive gender discrimination in patriarchal societies such as Korea. This sharing of lived experiences of gender injustice serves as a psychological basis for deep sympathy and strong motivation to contribute to the amelioration of social and cultural sources of gender inequality and structural violence against women.

## Imperial Japan's Military Comfort System

In this section, I provide a very brief summary of what distinguished the Japanese military comfort system from other instances of military prostitution.[3] Let us take a look at it at two levels: the structural and the organizational.

First, what is unprecedented about it is the active and systemic involvement of the imperial Japanese state—especially from 1938 on—in the establishment and management of comfort stations. This involvement sprang from a cultural order in which the state supported the actualization of a widely shared belief about sex as an essential recreational activity to help maintain troop morale. Masculinist sexual culture condoning the practice of military prostitution, of course, is not unique to Japan. The German military, for example, practiced forced prostitution for its military during World War II.[4] Most ironically, the postcolonial Korean military also operated a comfort women system during and after the Korean War from 1951 to 1954.[5] The main difference between the two military comfort systems is that the Koreans used women of the same nationality and mostly professional sex workers, whereas the Japanese relied primarily on Korean women, many of whom had no prior sexual experience and were either deceptively or coercively recruited. What was uniquely remarkable about the Japanese comfort system was the paternalistic interventionist role of the wartime *state* in its institutionalization, which resulted in the unprecedented duration of its operation and scale of the systematic, extensive exploitation of *colonial subjects*. It became, in the words of the Japanese historian Yuki Tanaka (2002: 167), the "largest and most elaborate system of trafficking in women in the history of mankind, and one of the most brutal."

Second, the organizational characteristics of comfort stations varied considerably, depending on a number of factors such as geographical location and temporal particularities in relation to the status of warfare as well as the military ranks of the primary users and the "race" of the women. The Japanese military comfort system was organized primarily under two separate categories during the so-called Fifteen-Year War (1931–1945): commercial enterprises owned and run by civilians and nonprofit facilities run directly by the military, which I have called "concessionary" and "paramilitary" comfort stations, respectively, and have analyzed elsewhere (Soh 2005). The concessionary comfort stations began in Shanghai as commercial establishments providing sexual entertainment and prostitution, which offered food and drinks served by mostly Japanese and some Korean women. From the middle phase (approximately 1938–1941) on, concessionary comfort stations of the standard type operated in both urban and remote areas as military brothels. The paramilitary category of comfort stations was set up and controlled by local military units as an essential amenity for the troops to quickly discharge their sexual urges, using predominantly teenage Koreans and other non-Japanese females. During the final phase (approximately 1942–1945) of the war, some facilities of the paramilitary category located on battlefronts degenerated into what I have called "criminal" comfort stations (Soh 2005), or centers of authorized gang rape and sexual enslavement of local women in enemy territory, recruited deceitfully by local collaborators or sometimes drafted coercively by the military.

## Marital Status and Childbirth among Korean Survivors: An Overview

The question of the wartime forced recruitment of Korean women as *ianfu* (comfort women, in Japanese) was first raised in the Japanese National Diet in June 1990 as a result of the women's movement in South Korea (Soh 1996). In 1991, two landmark events galvanized the Korean women's movement. In August, Kim Hak-sun (1924–1997) testified in public about her suffering as a former comfort woman in Manchuria, and subsequently thirty-five Koreans, including Kim and two other former comfort women, filed a class-action lawsuit against Japan in December. (In April 1992, six more ex-comfort women were added as plaintiffs to the lawsuit.) Kim's personal appearance in Tokyo as both a former comfort woman and a plaintiff in the lawsuit riveted the attention of both Japan and the world community in December 1991. Since then, more than two hundred Korean women have come out and officially registered as victim-survivors with the Department of Health and Welfare in South Korea. Almost all of them came from very poor families. More than a quarter of them have passed away.

The data analyzed in this essay derive primarily from the two collections of testimonies (HCTH 1993; Kang 2000) as well as from my interviews with activist survivors and their supporters. The 1993 volume, which has been translated into English as *True stories of the Korean comfort women* (Howard 1995), contains nineteen testimonies of survivors residing in South Korea. The 2000 volume by Kang Yong-kwŏn, a Korean researcher and permanent resident of the People's Republic of China, includes eight life-historical testimonials of Korean survivors who remained in the northeastern region of China after the end of the war. As noted earlier, a family history of destitution is a common feature of Korean survivors' life histories, which is unmistakably evidenced in nearly all the cases of the twenty-seven Korean survivors whose reproductive histories are analyzed here.[6] One distinctive feature in the postwar lives of the women, however, is the remarkably different proportion of the married versus single women between the two groups. Among the nineteen survivors living in South Korea, thirteen have married, whereas *all* eight Korean women residing in China married. Nearly all of them regarded marriage as a means of survival in a foreign land, and the majority (five) of them married Chinese men. Cho Yun-ok reminisced about the personal recommendation of her friend who, having married a Chinese, urged her to do the same, saying: "Chinese men are different from their Korean counterparts. The latter like to drink and harass women but Chinese men are extremely endearing to their wives" (Kang 2000: 351). Cho stated that she was indeed very happy to have taken her friend's advice and married a Chinese man with whom she had a loving conjugal relationship for twenty years until his death.

In contrast, nearly one-third of those in South Korea remained single: five of the nineteen never married, while a sixth married at the age of sixty, well past her reproductive years. She was divorced three years later, and her case is included in the single category since the purpose of this essay is to investigate the impact of sexual enslavement on women's reproductive ability. Moreover, among the thirteen married survivors in South Korea, only five were legally married (mostly to widowers or divorced men), while eight cohabited with married men (remaining "single" in the eyes of Korean family law). The unusually low ratio of married women in the Korean sample, I suggest, reflects the strength of the traditional cult of what one may call "virginal femininity," which mandated women's premarital sexual purity and postmarital chastity for their husbands.

Most victim-survivors seemed to have fully internalized the hegemonic ideology of virginal femininity, which among other things caused them to live in constant fear of having their past "shameful" lives discovered. Many considered themselves disqualified from lawful marriage. Some, like Pak Ok-nyŏn (whose marital status is discussed later), compromised to become a second wife or a mistress, and others remained single. When I interviewed an official at the Ministry of Health and Social Welfare in September 1997, I learned that 63 (or 40.1 percent) of the 157 comfort women survivors formally registered with the ministry never married. This is an extremely high rate, especially given the negative social evaluation of unmarried people in Korean culture.

An overview of childbirth experiences among the twenty-one married survivors showed that only eight had given birth. That is, the fertility rate among *all* married survivors residing in South Korea and China was 38 percent (8 out of 21), with an infertility rate of 62 percent, which is an abnormally high rate of childlessness. Since one woman who never married gave birth in January 1946 upon her return home from Japan, where she became a comfort woman for several months, the overall fertility rate of the group is 33 percent (9 out of 27), which is again abnormally low. The durations of sexual enslavement of the nine fertile women ranged between one month and four years, with an average of fifteen months. In comparison, the sexual enslavement durations for the thirteen married infertile women ranged between eight months and ten years, with an average of five years.

None of the testimonials of married infertile women include any specific diagnostic statement regarding the medical cause of their infertility. One notable exception was the case of Yi Ok-sŏn (b. 1927), who attributed her infertility to mercury smoke inhalation as prescribed by a military medical doctor to cure her of syphilis (Kang 2000: 318). It is impossible to determine whether these women's childlessness may be diagnosed as so-called primary infertility (no history of pregnancy) and whether that may be attributable to the sexual trauma suffered at comfort stations. Nonetheless, childless married survivors have simply assumed that their infertility is a result of the sexual abuse their bodies endured as comfort women. It is reasonable to assume that some of married infertile Korean survivors may have contracted chlamydia, which is a major cause of infertility among women. The disease is transmitted among the sexually active with more than one partner. According to Peter O'Hanley, an infectious disease specialist at Stanford University, 60 percent of women's infertility in the United States results from chlamydial infections of the tubes, and chlamydia is a probable major cause of infertility in the world.[7] Symptoms among women infected with chlamydial bacteria include itching, discharge, abdominal pain, and bleeding between periods. (Symptoms for male patients include discharge and burning while urinating.) It is significant, therefore, to note that Mun P'il-gi (b. 1925), who married but had no children, suffered from itching. Mun stated that many soldiers had crab lice *(phthirus pubis)* that were transferred to comfort women during sexual intercourse. Mun remembered how she and her friend helped each other to remove crab lice from their pubic hair (HCTH 1993: 114).

## Women's *Han* in Korean Society

Anthropological studies of human reproduction (e.g., Browner and Sargent 1990; Inhorn 1996) have noted that, in many societies throughout the world, a woman attains full adult status by childbearing. The depth of *han* owing to their childlessness that Yi Sun-ok (quoted in this essay's epigraph) and other infertile survivors have accumulated over their lifetimes can be fathomed only if one is familiar with the social psychological weight of the Korean cultural value placed on motherhood as the quintessential fulfillment of womanhood. In traditional Korea, for example, infertility was one of *Ch'ilgŏ-jiak* or "the seven cardinal sins" for which a husband was entitled to divorce his wife or take a concubine (Y.-C. Kim 1979). Moreover, a wife's failure to give birth to male offspring was tantamount to her being infertile. In other words, a Korean woman's achievement of full personhood hinged upon her reproductive health that enabled her to produce multiple children, especially sons. Since motherhood symbolized the fulfillment of womanhood, fertility has constituted the most fundamental source of married women's empowerment in the gender discriminatory structure of the Korean patrilineal kinship system. Unsurprisingly, one of the most prominent causes for many survivors to harbor deepest *han* turns out to be their inability to bear children.[8] For example, of the seven women whose testimonies specifically included the term *han,* five did not have children. Their *han* over childlessness is to be expected in the cultural context of Korean society, where marriage and motherhood continue to define women's social adulthood.

As noted earlier, the concept of *han* is a key emotional term widely used by Koreans. Yet it has received little scholarly attention until relatively recently (see Choi 1991; C. S. Kim 1992; Lee 1994). Feelings of *han* permeate the survivors' narratives, but there is no single word in English that can adequately convey its complex meaning. Researchers dealing with Korean culture and society have translated *han* variously, as "unrequited resentments," "bitterness and anger," and *"ressentiment"* (Kendall 1985; C. S. Kim 1992; and Lie 1998, respectively). *Han* is widely recognized as a major affective characteristic that many Koreans are said to harbor not only as individual actors but also as citizens of the Korean nation. One might say that *han* constitutes a core characteristic of the traditional Korean habitus (see Bourdieu 1990). Throughout its long history, Korea has endured numerous foreign invasions, seasonal famines, and social injustice under autocratic rulers in the premodern, monarchical systems, as well as in the tumultuous twentieth-century political upheavals resulting in, among other things, the division of the country.[9]

The concept of *han,* however, is not unique to Korean language and culture. The three East Asian nations of China, Korea, and Japan share the Chinese ideographs representing the concept. Nevertheless, the socially constructed meaning and linguistic usages of the term are incomparably more prominent in Korean culture and society in terms of psychological weight, frequency of use, and richness of the emotional vocabulary that includes the concept. In contemporary South Korea, media characterizations of the lives of comfort women survivors are often encapsulated by the idiomatic phrase, "a life filled with much *han*" *(han manûn salm)* or "a life knotted (or bound) in *han*" *(han maetchin salm).* For example, when Kim Hak-sun (who, as mentioned earlier, became the first Korean survivor to give public testimony to her life as a comfort woman in August 1991) passed away in 1997, a newspaper headline reported her death as "the closing of 'a life knotted in *han*'" [*"'han maetchin salm' magam"*] (*Han'guk Ilbo,* December 17, 1997).

The *han* complex, both Kim Yŏl-kyu (1981) and Jae Hoon Lee (1994) suggest, is formed through subjective experiences of social injustice and/or unfulfilled aspirations. There can be a variety of social and/or psychological causal factors for generating the feeling of *han* in the mind of a subject, which, once generated, is usually suppressed over a long period of time, developing into a complex of many related feelings such as resentment, regret, anger, resignation, longing, and sorrow. *Han* generally tends to fester inwardly since those afflicted with *han* lack social resources and political mechanisms to resolve its cause. Specifically, gender, class, and sexuality have been the major causal factors in generating *han* in individuals. Thus, more women than men,[10] more poor people than rich, and souls of maidens and bachelors who died without the consummation of marriage, were typically believed to suffer from the *han* complex. Women's literature of the Chosŏn dynasty (1392–1910), for example, was filled with the themes and emotional undercurrents of *han* felt by women about their duty-bound, constricted lives as mothers, daughters-in-law, concubines, and/or widows (Y. H. Kim 1994).

Customarily, those afflicted with the *han* complex would turn to healing rituals performed by shamans in order to seek the cathartic effect of unleashing their knotted emotions suppressed in their heart (see Y. Kim 1981; Choi 1991). However, because of the shame they felt and the social stigma they feared incurring for having been comfort women (since, until the international redress movement of the 1990s, comfort women were generally regarded as enforced prostitutes), they were unable to reveal their concealed *han* for nearly a half century. Moreover, hailing from very poor families, most of them received little formal education, and for some, this lack of education was a fundamental causal factor for their lifelong feelings of *han*.

### INDIVIDUAL NARRATIVES OF *HAN*

Despite a common theme of *han* about their subjection as comfort women and about the resultant loss of their virginity, however, not all survivors speak of their experiences in the same idioms of *han*. That is, within the general narratives of *han*, the specific causal factors for harboring *han* appear to vary among the survivors. Generally, the fundamental blame for unfulfilled womanhood as unmarried and/or infertile women is placed squarely on Japan for having subjected them to sexually abusive and socially stigmatized lives, which ultimately led to their low self-esteem and inability to live "normal" lives as wives and mothers. At the collective level, the survivors present postcolonial nationalistic narratives of *han*, demanding that Japan compensate for their "robbed virginity," which haunts them as the ultimate cause of their lifelong *han*-ridden suffering. Nonetheless, at the individual emotive level, the feelings of *han* that survivors, especially fertile ones, harbor are not directed exclusively toward the Japanese. Some survivors' narratives of *han* point to unlucky selves, as in the case of Kim Hak-sun.

### KIM HAK-SUN, A MARRIED FERTILE SURVIVOR

Kim Hak-sun was born in Manchuria in 1924.[11] Her father died soon after Hak-sun's birth, depriving her, among many other things, of the opportunity to receive the traditional celebration of *paek-il* (one-hundredth-day) feast for newborn babies. Hak-sun's mother apparently came to regard her daughter's birth as an omen of her own hard life ahead. Kim

Hak-sun recollected that when she behaved in an unruly manner, her mother would bewail her *sinse* (personal circumstances), accusing Hak-sun of having brought on her father's death. Her mother would also berate Hak-sun for being troublesome like her deceased husband, who had pestered her so much. After returning to Korea, her mother remarried when Hak-sun was fourteen. Hak-sun did not get along with her stepfather, and she felt estrangement in her *chŏng* (affect) toward her mother. Her mother then pawned Hak-sun as a foster daughter to a man who changed Hak-sun's name to the more feminine-sounding Kŭm-hwa and had her receive formal training in singing and dancing to become a *kisaeng* (professional entertainer). (Korean kisaeng, like Japanese geisha, received formal training in the arts of singing, dancing, and playing traditional musical instruments. They differed from licensed prostitutes in that their primary function was to entertain men with their artistic and social skills without necessarily engaging in prostitution.)[12]

When Hak-sun finished her training, she was unable to work as a kisaeng because of her minor status as a seventeen-year-old girl. Her foster father then decided to find a job for her in China. After receiving permission to do so from Hak-sun's mother, he left for China with Hak-sun and another girl (who had also been trained to be a kisaeng) in 1941. After they arrived in Beijing, they ran into Japanese soldiers who took the foster father away, suspecting him of being a spy. The two girls were then taken away in a truck by another group of soldiers. Hak-sun was raped by an officer even before they took her to a comfort house located next to a military unit. Hak-sun, however, is one of the rare cases of a woman who successfully escaped from a comfort station. One day, a Korean itinerant merchant of about forty years of age managed to steal into Hak-sun's room. After confirming that he was a fellow Korean, Hak-sun appealed to his sense of ethnic solidarity, begging him to take her with him. After servicing his sexual desire, Hak-sun desperately pleaded and was able to escape from the comfort house with him. They became man and wife, and Hak-sun gave birth to a daughter and a son before their return to Korea in 1946, when she lost her daughter to cholera.

Hak-sun had suffered so much psychological pain and emotional abuse from her husband that she did not feel much sorrow at his accidental death soon after the Korean War (1950–1953). For example, her husband, when drunk, would abuse her in front of their son by calling her a "dirty bitch" who prostituted herself for soldiers. A few years later, she lost her son to heart failure while he was swimming. Her son's death made her reflect on her luckless life that began from her childhood and continued throughout her adulthood as a wife and a mother, and she lost her will to live for several years. She tried to end her life several times and drifted for about two decades, drinking and smoking away all her hard-earned wages. Somehow she then came to realize that she should not waste her life. Eventually, she met an elderly woman who was a victim of one of the atomic bombs dropped on Japan in August 1945. Since this woman also had suffered as a result of Japanese colonialism and harbored grudges against Japan, Kim told her that she had once been a comfort woman. Led by the atomic bomb victim, Kim went to the office of Korean Church Women United in August 1991 and became the first of the survivors to give formal testimony.

When I first read Kim Hak-sun's published testimony prior to my meeting with her, I felt the primary tone was fatalistic resignation tinged with a sense of *han*. After my interview with her in 1995, I came away with the same conclusion about her fatalist subjectivity as an individual whose family life contained no memories of parent-child attachment bonds. The emotional abuse that the mother inflicted on the daughter may be understood as a release of the mother's own *han* about the untimely death of her husband soon after Hak-sun's birth, which may have indirectly caused a sense of guilt in the young daughter's mind. It is significant to note that Kim Hak-sun stated that her mother often scolded her for being obstinate and disobedient. According to Erikson's (1963) psychosocial development theory, children who fail to develop relations of basic trust with their primary caregivers are likely to acquire such personality traits as basic mistrust, defiance, and a sense of deprivation. For Hak-sun, mother-daughter relations, one may infer, were not conducive to the acquisition of basic trust and attachment during her childhood emotional development. Sadly, the bitter memories that Kim Hak-sun did not wish to "even recollect" included not only four traumatic months at two different comfort stations in China, but also her childhood resentment toward her remarried mother and her own unhappy marital life. She concluded that her "wretched fate" (*tŏrŏun p'alcha*) started with her unlucky relationship with her parents, which led to her luckless life in adulthood, not only with her husband but also with her children. She thought that neither the Korean government nor the Japanese state would pay much attention to the miserable life of a woman like her, once she passed away.

## YUN TU-RI, AN UNMARRIED CHILDLESS SURVIVOR

I wish to be born as a female once again. . . . When I was young, people praised my beautiful complexion and regarded me as a good candidate for the first daughter-in-law in a wealthy family. But I have never been married, and why is it? When I wake up at night, I start asking myself: Why am I sleeping all by myself? Why am I living alone? Who has ruined my life like this? Why did my country lose its sovereignty? These thoughts prevent me from falling back to sleep. Because I am unmarried and childless, my heart aches whenever I see people walking with their children in the street. I cannot help lamenting my lot and envying other people with children. . . . I cannot forget what I was forced to undergo until I die. No, I will not forget even after I die. (Yun Tu-ri, b. 1928)[13]

Yun Tu-ri is one of the few survivors who received a primary-school education. In contrast to some other survivors' testimony about their drunk and violent fathers, Yun's father did not drink and was very nurturing toward his children. He was a fairly prosperous builder before his untimely death when Yun was fourteen. Yun began to work to help her ailing mother make ends meet for the family. On the day of her abduction, Yun was returning home after visiting a glove-making factory to see if she could find a job there. Yun testified that a policeman abducted her into sexual slavery. Yun was forced to spend two years (1943–1945) at a comfort station that was located in her hometown, Pusan. When the war ended and Korea was liberated from Japanese colonial rule, Yun returned home and became the breadwinner for her natal family. When Yun was twenty-seven, her mother died expressing her regret for not seeing her daughter get married before her death. Yun never thought of getting married because she was "physically ruined." In her old age, as quoted above, she feels deep *han* about her childlessness and wishes to be reborn as a woman so that she may fulfill her womanhood as a wife and mother.

## Variables for In/Fertility among Comfort Women Survivors

It is reasonable to hypothesize a negative impact of long-term brutal sexual enslavement on the reproductive health of former comfort women who had been subjected to forced sexual intercourse with soldiers. In this regard, it is notable that Kim Hak-sun, Maria Rosa Henson, and Jan Ruff-O'Herne, the three women who became the first to give public testimony from among South Korean, Filipina, and Dutch survivors, respectively, all had married and given birth to multiple children (see Henson 1996; Ruff-O'Herne 1994). One commonality about their experiences as comfort women was the relatively short duration of their sexual enslavement (four months for Kim in China, nine months for Henson in the Philippines, and about two months for O'Herne in Indonesia), which I suggest was a crucial factor for their reproductive success in their postwar marital lives.[14]

Nonetheless, among the sample under study, some cases seemed, at first glance, to challenge my hypothesis regarding the correlation between survivors' infertility and the enslavement period. Four women who served between one and one-half and four years became mothers, while five married women who served between two and four years failed to reproduce. A close reading of their testimonials, however, does support my argument. The four fertile survivors received special treatment, which significantly lightened the intensity of their sex workload during the similar period of enslavement as the five infertile survivors. The special treatment, I hypothesize, significantly curtailed the frequency and brutality of forced sexual intercourse for them, thereby reducing the damage to the overall reproductive health of these four survivors in their postwar marital lives.

It turned out, for example, that one fertile woman with a four-year enslavement (Kim Kayoko) served as an "only" (Japanese slang referring to a mistress) of high-ranking military officers. Kim, who lived at a comfort station in Manchuria, primarily served two officers for about two years in each case. Neither of them used condoms and Kim became pregnant from her relationship with each man and gave birth twice. Her favored status as an officer's "private property" (in Kim's own words) empowered her to refuse serving other men without being punished by the comfort station manager. Kim believed that it was her beauty that made her life of sexual enslavement relatively comfortable and less taxing physically. After the war, she had two marriages to Chinese men and had five children altogether (see Kang 2000: 331–333).

A similar case is that of Kim Sun-dŏk,[15] who was able to have children in postwar married life despite her three-year history of sexual servitude. Kim Sun-dŏk formed an intimate relationship with a high-level officer in his fifties whose patronage provided her with a protective shield. She recounted that her personal characteristics of being "pretty and intelligent" (HCTH 1993: 53) were the reason why she was chosen to serve the officer. For her part, Kim came to regard him as a father figure and a loving husband at the same time. It was with his help that Kim was able to return home safely in 1940.

In the case of Yi Kwang-ja, a fertile woman with a two-year enslavement, the owner of the brothel forced her to work illegally only at night, serving officers who came for overnight stays (see Kang 2000: 370–382). Since the brothel management was unable to get a work permit for her due to her minor status, they decided to make her their "secret comfort woman." It was her youth and sexual inexperience that they exploited to make money by stealthily offering her illegal service to conniving officers only. Her illegal status as a comfort woman had the effect of limiting the number of men she had to service.

Last, in the case of Pak Ok-nyŏn,[16] who was enslaved for one and one-half years, the fact that she had been married and had given birth to a child before her servitude as a comfort woman may have meant that her reproductive organs had fully developed and were better able to withstand sexual slavery than in the cases of the majority of victim-survivors, who were recruited as sexually inexperienced teenagers and prepubescent girls. In addition, Pak's life at a comfort station in Rabaul was relatively shielded from rampant physical assault by numerous men, which many other survivors reported. After returning home to Korea, Pak herself anticipated that she would be unable to give birth any more, and reluctantly agreed to be a concubine. Therefore, it was to her great chagrin that she discovered herself to be with child soon after her sexual union with the married man. Legally, she was an unmarried woman and her three children, as offspring of a concubine, suffered discriminatory treatment from their father's family, which caused Pak a lifelong sense of *han*. She lamented her son's lack of education as the most egregious effect of her unlawful status of being a concubine, which in turn she attributed to her past life as a comfort woman.

## Conclusion

To sum up, the analysis of the individual experiences of Korean victim-survivors of the Japanese military comfort system introduced in this essay reveals that gender, class exploitation, and ethnic discrimination under colonialism were important intersecting variables for the military sexual enslavement inflicted on them as comfort women. Korean women constituted an overwhelming majority of the victims of enforced prostitution and sexual slavery for the Japanese imperial army. Most of them were sexually inexperienced young girls who came from impecunious families: the testimony of Korean victim-survivors shows that the majority were deceptively recruited by human traffickers—both Korean and Japanese—with promises of well-paying jobs.[17] The durations of their enslavement at comfort stations ranged from several months to ten years.

Among the twenty-seven women whose postwar lives were examined in this essay, twenty-one married, and the majority of them were infertile, with only eight (or 38 percent) bearing children. One notable common factor among the thirteen married but infertile women was that their sexual enslavement lasted for multiple years, ranging from two to ten years. There were, however, four exceptional cases of married and fertile women whose enslavement lasted from one and one-half years to four years. Nevertheless, because of their sexual attractiveness and other personal or situational characteristics, they received special treatment, serving a relatively small number of men, primarily high-ranking officers. Thus, despite the long duration of their enslavement, their sexual workload was incomparably lighter than that of other comfort women, which presumably helped to protect their sexual and reproductive organs, ultimately affecting their ability to reproduce in their postwar marital lives.

Finally, while infertility was a leading causal factor for the deep sense of *han* that Korean survivors harbor in their hearts, it must be noted here that the cases of Kim Hak-sun and Pak Ok-nyŏn (both of whom were able to marry and have children) underlined other important sources of former comfort women's *han*. They are inexorably rooted in the patriarchal ideology of male supremacy (expressed in the Korean aphorism *Namjon Yŏbi* [Men are revered, women debased]) and in the traditional sexual culture characterized by gender inequality. In this sense, one may argue that institutionalized practices of sexual inequality (such as an inordinate degree of son preference and daughter neglect permeating a woman's family life during her childhood, and the double standard of sexual purity prescribing virginal femininity as a prerequisite condition for females to achieve respectable womanhood) have contributed as fundamental causal factors of individual Korean women's personal *han* in general, and former comfort women's *lifelong* suffering in particular.

In recent years, the concept of *han* has been reified as a Korean national ethos, as noted in Soh (1998). For example, a South Korean folk model attributes the country's "economic miracle" to "Koreans' efforts to release the *han* caused by the chronic poverty for generations and the indignities suffered under Japanese colonial rule" (C. S. Kim 1992: 4).[18] Remarkably, in the midst of the national financial crisis, South Korea's President Kim Dae Jung asserted that the national ethos of *han* would help Koreans overcome the crisis (*Han'guk Ilbo*, July 1, 1998). Notably, the Korean women activists who spearheaded the transnational movement to seek redress for former comfort women have represented in a similar vein the issue of wartime military prostitution and sexual slavery as a historical injustice inflicted on the Korean nation as a whole by Japan as its colonizer. By dealing with lifelong sufferings of comfort women survivors as examples of the Korean national *han,* the movement leadership helped overcome the social stigma of sexual labor that the survivors had either personally experienced or constantly feared in their postwar lives.

As I have elaborated elsewhere (Soh 2004), however, the master narrative of contemporary Koreans about surviving comfort women as victims of *only* Japan's war crime in effect forecloses feminist critiques of sexism within the Korean patriarchy and scholarly analyses of victimized women's testimonial narratives in light of larger, emergent "modern" gender paradigms of the "new woman" in colonial Korea during the 1930s and 1940s. The victim-survivors' personal agency to leave home, whether in search of gainful employment or in daring pursuit of autonomy, should be examined in the emergent political economic system of class-based commodification and androcentric exploitation of female manual and sexual labor under burgeoning capitalism in late colonial Korea. The multifarious *han*-filled narratives of victim-survivors about their lifelong sufferings deserve postnationalist feminist analyses, in tandem with national and international recognition of their abject sexual enslavement perpetrated by imperial Japan for its wartime mobilization of colonial subjects. The challenge for feminist human rights activists of the movement for redress of comfort women is to move beyond the framework of ethnic nationalist discourse in order to confront and improve the insidiously persistent everyday realities of social injustice for many women, especially those working in the sex industry and trapped in what the Korean media have called "slave prostitution," who continue to suffer from gender inequality and social stigma by members of their own families and the nation in postliberation Korean society.

## Notes

A portion of this essay was presented at the American Anthropological Association annual meeting in Washington, D.C., November 28–December 2, 2001. The quotations in this essay are my translations of the testimonials of Korean former "comfort women" published by the nongovernmental organization Korean Council for Women Drafted for Military Sexual Slavery by Japan (HCTH 1993) and by Kang (2000). See HCTH (1993: 167–180) for Yi's testimonial. For information on the Korean Council, see Soh (1997).

1. *Han* in the Korean language has several homonyms, whose distinct meanings may be represented by different Chinese characters. The Chinese ideograph for the term *han* under discussion is 恨. It should not be confused, for example, with the homonym *han* ( 韓 ) in *han'guk* (Korea).

2. Additionally, there were twenty women who had been married *prior to* their recruitment. Among 178 survivors about whom childbirth information was available, sixty-five (36.5 percent) answered affirmatively. See *2001 nyŏn ilbon'gun 'wianbu' yŏn'gubogosŏ [2001 research report on Japanese military "comfort women"]* (Seoul: Ministry of Gender Equality) pp. 122, 125.

3. For descriptions of military prostitution for Western soldiers from the times of the Roman Empire to the present, see, for example, Enloe (1983; 2000); Hicks ([1994] 1995); and Truong (1990).

4. See Paul ([1994] 1996). Among other things, Paul's research uncovered that, between 1940 and 1942, Nazi Germany forced about thirty-five thousand women (including Eastern Europeans and Jews) into prostitution at various internment camps.

5. The Korean woman sociologist Kim Kwi-ok presented the first scholarly paper on the use of comfort women by the Korean military at an international symposium held in Japan in February 2002. She regards the comfort women issue of the Korean military as an "unfortunate offspring" of the Japanese colonial legacy (*Ohmy News,* February 26, 2002).

6. In some cases, poverty-stricken parents sold or gave away their daughters in order to decrease the number of mouths to feed. One former comfort woman stated that, having suffered from hunger a lot at home, she appreciated being fed regularly at the military comfort station. Toward the end of the war, when life became harder, however, she often experienced hunger again. See HCTH (1997: 184–197).

7. *Sexually Transmitted Disease,* a twenty-three-minute video produced by Films for the Humanities and Sciences, 1987. For the relationship between sexually transmitted diseases and adverse outcomes of pregnancy, see Hitchcock, MacKay, and Wasserheit (1999).

8. For example, see the testimonies of O O-mok and Yi Sun-ok in HCTH (1993).

9. For one recent introduction to Korea's modern history, see Cumings (1997).

10. This does not mean, however, that Korean culture constructs the emotion of *han* as female (cf. Lutz 1986).

11. For Kim's published testimonial, see HCTH (1993: 31–44).

12. For a historical study of kisaeng in English, see McCarthy (1991). For an anthropological study of geisha, see Dalby ([1983] 1998).

13. For Yun's published testimonial, see HCTH (1993: 285–298). Quotation from p. 298.

14. In the case of Ruff-O'Hearne (1994: 132), she had three miscarriages and underwent gynecological surgery before giving birth to two daughters. In contrast, another Dutch survivor, who lived in the same house for the same period as Jan Ruff-O'Hearne, stated during our interview at her home in the Netherlands in July 2000 that she experienced no complications in her two pregnancies and childbirths after her marriage.

15. Kim Sun-dŏk used a pseudonym (Kim Tŏk-chin) when she gave her testimonial published in HCTH (1993: 45–57). She now uses her real name.

16. Her testimony (HCTH 1993: 241–253) was given under a pseudonym (Pak Sun-ae), but she now uses her real name, Pak Ok-nyŏn.

17. Among 186 victim-survivors about whom information on the method of their recruitment was available, 99 stated that they had been recruited by Korean (64) and Japanese (35) human traffickers. *2001 nyŏn ilbon'gun 'wianbu' yŏn'gubo-gosŏ [2001 research report on Japanese military "comfort women"]*, p. 34.

18. This folk model contrasts with the specialist model that invokes Confucianism in the explanation of the rapid economic development in South Korea.

# References

Bourdieu, P. 1990. *The logic of practice.* Trans. Richard Nice. Stanford, Calif.: Stanford University Press.

Browner, C., and C. Sargent. 1990. Anthropology and studies of human reproduction. In *Medical anthropology: Contemporary theory and method,* ed. T. M. Johnson and C. Sargent. New York: Praeger.

Choi, K. 1991. *Han'gukin ŭi han.* Seoul: Yejin.

Cumings, Bruce. 1997. *Korea's place in the sun: A modern history.* New York: W. W. Norton.

Dalby, L. [1983] 1998. *Geisha.* Berkeley and Los Angeles: University of California Press.

Dutch Government. 1993–1994. *Report of a study of Dutch government documents on the forced prostitution of Dutch women in the Dutch East Indies during the Japanese occupation.* [Verslag van de Resultaten van een Onderzoek in Nederlandse Overheidsarchieven naar Gedwongen Prostitutie van Nederlandse Vrouwen in Nederlands-Indie tijdens de Japanse Bezetting]. The Hague: Tweede Kamer, vergaderjaar.

Enloe, C. 1983. *Does khaki become you? The militarisation of women's lives.* Boston: South End Press.

———. 2000. *Maneuvers: The international politics of militarizing women's lives.* Berkeley and Los Angeles: University of California Press.

Erikson, E. H. 1963. *Childhood and society,* 2d ed. New York: W. W. Norton.

HCTH (Han'guk Chŏngsindaemunje Taech'aek Hyŏpŭihoe and Chŏngsindae Yŏn'guhoe). 1993. *Chŭngŏnjip I: Kangje-ro kkŭllyŏgan chosŏnin kunwianpudŭl.* Seoul: Hanul.

———. 1997. *Chŭngŏnjip II: Kangje-ro kkŭllyŏgan chosŏnin kunwianpudŭl.* Seoul: Hanul.

Henson, M. R. 1996. *Comfort woman: Slave of destiny,* ed. S. S. Coronel, with illustrations by the author. Manila: Philippine Center for Investigative Journalism.

Hicks, G. [1994] 1995. *The comfort women: Japan's brutal regime of enforced prostitution in the Second World War.* New York: W. W. Norton.

Hitchcock, P. J., H. T. MacKay, and J. N. Wasserheit, eds. 1999. *Sexually transmitted diseases and adverse outcomes of pregnancy.* Washington, D.C.: ASM Press.

Howard, K., ed. 1995. *True stories of the Korean comfort women.* London: Cassell.

Inhorn, M. C. 1996. *Infertility and patriarchy: The cultural politics of gender and family life in Egypt.* Philadelphia: University of Pennsylvania Press.

Kang, Y. 2000. *Kangje chingbyŏngja wa chonggun wianbu ŭi chŭngŏn.* Seoul: Hae wa tal.

Kendall, L. 1985. *Shamans, housewives, and other restless spirits: Women in Korean ritual life.* Honolulu: University of Hawaii Press.

Kim, C. S. 1992. *The culture of Korean industry: An ethnography of Poongsan Corporation.* Tucson: University of Arizona Press.

Kim, Y. 1981. *Hanmaek wŏnlyu.* Seoul: Chuu.

Kim, Y.-C., ed. and trans. 1979. *Women of Korea: A history from ancient times to 1945.* Seoul: Ewha Womans [Women's] University Press.

Kim, Y. H. 1994. Women's literature in the Chosŏn period: *Han* and the songs of women. In *Korean studies: New Pacific currents,* ed. Dae-Sook Suh. Honolulu: Center for Korean Studies, University of Hawaii.

Lee, J. H. 1994. *The exploration of the inner wounds—Han.* American Academy of Religion Academy Series no. 86. Atlanta: Scholars Press.

Lie, J. 1998. *Han unbound.* Stanford, Calif.: Stanford University Press.

Lutz, C. 1986. Emotion, thought, and estrangement: Emotion as a cultural category. *Cultural Anthropology* 1: 287–309.

McCarthy, K. L. 1991. *Kisaeng* in the Koryŏ period. Ph.D. diss. Harvard University.

Paul, C. [1994] 1996. *Nazizumu to kyoseibaishun.* Japanese trans. of *Zwangsprostitution staatlich errichtete bordelle im nationalsozialismus.* Tokyo: Akaishi.

Ruff-O'Herne, J. 1994. *50 years of silence.* Sydney, Australia: ETT Imprint.

Soh, C. S. 1996. Korean "comfort women": Movement for redress. *Asian Survey* 36 (12): 1227–1240.

———. 1997. The Korean Council for the Women Drafted for Military Sexual Slavery by Japan. In *The historical encyclopedia of world slavery,* ed. J. P. Rodriguez. Santa Barbara, Calif.: ABC-CLIO Press.

———. 1998. Understanding the concept of *han.* Review of Jae Hoon Lee, *The exploration of the inner wounds—Han. Korea Journal* 38 (3): 340–346.

———. 2004. Aspiring to craft modern gendered selves: "Comfort women" and chŏngsindae in late colonial Korea. *Critical Asian Studies* 36 (2): 175–198.

———. 2005. Teikokunippon no 'gunianseido' ron: Rekishi to kioku no seijitekikattō (Theory on imperial Japan's "military comfort system": Political conflict between history and memory). In *Sensō no seijigaku [Political science of war],* ed. I. Kurasawa, T. Sugihara, R. Narita, et al. Vol. 2 of *Iwanami Kōza Ajia Taiheiyōsensō [Iwanami course in the Asia Pacific war].* Tokyo: Iwanami.

Tanaka, Y. 2002. *Japan's comfort women: Sexual slavery and prostitution during World War II and the U.S. occupation.* London: Routledge.

Truong, T.-D. 1990. *Sex, money and morality: Prostitution and tourism in Southeast Asia.* London: Zed Books.

Yoshimi, Y. 1995. *Jūgun ianfu.* Tokyo: Iwanami Shoten.

# PART TWO

# Seeking Sexual Pleasure

Seeking sexual pleasure openly is a political and transgressive act, as several decades of feminist and gay and lesbian thought have shown us. This remains the case today just as it was in 1960s and early 1970s. The essays in this part speak to the transgressive nature of sexual pleasure seeking in ways that demand critical reflection from even the most forward-thinking individuals, for whom the right to sexual pleasure is a foregone conclusion. Héctor Carrillo shows how HIV prevention campaigns can be harmful to the pleasure that individuals seek. Furthermore, in his case study he shows that, contrary to what many prevention campaigns propose, inequality and surrender to a sexual partner are sought after and necessary components of sexual pleasure.

The open and concerted effort many gay men put into their pursuit of pleasure at Circuit parties has aroused serious criticism from homophobic detractors as well as from community members who see in the Circuit parties a deliberate denial of HIV risk at least. Christopher Carrington asks what the subjective experiences are of the Circuit's participants to indicate that the men gain immense positive validation for themselves and for the community to which they belong. The pursuit of sexual pleasure by these men is not only their right; without understanding the deep meanings the Circuit holds for its participants, any health promotion effort is doomed to fail, since it cannot address the basic question: What constitutes health for these men?

A very different population, whose sexual pleasure has long been denied in public discourse, are Mexican women living in the United States. Gloria González-López shows how these women, caught in the now hackneyed dichotomy of mother/whore, known as marianismo, have expressed their sexual interests. In the face of oppressive social norms, most eloquently formulated by the Catholic Church, these women claim the right to experience sexual pleasure and negotiate in various ways the place of their sexuality in a life that is moral.

Russell P. Shuttleworth shows how disabled men are treated as children in this country, not entitled to pursue a fulfilling sexual life. The silence these men face with regard to their sexuality works to amplify only one message: It is not right for you to have sex, let alone to enjoy it. In the social science literature and in society at large, disabled men's right to sexual pleasure has received very little attention. Shuttleworth not only highlights this gap, he suggests a theoretical model to start conceptualizing this field of study.

The four studies in this part highlight how individuals and communities form strategies to enhance sexual pleasure in the face of great opposition. This opposition is formed not only by bigots, but also by those who are supposed to be allies. Without focusing on the subjective experiences and the expressed agency of these women and men, any attempt to promote greater health and justice is not only doomed to fail, it will be counterproductive.

# CHAPTER 5

# Where Does Oppression End and Pleasure Begin?

*Confronting Sexual and Gender
Inequality in HIV Prevention Work*

HÉCTOR CARRILLO

Two general strategies have become increasingly common in progressive
HIV prevention work. The first, of fairly recent adoption, is related to
the goal of promoting gender and sexual equality as a means to facilitate
the use of safety measures against HIV. The logic behind this strategy is
that a reduction in sexual and gender inequality would help eliminate
power differentials between partners in sexual and romantic relationships,
which would in turn facilitate greater individual empowerment to adopt
HIV prevention measures. A second strategy is related to the goal of creating a more "sex positive" sociocultural environment—to remove sexual taboos and to promote greater acceptance of sexuality and sexual desires. The premise is that a process of "sexual liberalization" ultimately
would facilitate sexual negotiation between sexual partners, as well as their
adopting the range of sexual practices commonly included in definitions
of "safe sex" or "safer sex."

How well do these strategies mesh with the lived experiences and erotic
sensibilities of the people whose health AIDS educators seek to promote?
Using qualitative data collected in Guadalajara, Mexico's second largest
city, I contrast the premises informing these two strategies with the expectations that Guadalajarans expressed about sexual interactions in
terms of sexual roles and sexual communication. I collected these data as
part of a larger ethnographic study of sexuality and HIV prevention that
took place between 1993 and 1995. My study consisted of participant observation in a variety of social settings in Guadalajara, three discussion
groups at a local clinic (two with elderly Mexicans), and sixty-four individual interviews. Participants in these interviews were men and women,

lower-middle- to upper-middle-class, ages eighteen to fifty-three, with homosexual, heterosexual, and bisexual orientations.[1]

I chose to use ethnographic research methods for this study because
I was interested in analyzing the influence of local sexual culture on individual decisions about sexual behavior and HIV prevention. Instead
of solely focusing on individuals' knowledge about HIV transmission
and prevention and their attitudes toward the use of protection, and conducting an inventory of sexual behaviors—which are the more typical
foci of much HIV-related behavioral research in Mexico and in other
places—I sought to achieve a more in-depth understanding of how Mexicans integrate HIV prevention measures in their sexual lives. I was interested as well in questions about cultural sensitivity—whether HIV prevention messages reflected Mexicans' sexual norms and values—and
cultural change about sexual issues. An ethnographic approach was particularly well suited to accomplish these research tasks because it provided me with many opportunities to engage participants in conversation and discussion about the topics of interest, and to contrast what they
had learned about HIV prevention with what they actually were doing
sexually.

## HIV Prevention Work in Mexico

Beginning in the mid-1980s, public health educators in Mexico initiated
efforts to inform individuals about HIV and its modes of transmission,
and to convince them to adopt protective measures (Pérez Franco 1988;
Sepúlveda 1993). This initial HIV prevention work took place in a social
context in which formal, open discussion about sex was scarce. In accordance with tradition and the perceived importance of respecting it, many
deemed open discussion about sexuality and homosexuality inappropriate, particularly in the realm of public discourse. As Altman (1993) has
suggested, under those conditions any efforts aimed at breaking the silence about the sexual transmission of AIDS, and to promote condom
use and safe sex were somewhat subversive. By initiating HIV prevention work in Mexico, public health educators were challenging the more
conventional silence about sexual matters and the traditional place of sexuality in Mexican society. Besides addressing an emerging public health
issue, the educators were also engaging in the project of promoting the
cultural modernization of Mexican sexuality. Their initial and most immediate goal, however, was to transform previously naïve individuals into

informed, aware, and self-sufficient people capable of protecting themselves and their sexual partners.

This cadre of AIDS educators in Mexico consisted of a combination of professionals trained in public health, medicine, and social psychology along with community activists—initially mostly homosexual—who were concerned about what appeared to be a potentially fast-spreading epidemic (Pérez Franco 1988; Díaz Betancourt 1991). Their efforts, however, did not remain uncontested. Despite the explicit support of the Secretariat of Health, initial educational efforts that strongly focused on condom promotion and the dissemination of information about AIDS were rapidly, and strongly, opposed by powerful socially conservative groups and individuals (Sepúlveda 1993). These conservative groups, which were associated with religious organizations and had already worked for years opposing governmental promotion of contraception, attempted first to silence the AIDS educators (González Ruiz 1994). Later, they shifted their strategy and constituted themselves as a different kind of "AIDS educator." They created their own messages and campaigns stating that fidelity within heterosexual marriage, and sexual abstinence outside of heterosexual marriage, were the only "morally valid" strategies to avoid the sexual transmission of HIV. In presenting these as the only two viable options, conservatives also made every effort to discredit condoms, safe sex, and even the more progressive AIDS educators who promoted them.

The tension between the progressive AIDS educators and the social conservatives resulted in charged debates and dramatic political maneuvers (Sepúlveda 1993). The strong opposition of the conservative minority to condoms and safe sex confirmed that the public health educators' efforts had greater social significance than just attacking a specific disease. The conservatives' adamant opposition also made the work of the public health educators difficult because they were placed in a defensive posture. The progressive AIDS educators could then anticipate that any future efforts to establish frank discussion of issues related to sexuality, and to promote options that the conservatives opposed, would generate a new conservative attack.

In this social and political context, the evolution of progressive HIV prevention work in Mexico since the mid-1980s has had the following general characteristics. A first phase focused on the creation of HIV-testing programs and the dissemination of information about HIV and condoms, with the goal of creating awareness and helping people to initiate behavioral changes (Pérez Franco 1988; Castro 1989; Sepúlveda 1993; Rico, Bronfman, and del Río-Chiriboga 1995).[2] A second phase resulted from the AIDS educators' realization that disseminating information was not enough to ensure that all Mexicans stayed protected against the virus. They added a focus on promoting the skills required to use condoms correctly and to negotiate their use with sexual partners. For instance, through role playing exercises, participants in educational workshops were taught how to put on a condom (on themselves or on a male partner) and how to convince a reluctant sexual partner of the advantages of safe sex and condom use (Martínez López 1998).[3] This new focus created room for the educators to begin paying attention to relational dynamics and power differentials that they perceived as reflecting Mexican *machista*[4] values, which appeared to prevent the less dominant partners in sexual encounters (mostly assumed to be women) from demanding that their partners use condoms. Awareness of these latter issues was beginning to filter into HIV prevention work around the time that I completed my ethnographic work in Guadalajara in the mid-1990s. AIDS educators had begun to think about how issues of gender and sexual equality could, and should, be considered in HIV prevention work. This change also coincided with the introduction of notions of empowerment (both of individuals and groups) into the local AIDS prevention discourse.[5]

Parallel to these developments, the progressive AIDS educators had also set themselves the goal of promoting a different kind of empowerment that they saw as being related to facilitating a better integration of sexuality and sexual desire in Mexican life. They were concerned about the silence that surrounded sexuality, the breaking of which had created such furor among social conservatives. They realized that the adoption of measures contained in the concepts of "safe sex" or "safer sex" required that Mexicans develop a greater acceptance of a wide range of sexual practices—beyond heterosexual vaginal intercourse—and that they eliminate the shame associated with open, formal discussion about sexual desires.[6] They saw this kind of "sexual liberalization" as an tool to help Mexicans have sexual encounters with full awareness of their sexual desires, the ability to enact those desires without shame, and the determination to set limits and negotiate with their partners how to engage only in practices that fall within the range deemed safe in terms of HIV risk.

The ideal scenario that would result from the combination of these two forms of empowerment would be the following: Empowered individuals would be capable of pursuing their sexual desires freely and of negotiating with one another, in a social environment characterized by sexual and gender equality. Their awareness of new norms of social and sexual interaction would create a level playing field in which all sexual partners par-

ticipate on an equal basis. Sexual practices and roles would be fully negotiated "up front," as open sexual communication and previously agreed conditions for sexual interaction would now be the rule. Finally, over time,
power differentials between sexual partners would be erased, as well as the
*machista* sexual and gender roles that those power differentials sustain.

## Theoretical Integration of Sexual/Gender Inequality in HIV Prevention Research

This sequence of stages in HIV prevention work might be recognizable
to readers who are familiar with the HIV prevention literature and the
history of similar activities in other places. Indeed, despite the fact that
the more conventional individual-based, information-based HIV educational programs remain dominant even today in the worldwide field of
HIV prevention, a minority of scholars and educators have proposed that
AIDS education efforts ought to transcend the level of individual behavior. They suggest paying close attention to issues of collective empowerment, relational dynamics, the meanings that sexual behaviors acquire
within them, and structural/environmental factors that may strongly
constrain (or enhance) individual sexual behaviors (Parker and Carballo
1990; Parker, Herdt, and Carballo 1991; Sobo 1995; Parker 1996; Campenhoudt et al. 1997; Díaz 1998, 2000; Mane and Aggleton 2000; Paiva 2000;
Parker, Barbosa, and Aggleton 2000; Parker, Easton, and Klein 2000; Carrillo 2002). This expansion of the focus of HIV prevention work has occurred mostly in fields of study (such as sociology, anthropology, and political science) that have remained somewhat marginal in HIV prevention
research in places such as the United States, where social psychology, public health, and medicine have been dominant.

Generally speaking, strategies that address inequality as a goal of HIV
prevention work pay attention to: (1) the role of macrolevel problems and
forms of social oppression—such as poverty, racism, homophobia, machismo, and gender inequality—in creating HIV risk for individuals and
communities; and (2) how to design interventions that may alleviate what
scholars call "structural violence" (Farmer, Connors, and Simmons 1996;
Parker, Easton, and Klein 2000), as well as structural barriers—such as
power differentials between sexual partners, particularly between men and
women—to the adoption of HIV prevention measures. Woven into
these approaches are (1) a sense that promoting the use of protection
against HIV cannot be done without attending to the social, cultural, and

political contexts in which individuals and sexual couples are embedded; (2) the recognition that attending to the larger macrostructural factors of HIV risk requires political will and a longer-term vision; and (3) an awareness that HIV prevention programs require simultaneously a short-term focus on the empowerment of individuals and communities and on the creation of new policies, as well as a longer-term focus on broader social, cultural, and political change.

The results of my study in Mexico are generally in agreement with the summary that I have presented here. The pressing need to confront gender and sexual inequality in Mexico, as well the importance of efforts to foster longer-term cultural and social changes, are indeed among the recommendations that resulted from my study (see Carrillo 2002). Yet, the data that I collected in Guadalajara also suggest that certain forms of difference, power differentials, and forms of inequality are perceived by people in Mexico as important ingredients for sexual pleasure and for the fulfillment of sexual desire. The value placed on such differences and inequalities poses a formidable problem for HIV prevention efforts—they create a need to distinguish between gender and sexual inequalities that hinder HIV prevention measures and sexual roles and forms of difference that may contribute to sexual pleasure, particularly within egalitarian relationships. As we will see in the following section, the problem is that it is often hard to establish whether chosen sexual roles and practices are an expression of internalized oppression or whether they are the simple reflection of mutual sexual desire, and whether the eroticization of difference is an indicator of sexual liberalization or merely a reflection of "traditional" or "old-fashioned" values that reproduce sexual and gender inequalities.


## Sexual Expectations

Generally speaking, participants in my study favored a style of sexual interaction that relied on spontaneity, seduction, nonverbal communication, and abandonment to the whims of sexual passion (Carrillo 2002). In the context of voluntary sex, they saw those characteristics as supporting the achievement of sexual pleasure and mutual surrender. The desire for mutual surrender was also accompanied by assumptions about highly valued, differentiated roles assigned to sexual partners. Participants often assumed that nonverbal seduction, spontaneity, and surrender most readily happened when one of the sexual partners—whom, for simplicity, I will call here the "dominant" partner—held the sexual interaction together and provided direction. The other partner—whom I will call the "responsive" partner—allowed himself or herself to be held, to be given direction, and to "be taken."

I must clarify that the dominant partner's directing during sex was expected to be resolute, although not necessarily forceful, and indeed it could be quite tender. The responsive partner's surrender was also often perceived to be far from passive or submissive, and the role sometimes reflected elaborate strategies that effectively turned the one "being taken" into the partner leading in the interaction. However, ideologically speaking, dominant roles were typically bound by perceptions of manhood or masculinity, and responsive roles by perceptions of womanhood or femininity.

To make matters more complicated, participants spoke of sexual roles in terms that suggest that those roles are not defined simply by gender expectations; social class, race, education, personality, and personal agency also figure in the equation. Furthermore, a person's adoption of a dominant or responsive role was not necessarily stable over time and it instead seemed to vary considerably with the situation and the relationship. For instance, Pablo, a young middle-class man who thought of himself as *gay* (I use here the Spanish version of the word), and who typically engaged in sex with other middle-class men who also identified themselves as *gay* or *homosexual,* described meeting a very masculine working-class *albañil,* a construction worker, at a site near his apartment. The two men exchanged glances several times when Pablo walked by on his way to the bus stop. One afternoon, when Pablo was returning home, he saw that the construction worker had finished his shift. Pablo approached him and offered him a glass of cold soda. The construction worker accepted and they walked together to Pablo's nearby apartment. As soon as they arrived, they began making out. Pablo described being extremely pleased by the man's masculine stance, and by his ability to direct the sexual encounter once it started. Pablo willingly adopted a responsive role.

When Pablo told me about this encounter, he was amazed that he could achieve such a level of surrender—that he could allow himself to be taken so thoroughly. His comments reflected not only admiration of his partner's masculinity, but also a certain fascination with—perhaps even exoticization of—his partner's working-class status and appearance. Pablo described this man as a *chacalón,* using a term that Guadalajaran homosexual men applied to masculine, working-class men with dark skin and Mexican Indian features. His comments implied that this man might not think of himself as a homosexual, but instead as a "regular" or "normal" man.

Despite his interpretation that he had played a responsive role in this sexual interaction, Pablo was the one who had pursued the seduction most aggressively and who ultimately initiated the sexual encounter. Pablo talked about the sexual encounter as if it had been his sole responsibility, and about his role in it as being fully chosen by him. Given his middle-class status and his ability to provide the physical space for the sex to happen, Pablo could be seen as having much more power to shape the outcome than his partner. But in practical terms, the one determining the sequence of events during sex itself was the working-class, masculine partner. In his desire to allow his partner to be dominant, Pablo willingly gave up his power to decide what happened, in part because he found his partner's forcefulness once sex started as an important ingredient for his own sexual pleasure.

In another example, Martha, a young middle-class woman, gave into having sexual intercourse with her boyfriend after a long period during which he insisted and she resisted. This man eventually told Martha that he loved her, which she thought provided enough justification for engaging in sexual intercourse. Martha said, "We had some drinks, became aroused—a little kiss here, a caress—and all of a sudden he saw me and said, 'You know what, I want to be with you.'" Soon after first having sexual intercourse, Martha's boyfriend abandoned her.

This could be seen as a case of a man who is seeking to have sex and who declares his love as a way to obtain it, and of a woman who is misled in the process. This interpretation is most likely fairly accurate. However, Martha also had played a role in creating the sequence of events. She felt that her resistance was expected as a means of protecting her reputation. But such resistance did not necessarily mean that she herself did not want to have sex or was not aroused by the interactions. In accordance with the prescribed roles for a "virginal" young woman like Martha, the only avenue for her to become sexual outside of marriage without being stigmatized was the one that she had followed. When Martha's boyfriend finally declared his love, the couple was opening the door for her to accept having premarital sex, which she, at the time, thought of as a preamble to marriage.

Since that time, Martha had considered the possibility of her becoming sexually active again. This did not mean, however, that she was living her sexuality more openly. When I interviewed her, she had a new boyfriend and she strongly desired to have sex with him, but so far she had resisted all his advances. Her logic was that showing resistance was still a necessary step to protect her reputation, to avoid being seen by her boyfriend as "loose." As their sexual involvement grew, with sexual caresses and playful interactions that seemed to be bringing them closer to sexual penetration, the couple seemed to have an unspoken agreement that sexual intercourse was eventually going to happen. Based on her boyfriend's insistence and on Martha's resistance, when sexual intercourse finally happened they would both have social justification for their actions. He could claim that she succumbed to his sexual prowess, confirming his dominance and masculinity. She could allege that she only gave into having sex once she could resist no longer, and thus continue to protect her reputation as a "decent" or "sexually modest" woman. By resisting, Martha understood that she was making it clear to her boyfriend not only that she was someone decent enough to be a good candidate for marriage, but also that she had some expectations about the role that he ought to take during sex (a role that also supported hers).

Her strategy was similar to those of other women in my study who said that they were proactive and often dominant during sex, and that they could determine the course of a sexual encounter. But in order to take that role, they were also careful to make it look as if their male sexual partner was the one who was dominant. Lola, another young woman, said that her taking the initiative during sex "was surprising to men . . . as if they thought, 'Why are you so experienced?' And in fact many women are inhibited . . . we are inhibited in a first relationship due to the reactions of men [who tend to think] 'Oh, you are a woman of the world.' The reaction is that you have been around the block." Lola tended to be quite dominant during sex, and she said that her sexual partners liked that so long as she also presented her dominating role as happening in response to the man's desire for her to take that role.

Comments from some heterosexual men certainly supported this notion. Javier, talking about his wife, said that when he first met her in a place where it was easy for him to meet women for sex, he had been impressed by her initial resistance to having sex with him. "Maybe that is what I liked," he said. "That she was different from the rest." Before marrying her, he wanted to make sure that she would not be sexually uptight. He pursued performing oral sex on her, through which he led her several times to orgasm. She never touched or saw his genitals before marriage, which he took as further evidence that she was sexually modest. I don't know what Javier's wife thought about these events, but her situation seemed comparable to that of Martha's. It appears that at the same time that Javier's wife sent out messages about her sexual modesty, she also obtained sexual pleasure without risking that Javier would label her as "loose," and thus as someone whom he would not want to marry.

## Sexual Desire versus Sexual/Gender Oppression

In these cases, the internalization of oppressive forms of gender and sexual inequality, the transgressive strategies that become available in order to circumvent cultural proscriptions, and the eroticization of forms of difference, may be tightly intertwined.[7] In HIV prevention terms, the negative effects of the roles that people like Pablo and Martha played were rather evident. Once sex began, Pablo had had no say about what happened during the encounter with the construction worker. Going against his own desire to use condoms, he had felt compelled to allow his working-class, masculine, dominant partner to anally penetrate him without one. In Martha's case, although she desired to have sex with her new boyfriend, she was incapable of initiating sex out of fear of ruining her reputation. She saw her role as exclusively responsive and felt that she should have to wait for her boyfriend to push far enough for the sex to be justified (at least in her own mind). As part of this reactive role—combined with a sense that love is needed to justify sex and that the willingness to self-sacrifice is an indicator of love—Martha was also incapable of asking her boyfriend to use a condom. Apart from the fact that her attention was placed on the careful management of her role, which meant that AIDS concerns did not figure prominently in her list of priorities, asking for a condom would betray the role that she was crafting for herself because it would present her as "sexually experienced."

Neither in Pablo's nor Martha's case were the conditions to enact HIV prevention measures adequate, and much of the problem had to do with incompatibilities between widespread scripts governing gender roles and the need for condom negotiation—verbal or nonverbal—during sexual encounters. Furthermore, such incompatibilities may be seen as related to forms of gender and sexual inequality that are at least somewhat reflected in the scripts informing the decisions that Pablo and Martha made in each case.

On the other hand, in these cases we can also see some expressions of personal agency and power on the part of Pablo and Martha, as well as the expression of their and their partners' sexual desires. Particularly in Pablo's case, there are also clear signs of the eroticization of difference and of appreciation for the forms of dominance and surrender that directly resulted in sexual pleasure. Moreover, Pablo, as the middle-class partner certainly played a significant role in shaping the conditions of the interaction, including providing the physical space—his own apartment—in which it could unfold.

Although Pablo felt frustrated about his failure to suggest the use of protection during anal sex, out of fear of possibly "killing the moment" and of the reaction that his partner might have, he was also extremely appreciative of the surrender, spontaneity, and passion that ensued as a result of the roles that he and his partner had assumed. In fact, when he called me to talk about this sexual encounter, he was seeking a way to adopt HIV prevention measures without giving up what he thought was most attractive about the encounter. He was puzzled about how to allow a man to take a thoroughly masculine and dominant stance, while at the same time being able to ensure that no unprotected anal intercourse happened.

In a way, Pablo's open acknowledgment of his preference for strong role differentials—defined in terms of masculinity and dominance/surrender—could be seen as consistent with "sexual liberalization," what I described at the outset as the second recent strategy in progressive HIV prevention work. Indeed, aside from the unprotected anal sex, the pleasure and playfulness created within the sexual scenario that Pablo described could be seen as being consistent with the kind of eroticization that AIDS educators have advocated.

It seems clear that attending to the lack of HIV prevention measures in the cases that I discussed would require addressing the gender and sexual inequalities that put Martha in a position in which she cannot live her sexuality more freely, as well as the circumstances that prevented Pablo from being able to demand condom use when having sex with a man whom he deemed highly masculine and who was of a different social class. The question remains, however, whether promoting empowerment would require the *elimination* of all forms of difference betweens sexual partners. For people like Pablo and Martha, such elimination would most certainly not be appealing.

Clearly, the task at hand may be more complicated: It may mean promoting greater gender and sexual equality as a means to increase self-determination, but without implying that empowerment of all sexual partners ought always to mean complete equality in sexual roles and the absence of any eroticized form of difference. Indeed, there is also a need to conceive of ways of integrating the voluntary eroticization of difference within egalitarian relationships into the repertoire that may support "sexual liberalization," cultural change, and safe sex. At the crux of the issues considered throughout this essay is how to confront gender and sexual inequality as part of HIV prevention work without stripping sex completely of sexual roles and forms of interaction that people such as those in my study in Mexico valued highly.

# Notes

1. For an expanded discussion of the perceptions of sexual identity of participants in this study, see Carrillo (2002).

2. This initial emphasis on disseminating information was not exclusive to Mexico. See Bandura (1987); Aggleton (1989); Freudenberg (1990); Patton (1990); and Kippax and Crawford (1993).

3. Strategies oriented toward promoting HIV skills stemmed from behavioral theories, such as social cognitive theory, that suggest that individual behaviors are greatly dependent on individuals believing that they have the "self-efficacy" to enact them. "Self-efficacy," the theory suggests, is acquired through modeling, skill-building, and incremental experimentation with the desired behavior. See Bandura (1977).

4. Spanish words appear in italics throughout the chapter.

5. For discussions of the general concepts of self- and group empowerment, see Freire (1988); Aggleton (1989); Minkler (1997); Wohlfeiler (1997); Paiva (2000); and Parker, Barbosa, and Aggleton (2000).

6. Initially, notions of "safe sex" and the variety of sexual practices that the concept includes were promoted in Mexico almost exclusively to those population groups—such as homosexuals—that were presumed to engage in sexual practices outside of the realm of heteronormative vaginal intercourse.

7. On the general topic of the eroticization of transgression, see Watney (1993) and Kendall (1995).

# References

Aggleton, P. 1989. Evaluating health education about AIDS. In *AIDS: Social representations and social practices,* ed. P. Aggleton, G. Hart, and P. Davies. New York: Falmer Press.

Altman, D. 1993. Expertise, legitimacy and the centrality of community. In *AIDS: Facing the second decade,* ed. P. Aggleton, P. Davies, and G. Hart. London: Falmer Press.

Bandura, A. 1977. *Social learning theory.* Englewood Cliffs, N.J.: Prentice Hall.

———. 1987. Perceived self-efficacy in the exercise of control over AIDS infection. Paper presented at the NIMH drug abuse conference "Women and AIDS: Promoting Health Behaviors," Bethesda, Md.

Campenhoudt, L. V., M. Cohen, G. Guizzardi, and D. Hausser. 1997. *Sexual interactions and HIV risk: New conceptual perspectives on European research.* London: Taylor and Francis.

Carrillo, H. 2002. *The night is young: Sexuality in Mexico in the time of AIDS.* Chicago: University of Chicago Press.

Castro, R. 1989. La educación como estrategia prioritaria contra el SIDA: Retos y dilemas. In *SIDA, ciencia y sociedad en México,* ed. J. Sepúlveda Amor, M. N. Bronfman, G. M. Ruiz Palacios, E. C. Stanislawski, and J. L. Valdespino. Mexico City: Fondo de Cultura Económica.

Díaz, R. M. 1998. *Latino gay men and HIV.* New York: Routledge.

———. 2000. Cultural regulation, self-regulation, and sexuality: A psycho-cultural model of HIV risk in Latino gay men. In *Framing the sexual subject,* ed. R. Parker, R. M. Barbosa, and P. Aggleton. Berkeley and Los Angeles: University of California Press.

Díaz Betancourt, A. 1991. De la lucha contra el SIDA: Ser y quehacer de las ONGs en México. *Sociedad y SIDA* (March): 5.

Farmer, P., M. Connors, and J. Simmons, eds. 1996. *Women, poverty, and AIDS : Sex, drugs, and structural violence.* Monroe, Me.: Common Courage Press.

Freire, P. 1988. *Pedagogía del oprimido.* Mexico City: Siglo Veintiuno Editores.

Freudenberg, N. 1990. AIDS prevention in the United States: Lessons from the first decade. *International Journal of Health Services* 20 (4): 589–599.

González Ruiz, E. 1994. *Cómo propagar el SIDA: Conservadurismo y sexualidad.* Mexico City: Rayuela Editores.

Kendall, C. 1995. The construction of risk in AIDS control programs. In *Conceiving sexuality: Approaches to sex research in a postmodern world,* ed. R. G. Parker and J. H. Gagnon. New York: Routledge.

Kippax, S., and J. Crawford. 1993. Flaws in the theory of reasoned action. In *The theory of reasoned action: Its applications to AIDS-preventive behaviour,* ed. D. J. Terry, C. Gallois, and M. McCamish. Oxford: Pergamon Press.

Mane, P., and P. Aggleton. 2000. Cross-national perspectives on gender and power. In *Framing the sexual subject,* ed. R. Parker, R. M. Barbosa, and P. Aggleton. Berkeley and Los Angeles: University of California Press.

Martínez López, J. 1998. "'Capacitación sobre SIDA': Un modelo aplicado dentro del área educativa del Comité Humanitario de Esfuerzo Compartido contra el SIDA, A.C. (CHECCOS, A.C.), en la ciudad de Guadalajara, Jal." B.A. thesis, National Autonomous University of Mexico.

Minkler, M. 1997. Community organizing among the elderly poor in San Francisco's Tenderloin District. In *Community organizing and community building for health,* ed. M. Minkler. New Brunswick, N.J.: Rutgers University Press.

Paiva, V. 2000. Gendered scripts and the sexual scene: Promoting sexual subjects among Brazilian teenagers. In *Framing the sexual subject,* ed. R. Parker, R. M. Barbosa, and P. Aggleton. Berkeley and Los Angeles: University of California Press.

Parker, R. G. 1996. Empowerment, community mobilization, and social change in the face of HIV/AIDS. *AIDS* 10 (Suppl. 3): S27–S31.

Parker, R. G., R. M. Barbosa, and P. Aggleton, eds. 2000. *Framing the sexual subject: The politics of gender, sexuality and power.* Berkeley and Los Angeles: University of California Press.

Parker, R. G., and M. Carballo. 1990. Qualitative research on homosexual and bisexual behavior relevant to HIV/AIDS. *Journal of Sex Research* 27 (4): 487–525.

Parker, R. G., D. Easton, and C. H. Klein. 2000. Structural barriers and facilitators in HIV prevention: A review of international research. *AIDS* 14 (Suppl. 1): S22–S32.

Parker, R. G., G. Herdt, and M. Carballo. 1991. Sexual culture, HIV transmission, and AIDS research. *Journal of Sex Research* 28 (1): 77–98.

Patton, C. 1990. What science knows: Formation of AIDS knowledges. In *AIDS: Individual, cultural and policy dimensions,* ed. P. Aggleton, P. Davies, and G. Hart. London: Falmer Press.

Pérez Franco, L. 1988. El Centro Nacional de Información de CONASIDA: Entrevista con Gloria Ornelas. In *El SIDA en México: Los efectos sociales,* ed. F. Galván Díaz. Mexico City: Universidad Autónoma Metropolitana.

Rico, B., M. Bronfman, and C. del Río-Chiriboga. 1995. Las campañas contra el SIDA en México: ¿Los sonidos del silencio o puente sobre aguas turbulentas? *Salud Pública de México* 37 (6): 643–653.

Sepúlveda, J. 1993. Prevención a través de la información y la educación: Experiencia en México. In *SIDA, su prevención a través de la educación: Una perspectiva mundial,* ed. J. Sepúlveda, H. Fineberg, and J. Mann. Mexico City: Editorial el Manual Moderno.

Sobo, E. J. 1995. *Choosing unsafe sex: AIDS-risk denial among disadvantaged women.* Philadelphia: University of Pennsylvania Press.

Watney, S. 1993. Emergent sexual identities and HIV/AIDS. In *AIDS: Facing the second decade,* ed. P. Aggleton, P. Davies, and G. Hart. London: Falmer Press.

Wohlfeiler, D. 1997. Community organizing and community building among gay and bisexual men: The Stop AIDS Project. In *Community organizing and community building for health,* ed. M. Minkler. New Brunswick, N.J.: Rutgers University Press.

CHAPTER 6

# Circuit Culture

*Ethnographic Reflections on Inequality,*
*Sexuality, and Life on the Gay Party Circuit*

CHRISTOPHER CARRINGTON

The truest expression of a people is in its dances and its music.
Bodies never lie.

Agnes DeMille, American dancer and choreographer
*New York Times Magazine,* May 11, 1975

Midnight approaches on a warm desert night in Palm Springs, California, and from the booming music and light spectacle emanating from the cavernous Palm Springs Convention Center, one can tell the Circuit has come to town. Ten thousand people, mostly gay and mostly male, have gathered to dance and rejoice. The convention hall glows with an intense, captivating light generated by the latest software and laser technology. The lights and the music unite in perfect sync. The music, a fierce combination of trance, epic, and progressive house, infuses one's body, erasing the line between one's self and the music pulsating through it. For this event, the tenth anniversary of the White Party in Palm Springs, the producers have choreographed an eerie and captivating ritual opening to the main Saturday night party. Just before midnight, the doors to the convention hall open, and the attendees, adorned in the traditional white clothing from which the White Party takes its name, line the edges of the dance floor. The convention hall is completely dark. At one corner of the convention hall, a series of spotlights illuminate the sails of what appears to be a ship moving across the empty dance floor. As the ship reaches the center, out of its cargo hold arises an enormous disco ball that ascends to the ceiling. The crowd breaks into applause. To accompany the arrival of

123

the disco ball, the DJ has sampled and remixed many of the classic disco, new wave, and new romantic tunes of the late 1970s and the early 1980s. A wave of nostalgia takes hold of many in the crowd. The symbolic return of the disco ball from the darkness perfectly mirrors how many Circuit participants think about the history of gay party culture and of gay life in general. The darkness signifies the specter of AIDS and the demise of dance and party culture during the AIDS era. To many Circuit boys, the return of the disco ball represents the hope of the post-AIDS era and the aspiration that the party culture of 1970s lore might return.

As we stand waiting, my stomach aching in anticipation, I look up into the eyes of my friend Trevor, a forty-two-year-old, 230-pound, six-foot-four Caucasian guy with a muscled body and a painfully shy demeanor often misread by others as "attitude." A tear wells up in his eye as we both remember when we first heard such music at The Saint disco in New York City in the early 1980s. Suddenly, smoothly, and in perfect coordination, the attendants remove the ropes holding the crowd at the edges of the dance floor. The dancers converge under the disco ball, and as they do, a bright, crystalline light engulfs the dance floor. Victor Calderone, one of the preeminent Circuit DJs, leads the revelers tonight. As the dancers converge, he makes a perfect transition from the music of yesteryear to music of the moment—paradise regained. The intense light illuminates the faces of dancers in every direction. Dancing under the disco ball, and looking out into the mass of faces that now surround us I recognize many faces, both my inner tribe of friends who surround me, and hundreds of others with whom I have danced for decades.

Squeezed onto the dance floor, bodies entangled closely together, one realizes that many of the rules governing everyday social interaction between autonomous individuals no longer prevail. In fact, the boundaries between self and other seem to evaporate with every passing beat and every new eye contact. Add the tantalizing and empathy-enhancing drug ecstasy (4-methylenedioxy-N-methamphetamine or MDMA) to the infectious musical beat, the close proximity of many gym-toned human bodies, and captivating laser light displays, and it becomes perfectly clear why Circuit devotees find it difficult to articulate in words the sense of wonder and awe that they experience at Circuit parties. While sitting next to the pool the next day and talking about the party, a twenty-two-year-old Circuit boy from Dallas commented: "It's indescribable. I try to tell my friends about it and I just can't think up the right words, it's like a religious thing, but you don't feel guilty, you just feel at one with yourself and the world around you. You feel safe and you feel free."

The Circuit has emerged as a central feature in the cultural scene of urban gay life in the United States, Canada, Australia, England, Switzerland, Germany, and, increasingly, other parts of Europe as well, particularly resort communities such as the Greek island of Mykonos and the Spanish island city of Ibiza. Similar events have emerged in the Mexican coastal city of Puerto Vallarta. Most major North American and Australian cities with substantial gay populations now host at least one, if not multiple Circuit events each year. The Circuit consist a series of huge dance and party weekends that recur on an annual basis. Circuit events can last from two to seven days and draw thousands of participants. These events have become central to the life stories of many urban gay men. Hence, Circuit events now serve as the social stage for coming out of the closet, for meeting friends and lovers, for celebrating major holidays, and for raising funds for gay organizations and institutions. Many gay men now routinely make social distinctions between Circuit boys and others gay men, signifying subcultural differences in sexuality, substance use, friendship, dancing, grooming, and, of course, music. Participants travel from around the region, the country, and, in some cases, the globe in order to attend these events, often traveling with close friends and lovers. Once there, participants gather with friends and lovers for meals, lie by the pool or on the beach, attend the dances, consume both licit and illicit psychoactive substances, dance for extended periods to house music, and encounter one another emotionally, physically, and sexually.

Not surprisingly, this homoerotically charged environment draws attention from many quarters. Public health advocates focus on the potential for unsafe sex, especially under the influence of alcohol and drugs (Halkitis, Parsons, and Stirratt 2001; Gorman 1996). Social conservatives take issue with the flagrant display of homosexuality itself present at Circuit events. Gay conservatives take issue with such display, as they dislike the public image of gay men created by Circuit events, a critique strikingly similar to the one leveled against drag kings and queens.

In the main, most observers, scholarly and otherwise, focus on the risks, dangers, norm violations, and political costs associated with the Circuit. Few observers take seriously the experiences and perspectives of the Circuit participants themselves. I consider this unfortunate in several important respects. First, those with particular concerns about the health of gay men would do well to take seriously the mostly positive and enriching aspects of the Circuit as articulated by most participants. Understanding what draws gay men to the Circuit would undoubtedly enhance the efforts of those working to reduce the potential for harm. Second, we must come to terms with the huge gap that exists between what scholars and researchers think about the Circuit as compared with what most Circuit participants themselves think about it. Third, we must acknowledge the inherently political character of how people portray or conceive of the Circuit, both the conceptions of those who study the scene "objectively" (i.e., from a distance) and of those who, like me, study it up close. Too many scholars and researchers fail to acknowledge how their own values and political commitments color what they observe in the Circuit. None of this implies that I consider the problems associated with the Circuit culture completely benign, particularly the misuse and abuse of various psychoactive substances.

However, such problems appear, in my view, at the margins, not at the center of Circuit culture. Further, my fieldwork and a careful reading of the research literature as well as of journalistic accounts of the Circuit lead me to conclude that many Circuit observers conflate genuine pathology with a host of sexual and gender norm violations. C. Wright Mills, the noted sociologist and social critic, long ago warned scholars of the social-scientific tendency to turn genuine social differences and deviation from widely embraced norms into pathology (Mills 1943). Many contemporary scholars of the Circuit would do well to reread Mills and thus to pay more attention to the experiences of the wide and substantial majority of Circuit participants, people who break various social taboos but who rarely harm either themselves or other people via their participation in the Circuit.

In light of these social characteristics, it seems most appropriate from a sociological standpoint to conceive of the Circuit as a "marginal subculture" or as a "world within a world" (Gordon 1947). The Circuit exhibits many of the qualities of a distinct subculture: rituals, attitudes, values, shared communications, shared symbols, distinct social spaces, and the like. I use the term *subculture* because it captures the in-between quality of the Circuit. For instance, the Circuit culture shares many dominant cultural values (e.g., the work ethic, materialism, consumption, the importance of leisure), but in other respects the Circuit violates dominant cultural values (e.g., drug use for pleasure, sexual attitudes and practices, gender-role violations). In fact, the term *counterculture* (Yinger 1982) or perhaps even the term *spectacular subculture* (Hebdige 1979) seems appropriate. Hebdige argues that subcultures constitute a form of cultural "noise," a noise violating authorized and dominant rules and social mores. Occasionally, Hebdige notes, subcultures violating socially sanctioned rules elicit ambivalent and, sometimes, even hysterical social responses. The social responses to subcultures violating such rules "fluctu-ate between dread and fascination, outrage and amusement" (Hebdige 1979: 90). Hebdige refers to the subcultures that educe such responses as *spectacular subcultures*. As I will show, the Circuit culture, in ways quite similar to the rave scene, elicits such responses.

At first glance, the gay Circuit scene resembles the infamous rave scene, given the musical affinities, the dancing, and the psychoactive substance use, but first impressions can be deceiving. Sometimes referred to as the "gay raves," the Circuit shares many elements with the British and American rave scenes, but stark differences also exist. Similar to the rave scene, the Circuit appeals to a predominantly, though not exclusively, white crowd. Data collected by Mattison et al. (2001: 122) at the White Party, Palm Springs, reveals that 75 percent of the respondents were white. The Circuit shares many of the institutional characteristics of the rave scene, including party promoters and the centrality of DJs, magazines, Web sites, and intricate cyberspace communications. Both the rave and Circuit scenes feature similar recreational drugs such as ecstasy, Special K (ketamine hydrochloride), GHB (gamma hydroxybutyrate), and crystal (methamphetamine).

The rave and Circuit worlds both feature devotees who sometimes travel great distances to attend. In the rave scene, these devotees are of-ten called "ravers" or "punters" (Fritz 1999), whereas in the Circuit scene, they are called "Circuit boys" or "Circuit queens." In addition, the two scenes share a rich musical history, frequently cross-pollinating each other, but with distinct musical emphases (Silcott 1999; Gilbert and Pear-son 1999: 99). House music, the central musical stream of rave, as well as HiNRG, a central musical stream in the Circuit, flow from the disco move-ment of the 1970s (Reynolds 1998: 57; Collin 1997). In both streams, the DJ cult prevails, or as Sarah Thornton, a media scholar and the author of *Club Cultures* puts it, "Disc jockeys have had a decisive role in conduct-ing the energies and rearranging the authenticities of the dance floor" (1996: 58). The DJ bears the responsibility for taking participants on a journey over the course of the night. In both the rave and the Circuit scene, DJs develop characteristic styles and followings. In many instances, Cir-cuit participants conceive of music using references to the DJs who mix and spin the songs, rather than to the musicians who actually composed and/or performed the tunes. In some senses, this cult of the DJ decen-tered the corporate musical star system dominating late twentieth-cen-tury musical production and enabled the emergence of somewhat inde-pendent cultural production (Hill 1998; Vontz 2002), an independence embraced by many ravers as well as some Circuit boys. Suffice it to say, however, that the Circuit scene maintains the traditional gay allegiance to divas (e.g., Madonna, Cher, Whitney Houston, Jennifer Lopez).

The Circuit scene, unlike raves, appeals to a decidedly older, gayer, male, and perhaps more body-conscious crowd. Outside observers often express surprise at the relatively mature age of most Circuit participants, an average age of thirty-three (Mattison et. al. 2001: 122). Naïve observers of the Circuit frequently misread the age of Circuit boys, in part as a result of stereotypes about bodies and age, but also owing to gay men's efforts to look attractive. In general, the Circuit features a much more stereotypically masculine presentation of the body than one would encounter in the rave scene. Many, and perhaps a majority of self-identified Circuit boys work out at the gym. The social networks and friendship groups common in many urban gay gyms often overlap with dance and Circuit venues. Not surprising, gyms and nutritional supplement companies frequently serve as major commercial sponsors of Circuit events. The focus on body fitness and muscular development intimidates many observers of the Circuit, and frequently draws a good deal of criticism from those who consider the disciplined, sculpted body as an expression of "body fascism" instead of beauty. Many Circuit newcomers report much hesitancy about entering the dance floor, fearing rejection from the beautiful. Providing a common account I hear in most interviews with Circuit participants, Lenny, a thirty-eight-year-old self-proclaimed Circuit boy explains:

As a young, shy boy in my early twenties, and new to the gay scene, I was hesitant to jump in and join the mass of flesh and sweat at my first Circuit party, the Morning Party at Fire Island. In fact, I stood on the edge, terrified of rejection. I think back now and realize how ridiculous this was, but it took me a while to feel comfortable. Most boys won't reject you just because you aren't all muscled up and shit. I remember a guy who cruised me hard at that party and started talking to me for a few minutes. He invited me to come out and dance with him and his friends, but I couldn't do it, I was just too freaked out. I was fascinated though, because I really found a lot of those guys in the center of the dance super hot. A few parties later, I finally got connected and with the encouragement of friends finally overcame all of my fears.

This fear grows from what the newcomer anticipates other gay men will expect of him. In practice, much of this fear appears to be more a self-imposed psychodynamic than any uniform standard imposed by the other dancers, although nasty or "catty" comments about body size or body hair are sometimes heard on the dance floor. Without doubt, many Circuit participants avoid large and rotund people. However, many Circuit events draw what natives would call a "bear" crowd. "Bears" are gay men who celebrate larger and hairier bodies. Some Circuit events (e.g., the Magnitude Party in San Francisco) definitely appeal to bears. Intolerance of bears, like intolerance of "chickens" (i.e., thin, hairless, skinny guys), exists across the Circuit culture. Finally, the Circuit appears to take on a more erotic and sexual cast than the rave, but this seems more a matter of degree than a sharp contrast, although stories of dance floor sexual encounters are quite common among Circuit boys.

The Circuit has now become both an institution in its own right and a part of a wide variety of other gay social institutions, ranging from gay and lesbian pride events to gay media to gay-oriented cyberspace to gay and lesbian politics. Circuit events function as important fundraisers for a wide variety of lesbian and gay political and social causes, as well as for HIV/AIDS organizations. For example, the Pines Party, a Circuit party held on Fire Island, New York, each summer, raised six hundred thousand dollars for the Stonewall Community Foundation and the Fire Island Pines Property Owners' Charitable Foundation in 2002. The Stonewall Community Foundation in 2002 provided ten thousand dollars to each of the following organizations: the Center for Anti-Violence Education; the Bronx Lesbian and Gay Health Resource Consortium; Latino Gay Men of New York; MIX: The New York Lesbian and Gay Experimental Film Festival; the New York Association of Gender Rights Advocacy; Senior Action in a Gay Environment (SAGE); and the Queens Pride House. Further, in 2002, the Stonewall Foundation provided forty thousand dollars to each of the following organizations: the Institute for Contemporary Psychotherapy; the Lesbian, Gay, Bisexual, and Transgender Community Services Center; the Lesbian and Gay Immigration Rights Task Force; the New York City Gay and Lesbian Anti-Violence Project; and the Positive Health Project. Suffice it to say that many important lesbigaytrans institutions benefit from the dollars raised at Circuit events.

While the Circuit functions as an important source of fundraising , the Circuit also functions, in ways similar to gay/lesbian pride parades, as a form of cultural self-assertion or a way of laying claim to cultural time and space, if only for short duration. Participants at the White Party in Palm Springs often conceive of the event as transforming Palm Springs into a gay town, if only for one weekend. Partiers frequently revel in the disorientation that unsuspecting heterosexuals experience during these weekends. Depending on the person, the heterosexual experience of suddenly finding oneself surrounded by gay passengers on an airplane, or by gay customers in a restaurant or by twenty thousand gay dancers in the convention center can prove quite disorienting, if not fear- and angst-producing. The effect can prove even more disconcerting when the gay crowd consists of muscled and/or lean twenty- to fifty-year-olds who exude an unapologetic sexual energy expressed through embracing, dancing, teasing, and cruising one another. Interviews I conducted with heterosexual security and service personnel who work at the various party venues during Circuit party events reveal palpable levels of fear and unease. One twenty-nine-year-old heterosexual security guard who worked the Saturday night party in Palm Springs in 1998 confessed to me that his heart raced and he felt frightened while watching so many men dancing together:

*CC: Tell me about your reaction to seeing all of these men dancing together in the convention center.*

W.R.: Well, I gotta tell you, it kind of freaked me out. I mean, I think being gay is cool. I like a lot of you gay guys, but I felt kind of scared that night. It seemed like the world was no longer under control. I mean, it's hard to say, but like all the normal world had disappeared. My heart was pounding. I remember saying to this other guard, I said to him, "Jesus Christ, this is freakin' me out." And the guy said, "You're not kidding."

Circuit events are unapologetically gay in their emphasis on gay male desire. In this sense, dancing takes on a decidedly political quality. As one noted scholar of dance observes: "dance may often be a vehicle of self-assertion symbolically establishing identity as a counter to . . . a dominating power" (Hanna 1987: 142). The gay dance and Circuit scene signifies, if only for a few hours, a fissure in the heteronormativity of everyday life, a point I will return to in discussing the appeal of the Circuit for so many gay men.

## Method

In ethnographic terms, mine has been a complete membership role (Adler and Adler 1987). The data for this essay emerge from ethnographic research conducted over the five-year period 1996–2001. Participant observation, in-depth interviews, and content analysis of both written and Web materials constitute my primary data sources. From 1996 to 2001, I attended fifty-three Circuit events in the United States, Australia, Canada, and Mexico. However, as I indicated earlier, my participation in the Circuit scene and its antecedents spans two decades. In 1996, I began taking systematic field notes, conducting unstructured ethnographic interviews (Denzin and Lincoln 2000: 652–656), and gathering materials for content analysis. In 1999, I began conducting in-depth interviews with a wide range of Circuit participants. As of this writing, I have interviewed eighty-nine individuals. In selecting people to interview, I used a theoretical sampling strategy (Denzin and Lincoln 2000: 519), attempting to reach participants who I suspected might hold substantively different perspectives about the Circuit based on salient identities (e.g., ethnic, racial, gender, sexual, regional, class, or occupational) and experiences (e.g., newcomer, long-term participant, promoter, security guard).

Given my depth of participation, history, and affinity with gatekeepers (e.g., promoters, DJs, security guards), I have faced few problems gaining access and building trust with people in the scene. I experience much more contested relations with outsiders. For instance, when I presented my work to the National Gay and Lesbian Health Conference, another panel participant took to referring to me as the "Circuit poster boy." Ironically, this panelist introduced my talk, heaping praise on my earlier scholarship (Carrington 1999), and noting the "mature" and "wise counsel" that readers would encounter in that scholarship. Obviously, critics of the Circuit scene consider me too closely identified with it. Despite the protestations of such detractors, my capacity for critical judgment remains intact. I consider my insider status an advantage, one that allows me to understand the Circuit phenomena by its own logic. Indeed, given the ease with which people scapegoat Circuit boys (Rofes 1998: 167–210), the resentment that many people feel toward them, and, in particular, the tendency to dehumanize them (e.g., as "Stepford homos"), I spend a good deal of energy using that critical judgment to confront stereotypes, debunk myths, and place the supposed risk taking of Circuit boys in appropriate context.

In contrast to this constant search for problems, this essay attempts to explain and analyze how Circuit boys themselves make sense of their participation and to account for the rather positive views they hold about their own Circuit experiences. And, in marked contrast to much of the extant literature, this essay attempts to take seriously the positive aspects of Circuit events I have encountered both in my fieldwork and in the in-depth interviews. If one listens carefully to the stories offered in retrospect about Circuit events, some events dating back many decades, the level of nostalgia and the joy with which Circuit boys recall their Circuit days is rather striking, a point I will return to and develop shortly.

I have played a variety of roles in the Circuit scene, and in these various roles, I have interacted with Circuit promoters, DJs, security, janitorial staff, medics, and thousands of Circuit participants. Over the years, I have been involved in producing and promoting various Circuit events. I have recruited volunteers and solicited funds from donors. I have hosted events for volunteers. Some Circuit participants and promoters know me as a health educator / harm-reduction activist. In 1995, I co-founded the Harmony Project, an organization committed to educating Circuit participants about the drug GHB, a central nervous system depressant that became quite popular in the mid-1990s. GHB can be quite dangerous when mixed with other central nervous system depressants such as alcohol and Valium, and when mixed with opiates. The Harmony Project produced and distributed brochures explaining the effects and potential dangers involved in using GHB and mixing it with other substances. The San Francisco Public Health Department adopted the Harmony GHB brochure and distributed it to city clinics and health agencies. Due to this activism, I have often found myself taking care of individuals misusing GHB, accompanying them on ambulance rides to emergency rooms, and explaining the drug to paramedics and emergency room doctors. As strange as this might seem, many medical personal in the mid-1990s knew little about GHB, whereas I knew a great deal. This situation allowed me to interact with paramedics and emergency room doctors, as well as law enforcement personnel, in a unique fashion. Unlike many partiers who end up in emergency rooms, I knew the language, could accurately describe symptoms, and could recommend reasonable medical protocol to confused medics. This led such professionals to treat me as a peer, as well as to treat me as a conduit for information. On one occasion, an emergency room doctor at San Francisco General Hospital spent the better part of an hour lecturing me on the public health dangers of having so many ambulances tied up at gay clubs and the need for the gay community to get a handle on GHB. I took her lecture to heart and became involved in organizing the Harmony Project. I also asked her for a follow-up interview. My health activism has at times strained my relationships with some Circuit party promoters because I came to believe that promoters should take a proactive stance toward drug education and harm reduction. Suffice it to say that law enforcement often views drug education as drug promotion, not as harm reduction, and only the courageous, and perhaps naïve, promoter would become formally involved in explaining to patrons how to avoid and/or reduce harm when using psychoactive substances. To be sure, the supposed danger associated with the use of these substances remains the subject of intense and protracted debate and conflict. See Beck and Rosenbaum (1994), Hammersley et al. (2002), and Holland (2001) for critical appraisals of the supposed dangers of MDMA, and Dean et al. (1997) on the risks associated with GHB.

Over the course of two decades, I have used most all of the illicit and licit substances available in the scene. Over time, I became savvy in the use recreational drugs and developed a clear understanding of the risks and benefits of each. I took my first ecstasy (MDMA), which was then legal, in January 1983 at the Saint Disco in New York City. It was my twenty-first birthday. It is a memory I now cherish beyond words. It was the first time in my life when I felt no fear about being gay and felt free to express affection and emotion to other gay men (see Bravo 2001 for a description of the effects of MDMA). For me, ecstasy and the gay club scene provided a glimpse of what life might be like outside of the shadow of heterosexism and sexual prejudice (Herek 2000a, 2000b). Tragically, all of the guys with whom I shared that moment, including my first boyfriend, are now dead, all of them succumbing to AIDS during the 1980s. Throughout much of late 1983 and 1984, I believed that I too would die in the epidemic. Unaware of the true source of AIDS (i.e., the HIV virus), I thought that ecstasy was the probable cause of the disease, and that my days were numbered. In fact, ecstasy does not cause AIDS, and I learned an elementary lesson in distinguishing correlation from cause and effect. I do not mean to argue that psychoactive substances might not act as cofactors in transmission (in some cases, they do), but they do not cause the illness itself. In later years, my usage of psychoactive substances decreased markedly as particular substances became illegal (MDMA became illegal in the United States in 1985; GHB in 1990; ketamine in 1999; and GBL in 2000) and I could no longer afford to feel the Tuesday blues (MDMA often creates acute depression on Tuesday following Saturday night usage).

For purposes of the semistructured interviews, which I began in 1996, all interviewees were informed of my interest as a researcher, and all participants of interviews were assured of their anonymity and the confidentiality of their responses. I analyzed field materials using the precepts of grounded theory (Glaser and Strauss 1967).

## THE SOCIAL MEANINGS OF THE CIRCUIT

In the intense feelings it provokes, the rules it violates, and the aspirations that it represents, the Circuit embodies not just a rift between the predominant heterosexual culture and gay culture, but a cultural rift that tears across the contemporary lesbian and gay movement itself. While much of the Western gay and lesbian movement of the late twentieth century aspires to bourgeois respectability with its emphasis on attaining legal marriage and military service, and removing the barriers to job and career success, the Circuit moves in a seemingly counter direction. With every step toward assimilation into the cultural mainstream, the Circuit has become a vast symbolic counterweight reminding gay men of their essential difference. The now proverbial Circuit boy—a guy with a gym-toned body, dressed in athletic pants and tennis shoes, tattooed with a tribal insignia, holding on tightly to a glow stick or to a clan of other men, while dancing for hours, or even days, under the influence of recreational drugs such as ecstasy, ketamine, crystal, and GHB, all the while questing for his next sexual encounter—has now become emblematic of what Frank Browning (1993) identified as the culture of desire. The Circuit boy now functions as another icon of gay identity, taking his place next to the drag queen and the leather daddy. Like the drag queen and the leather daddy, the Circuit boy represents an alternative vision of what a gay man can aspire to in life. In many ways, the Circuit queen is the direct descendant of the dancing queen of 1970s cultural lore, but with a much more muscled body.

In some circles, the Circuit represents liberation, a return to the themes of the gay liberation movement of the late 1960s and 1970s. For others, the Circuit operates as the dark and forbidden escape from their closeted ordinary lives. For these men, the Circuit becomes a secret delight, but something to hide and deny. For others, the Circuit embodies all the ills of contemporary gay life: use and misuse of illicit substances, unregulated sexuality, and flamboyant rebelliousness against dominant cultural ideals of masculinity and femininity. Hence, many social groups (e.g., the religious right, AIDS activists, prominent gay intellectuals, public health officials, and law enforcement agencies) depict Circuit boys and Circuit scene as *deviant* and pathological. Circuit boys themselves often accept this deviant label, taking it as a badge of honor, a statement of their willingness to swim against the tide. This willingness is not absolute, however, for in the wide majority of cases, Circuit boys swim against the tide of cultural conformity during three-day weekend Circuit parties and lead rather bourgeois lives the rest of the week. Notwithstanding, interpretations of the Circuit are highly contested, and they often reflect the distinct sociocultural attributes and political interests of the interpreters. My own interpretations reflect a long and joyful association with the Circuit culture and exhibit a marked hostility toward supposedly "neutral" outsiders attempting to pathologize, stigmatize, and criminalize the scene. None of this should suggest that I am not aware of the potential risks associated with the scene. I am well aware that some participants develop horrendous drug addictions and act in ways harmful both to themselves and to others. Yet, as every social scientist knows, correlation does not equal causation, and I am not convinced that these same participants would not develop abusive patterns in other venues with other substances.

Regardless of how one makes sense of it, the Circuit has grown phenomenally over the course of the last decade. The major Circuit events today draw tens of thousands of partiers. Originally organized in the late 1980s as fundraisers for AIDS-related organizations, many of the events evolved into massive fundraisers for a variety of lesbian/gay-oriented causes. Because of the continuous controversy over the use of recreational drugs, some of the major events dropped their AIDS-related focus and became fundraisers for other gay and lesbian causes. The Morning Party on Fire Island, New York, serves as a good example of this. Originally conceived as a fundraiser for the Gay Men's Health Crisis (GMHC) in New York, the party raised a half-million dollars in 1998. After a drug overdose in 1998 at a private home during the Morning Party weekend, critics of the event successfully ended the relationship between GMHC and the Morning Party. Shortly thereafter, organizers in New York City and on Fire Island organized a new Circuit event called the Pines Party, the event I mentioned earlier. In spite of the organizational setback, one should note that the event survived and continues to thrive. These events have become something much larger than fundraisers for good causes. The Circuit has taken on a cultural life of its own. Somewhat ironically, breaking the link between an AIDS organization such as GMHC and the Morning Party also played well to the aspirations of those who want to move into a post-AIDS culture and identity, to break the link between gay life and the specter of HIV.

Almost without exception, popular and gay press accounts, as well as books concerning themselves with the Circuit by prominent gay intellectuals, including Michael Signorile's *Life Outside* (1997), Andrew Sullivan's *Love Undetectable* (1998), and Gabriel Rotello's *Sexual Ecology* (1997: 93–94), portray the Circuit in problematic and pathological terms. Devotees and defenders of the Circuit often refer to these three thinkers as the "troika" or as the "three horsemen of gay conservatism," as one Circuit promoter described them to me. These three thinkers deploy a set of theoretical perspectives that are quite familiar to sociologists of deviance and conformity, relying on pathological, social disorganization and/or social learning theory (see Pfohl 1994 for a description and critique of each view) to explain the rise and reach of the Circuit. These thinkers portray the Circuit as a nemesis to social order, as a breeding ground for sexually transmitted infections (STI) and diseases, and as a meaningless quest for the magic dragon. Andrew Sullivan recounts his experience of a Circuit event:

There was a numbness to it, as well. The first few times I went to these events, I made an elementary mistake of trying to engage my fellow partiers, of trying to catch their eyes or strike up conversation. But they were anesthetized, almost as if this display was only possible by distancing themselves from their mental being, pushing themselves into a drug-induced distance from their minds and others', turning their bodies into images in the catalogue whose pages they turned, in a bored, fitful trance (Sullivan 1998: 13).

In a similar vein, Michael Signorile comments that he found it quite difficult to find Circuit participants who would reflect on the Circuit in a "political, social, or intellectual capacity" (1997: 94). He comments:

For far too many of the men I speak with . . . on the Circuit, it appears that a basic discussion about the scene, its physical paradigms, and its negative or positive effects—including drug abuse and unsafe sex—is a discussion they've simply never had; to most, the idea hasn't even crossed their minds. When engaged about these issues, these men offer only blank stares or frightening conditioned, robotic responses. They are, for all practical purposes, the Stepford Homos (Signorile 1997: 94).

These journalistic interpretations of the Circuit strike me as cursory. They appear uncannily reminiscent of a late nineteenth-century "verandah anthropology" in which objective observers scanned the cultural worlds of savages from a safe and civilizing distance. Sullivan's portrayal of gay men who showed little interest in conversing with him or Signorile's portrayal of these men as "Stepford Homos" tells us more about the respective cultural politics of Sullivan and Signorile than about the lives of the gay men who populate the Circuit. Not surprising, as a field researcher enmeshed in the Circuit culture for much of the last two decades, I find Signorile's assertion of a dearth of earnest reflection among Circuit boys almost comical in its naïveté. Clearly, many Circuit participants will not regale one with rational accounts of their behavior and attitudes, but the idea that they cannot critique or offer compelling self-analysis of their motivations reflects more a research failure to gain the trust and understanding of Circuit boys than it reflects any widespread flaw among them.

Unfortunately, much of the extant social science literature suffers not from the politically motivated assault of the gay conservatives, but rather from an obsession with mechanistic and overly empirical descriptions of how many people have sex, what particular sex acts they engage in, what drugs they use, and how often they use them (Colfax 2001; Klitzman, Pope, and Hudson 2000). Rarely does this literature allow the participants to make sense of their own behavior; instead, researchers infer meaning from behavior. In much of this research, the centrality of local context and the nuanced quality of individual decision making and interpersonal negotiation disappears from view and from the social scientific analysis. Of course, epidemiological concerns about gay men and their unsafe sexual behaviors frame this literature (Colfax 2001). Much of the research intends to identify vectors of risk and strategies of social control to stymie the spread of HIV. Although these are noble goals, much of the literature emphasizes the risks rather than the gains, and not surprisingly, given its focus, conceptualizes the Circuit as risky, escapist, and pathological. Even researchers who bother to make important empirical distinctions between drug misuse and Circuit-party attendance find that media sources insist on conflating the two (Colfax 2001). One notable exception to this general research pattern is the work of Lewis and Ross (1995). Their ethnographic study of the dance and party scene in Sydney, Australia, offers a needed corrective to research that concentrates on behavioral frequencies to the exclusion of the social and cultural meanings that participants apply to their own behavior. Lewis and Ross (1995: 197) offer a compelling analysis of the important support role that the dance and party culture played in response to the decimation of HIV/AIDS during the 1980s and early 1990s, as well as a persuasive case that dance played a crucial role in coping with the suffering and grief attendant on the HIV/AIDS epidemic. My research repeats this central finding of Lewis and Ross, although many Circuit participants no longer experience HIV/AIDS in such an immediate and crisis-oriented way. Accordingly, my research builds on Lewis and Ross's, emphasizing the social and psychological import of the Circuit. Scholars and activists need greater appreciation and awareness of the ways that the Circuit functions as a response to and respite from social inequality, the fear of sexuality, and pervasive heterosexism. A good deal of the published research literature concerning the Circuit ignores the positive meanings that gay men attach to Circuit events or pays them perfunctory attention. When considering the understandings and interpretations of Circuit participants themselves, one begins to glimpse the multidimensional, and most often valuable, meanings that gay men experience via the Circuit. Research that truncates these experiences from the analysis clouds our understanding and, not surprisingly, often legitimates political interpretations intent on scapegoating Circuit boys (Rofes 1998) and contributing to moral panics (Cohen 1972; Goode and Ben-Yahuda 1994; Thompson 1998). By obfuscating or devaluing the positive experiences of most Circuit boys and emphasizing the flippant and exceptional cases, scholars may be inadvertently facilitating repressive social policy directed at harming the Circuit scene and, in the process, diminishing a social experience that contributes handsomely to the well-being of thousands, and perhaps millions, of gay men.

## Emergent Themes: Explaining the Appeal of the Circuit

In the secure environment it creates, the stress it alleviates, the emotions it elicits, the social bonds it forges, and the political resistance it embodies, Circuit culture meets important social and social psychological needs for many gay men, in ways markedly similar to a wide range of other social institutions, including religious organizations.

### THE CIRCUIT AS HOMOEMPATHIC ENVIRONMENT

Without fail, Circuit boys articulate the appeal of an all-gay social environment as a central component of their attraction to the Circuit scene. Perhaps paradoxically, many of them emphasize a sense of safety that they draw from this social scene. During an interview, Lance, 31, who has been involved in the Circuit for much of the last five years offers the following reflection:

The beauty of the Circuit for me is that it's an all-gay, totally safe, alternate reality from the world we live in. People are free to be who they want to be, and one would not even think twice about embracing or kissing another guy. It's our world, it's one of the few worlds where gay people set the rules. And you know, even gay bars can't match it, because, even in a gay bar, unless you're totally drunk, you still don't let yourself go, and say what you feel, and hold, and touch the people you love. In fact, in the Circuit setting, and especially when you are in the midst of your tribe, the opposite rules apply: you must touch, you must express your feelings for one another.

Blake, thirty-three years old and a self-defined participant, expresses a similar sentiment:

*CC: What draws you to the Circuit?*

Blake: It is kind of hard to describe what is so attractive about the Circuit to me. It will sound kind of corny, but I think that beyond the obvious, the amazing music, the sense of being a part of something bigger, and your friends, I think the thing that is so attractive is the safety, the fact that gay people finally rule. Even if it's only for seventy-two hours, we are in charge, and straight people are pushed to the margin. All of that straight energy is gone. It's not that we are mean to straight people, it's just that their way of living doesn't determine everything.

*CC: Can you think of an example of this?*

Blake: Yes, at the Morning Party in August, there was this moment, when I was with my friends, the whole tribe, and Julian Marsh [the DJ] played this remix of an old Carpenters song. All of the guys were singing, I mean, here we are, all of these fags, singing this song that we loved as kids, but would never dream of even saying that we know the song in front of most straight guys. I was so happy, I came close to crying. My friend Ricardo was next to me, holding onto me so tight, and I just remember him smiling, and I remember kissing him so hard. You know, that kiss of love. That could never happen with straight people around.

Kevin, fifty-four years old and a self-described Circuit senior, describes the draw of the Circuit:

I guess, for me, the Circuit is about being myself, and people accepting me for who I am, as a gay man, without the judgments or the fear of rejection. It's harder as you get older; you don't get as much attention, sexual attention, that is. I usually go to Circuit parties with friends, and I find that we are often so kind with one another at these events. Somehow, and I don't know if it's the drugs or the celebratory atmosphere or what, or the tone of the event, but I can always say what I feel. It's a bonding thing really. And, it's a kind of community. There are not a lot of guys my age 'cause most of those guys died in the epidemic, and most of my friends are younger than I am, but they really embrace me at these events. And, you know, unlike many of my coworkers or even some other gay men with whom I spend time, the guys who I know in the Circuit don't desexualize me because I am older. There's something about an all-gay environment where its ok, even expected, that you will feel randy.

As these comments illustrate, the unapologetically homoerotic character of Circuit events appeals to many. Given the heteronormative character of much of social life, the intensity and the sense of safety that participants experience does not seem that surprising. In a sense, the Circuit compensates for the exclusion of gay experience, particularly gay desire, in the broader society.

## THE CIRCUIT IN RESPONSE
## TO THE DECIMATION OF AIDS/HIV

Many astute observers of gay life and of the dance scene note the importance of HIV/AIDS to understanding the scene (Lewis and Ross 1995). However, the importance of HIV/AIDS to the Circuit eludes easy classification. For some individuals, particularly in the late 1980s and early 1990s, HIV became the rationale for throwing caution to the wind and led many a Circuit boy to live life with complete abandon—carpe diem. Given the depressing short- and long-term prognosis at the time, many HIV+ guys decided to enjoy their final years partying with gusto. I frequently encountered Circuit boys who held this view in the late 1980s. Many developed serious substance abuse issues along the way, and some certainly hastened their deaths through drug overuse and misuse. Protease inhibitors appeared in the mid-1990s, and consequently, HIV disease evolved into a long-term chronic condition, instead of a death sentence, at least for those who could afford treatment and maintain the treatment regimen. Consequently, the carpe diem attitude detected by earlier studies of the Circuit scene (Lewis and Ross 1995) receded, but the specter of HIV infection remained. Social thinkers have long noted that times of plague often elicit collective social behavior, including dance, as one means of coping with potential immanent death (Camus 1947). Consider the following observations of Daniel, a forty-one-year-old Circuit participant who has been involved in the scene for more than a decade:

*CC: Tell me about what draws you to the Circuit.*

Daniel: (pause) Healing. I know people don't believe it, but the bonding with your friends, the only people who really understand you and us. You know, I remember when my friend Billy told me he had seroconverted. He told me at the Tea Dance at the White Party back in 1993. I was the last in our tribe to know, he didn't want to tell me, because he knew how upset and how angry I would be. And I think if he would have told me somewhere else, I would have been angry.

*CC: How come?*

Daniel: Because, he knew better. He knew better! He lapsed and he let some guy fuck him without a condom that he should not have. He knows better. But you know, something strange happened at that Tea Dance. I really can't explain it because it doesn't make any sense.

*CC: Give it a try.*

Daniel: Well, it's like this. Here we were, after three days of partying our asses off. I hadn't slept in days. We were raging, and it was so much fun.

All of the people I love more than I can even say. So, here we are at the Tea Dance. I decided to do some more ecstasy at around 4. We get to the party, and we found a great place to dance. We started dancing, Billy was next to me, and we all started to roll. All of us were there, Chad, Greg, Carlos, Antonio, Fernando, and Stephen. I am looking into his face, Billy's face, and I sensed that something wasn't quite right. I thought that maybe he was sad that he hadn't gotten laid, or that we were not paying enough attention to him. Suddenly, he started to cry. I was kind of confused. I was thinking, wow this is powerful X. And then I looked over at Carlos, and he was crying. I start asking Billy, what's up, hon? He tells me he has something to tell me. And I'm like, what? He tells me that he turned positive about a month ago. I felt intense anger and I left them for the side of the dance floor. I had so many things going on in my head. I just wandered in the gay mass. I would run into people I knew and dance with them, and suddenly I was overwhelmed with pain. I didn't know what was what, so many thoughts were going through me. I knew I had to get back to them, I realized, I had to get back to him. Those were my guys. I came up to them all in the crowd; they were all in a huddle, completely intertwined in a ball of human flesh. At first, I couldn't get in, they were so tight together. So, I just danced behind them with my arms on their backs and shoulders. Finally, Antonio sees me, and his face is filled with tears. They all opened the circle and embraced me, and I am telling you, I was overwhelmed. Everyone was crying, and telling each other how much we loved each other. I can't even tell you what happened then. I do remember that the DJ played a remix of that music from *Schindler's List*.

*CC: Oh yeah, you mean Barber's "Adagio for Strings"?*

Daniel: Yep, and you know, suddenly nothing else mattered. I thought to myself, we could all die at this moment, and you know that would be just fine because there could be no moment that could ever match the love that flowed between us on that dance floor. I felt so safe. It was like we were at one, that there were no boundaries between us. We completely understood one another, and we had forgiven each other, and we could face whatever was to come. And you know, I don't think we talked very much again that night, not verbally anyway, but we spoke with our bodies and eyes. My anger evaporated; it was like I had gone through all of the stages of grieving in the course eight hours of dancing. Words just weren't helpful. Oh God, I can't tell you how much that night meant to me. And every year, we go back. And if, and when, Billy passes on, we have all vowed that we will honor him at the White Party, even if it's fifty years from now!

Obviously, as the previous comments suggest, Circuit events provide solace and they create a social venue for the expression of grief. The continuous appeal to the metaphor of "safety" by Circuit participants suggests that the scene provides a safe space for expressing sentiments and feelings.

## THE CIRCUIT AND THE FEAR OF HIV

*A life lived in fear is a life half-lived.*
—Spanish proverb

The advent of HIV/AIDS transformed gay male sexuality during the course of the past two and a half decades. Empirical research confirms dramatic declines in STI incidence (www.cdc.gov/std/2000Slides.htm) from the early 1980s to the mid-1990s. The fear of HIV infection propelled gay men to dramatically alter their sexuality. Strikingly similar to Victorians who winced at the ominous threat of syphilis, gay men live in constant fear of HIV. Any discussion of gay male substance use and abuse must consider the pervasiveness of this fear. My research reveals palpable fear and a constant struggle to reconcile it with desire. During an in-depth interview in which I ask him to talk about his use of ecstasy, Tucker, a twenty-nine-year-old Canadian from Vancouver and a newcomer to the Circuit scene, comments:

One of things I love about ecstasy is that it lets me let go of some of the fear I have of sex. When I am sober and having sex with a guy, even if its safe sex, I am always thinking about HIV. Somehow, X allows me to calm down a little and not be so frightened. Maybe, that's not so good, but I have come to see that some of my fear is overdone.

*CC: Tell me more about that, your sense of fear as "overdone."*
Tucker: Well, like for instance, oral sex. I used to think that oral sex was a huge risk for HIV and now I know it's not. But, even though I know this, I am still kind of panicky about it. So, when I get a little high, I don't feel so frightened. I think the X allows me to deal with that fear. Now, I know that a lot of people would prefer that gay guys stay terrified of their sexuality, and I hear that argument, but you know, I want to be happy too. I mean, if you let that fear run your life, why bother living? Ya know?

As Tucker's comments suggest, some of the use of psychoactive substances stems from a desire to deal with widespread fear of HIV. For some gay men, such as Tucker, the Circuit scene counters the wider discourses (e.g., sex education in schools, public service campaigns, mass media coverage of HIV) encouraging gay men to fear sexual contact.

## THE CIRCUIT AS RESISTANCE TO ASSIMILATION

Many Circuit boys view the Circuit as a countercultural force, a force powered by different engines and by different degrees of resistance. Some scholars diminish the sexual and erotic aspects of Circuit life (Sullivan 1998), but my research suggests wide affirmation among long-term Circuit participants that desire propels the Circuit. Consider the following comments from Gregor, a thirty-seven-year-old participant who attended his first Circuit event in 1990:

*CC: Tell me about the sexual aspects of a typical Circuit weekend for you.*
Gregor: Typical for me, or for others?

*CC: For you.*
Gregor: OK. Let's see. The first night usually is Special K night. That usually means that I am numb and couldn't have sex even if I wanted to. Most of us try to sleep on Friday night, to get prepared for going without sleep on Saturday night. Saturday night, the main dance, is usually about your friends. You might meet someone for sex, but usually I stick with my clan and we party. We are usually doing E [ecstasy] then anyway, and E can be great for sex, but it's also great for bonding with your friends. The after-hours party on Sunday morning starts to get more sexual. A lot of times, guys will be having sex on the dance floor. Depending on the venue, they might have sex on the edges of the party or in the bathrooms. I have connected with a lot of guys at the after-hours. We go back to the hotel rooms and party and have sex. Depending on who I am staying with, or who else I meet on the dance floor, it might be sex with just one guy, or maybe a group, depending on who's around, and whether we connect or not.

*CC: And then?*
Gregor: We party or have sex for a few hours. I usually can't cum then anyway because of the E or whatever. So, you cuddle and kiss and just hang out and talk. Then you prepare for the Tea Dance. The Tea Dance is the hunting ground. This is when the boys are really horny and looking for sex. Most people have come off their X, and now they can cum. The hours between the Tea Dance and closing dance for me have always been filled with sex.

*CC: Safer sex?*

Gregor: Oh yeah. I'm no idiot. I mean, I'm not perfect, like a condom every time, but I know the basics, and most boys on the Circuit do too. Some guys get into trouble with crystal with this, but not me. Even in a crystal binge, I don't let anyone fuck me without a condom.

*CC: How do you think the outside world would think about the sexual aspects of the Circuit?*

Gregor: They hate it, or envy it. I don't know which, but I know gay boys, or at least Circuit boys, don't accept the view of outsiders. That's their culture, this is ours. And I don't want our culture to become like theirs. For a while in the '80s, I felt different. We were dealing with so much death, and it just seemed more sensible to cool it down, the sex stuff. But now, I don't buy that anymore. We have safe sex, and we know how to protect ourselves, and so I think it's time to reclaim sexual freedom.

Many Circuit boys conceive of the Circuit as a kind of rebellion against the dominant cultural attitudes about gay sex, discourses emphasizing risk and danger. In the Circuit, one encounters a marked effort to reclaim gay male sexual desire and to escape the dominant view of gay sex as always dangerous. Although this countercultural view may well increase the risks of STI—a point well made and constantly repeated by media, social scientists, and public health entities—it seems clear to me that many Circuit participants, such as Gregor, wish to balance the risks and benefits of participating in scene. Gregor is not unique, given that his nuanced appraisal of the potential risks and benefits closely resembles the perspectives of many other gay men I have interviewed and come to know in the Circuit scene.

## Conclusion

Analyses of the Circuit culture must take seriously the perspectives of Circuit participants themselves and recognize that for many gay men, the Circuit functions to meet a variety of important social and psychological needs for participants. This includes the importance of creating homosocial spaces and accentuating male homoerotic desire. Such desire rarely appears in the broader culture, and hence, the Circuit often compensates. The Circuit unashamedly embraces gay male desire and constructs, maintains, and celebrates collective social bonds, bonds of great import to many gay men but underappreciated or vilified by many observers. The homoeroticism encountered in the Circuit culture creates palpable fear in some observers, particularly some heterosexual men who encounter these events, usually while working as security guards or paramedics. Such fear underscores the potent political character of Circuit parties, for these events challenge the heteronormative quality of everyday life and they unrepentantly affirm the worthiness and beauty of gay male homoerotic desire.

The metaphor of "tribe" recurs throughout my fieldnotes, interview transcripts, Web discussion groups, and printed Circuit-related materials. Scholars should take this metaphor seriously for it reflects genuine sentiments and real social and familial bonds. Most of the Circuit boys encountered in my research point to the importance of friendship bonds within the Circuit scene, particularly the longer-term participants. Many trace the origins of their relationships and friendship circles to Circuit events. Many others treat Circuit events as special occasions for celebrating friendship bonds. Typically, Circuit boys attend Circuit events as part of a friendship circle or "tribe." In many respects, scholars should conceive of these friendship bonds as communities of care, solidarity, and even resistance to the broader dynamics of heterosexual and sexual prejudice. Failure to do so misrepresents the lives of such men. Undoubtedly, some gay men attend Circuit events and harm themselves or others through the misuse of recreational drugs or through engaging in riskier forms of sexuality. Social science has well documented these dynamics (Colfax 2001; Halkitis, Parsons, and Stirratt 2001; Gorman 1996). That said, a bigger and more important sociological story emerges from this ethnographic research. It is a story about gay men loving one another in the face of enormous hostility and prejudice, of dancing together in the face of a pandemic, of celebrating homoerotic desire in a cultural context that increasingly conceives of gay male sexuality as pathological, of embracing safer sexual expression as worthy and wholesome against the backdrop of pervasive and even irrational fears of contracting HIV, and, finally, of forging social and collective bonds that provide some protective cover for individual gay men against the ubiquitous forces of social inequality and heterosexism.

## References

Adler, P., and P. Adler. 1987. *Membership roles in field research.* Newbury Park: Sage.

Beck, J., and M. Rosenbaum. *Pursuit of ecstasy: The MDMA experience.* Albany: State University of New York Press.

Bravo, G. 2001. "What does MDMA feel like?" In *Ecstasy: The complete guide,* ed. J. Holland. Rochester, N.Y.: Park Street Press.

Browning, F. 1993. *The culture of desire: Paradox and perversity in gay lives today.* New York: Crown.

Camus, A. 1947. *The plague.* New York: Penguin.

Carrington, C. 1999. *No place like home: Relationships and family life among lesbians and gay men.* Chicago: University of Chicago Press.

Cohen, S. 1972. *Folk devils and moral panics: The creation of mods and rockers.* London: MacGibbon & Kee.

Colfax, G. 2001. Drug use and sexual risk behavior among gay and bisexual men who attend circuit parties: A venue-based comparison. *Journal of Acquired Immune Deficiency Syndromes* 28: 373–379.

Collin, M. 1997. *Altered states: The story of ecstasy culture and acid house.* London: Serpent's Tail Press.

Dean, W. 1997. *GHB: The natural mood enhancer.* Petaluma: Smart Publications.

Denzin, N., and Y. Lincoln. 2000. *Handbook of qualitative research,* 2d edition. Thousand Oaks, Calif.: Sage.

Fritz, J. 1999. *Rave culture: A primer for the global rave phenomenon.* Montreal: Small Fry Press.

Gilbert, J., and E. Pearson. 1999. *Discographies: Dance music, culture, and the politics of sound.* London: Routledge.

Glaser, B., and A. Strauss. 1967. *The discovery of grounded theory: Strategies for qualitative research.* Chicago: Aldine.

Goode, E., and N. Ben-Yehuda. 1994. *Moral panics: The social construction of deviance.* London: Blackwell.

Gordon, M. 1947. The concept of sub-culture and its applications. *Social Forces* 26: 40–42.

Gorman, M. 1996. Speed use and HIV transmission. *Focus* 11 (7): 4–8.

Halkitis, P., J. Parsons, and M. Stirratt. 2001. A double epidemic: Crystal methamphetamine drug use in relation to HIV transmission among gay men. *Journal of Homosexuality* 41 (2): 17–35.

Hammersley, R. 2002. *Ecstasy and the rise of the chemical generation.* London: Routledge.

Hanna, J. L. 1987. *To dance is human: A theory of nonverbal communication.* Chicago: University of Chicago Press.

Hebdige, D. 1979. *Subculture: The meaning of style.* London: Methuen.

Herek, G. M. 2000a. The psychology of sexual prejudice. *Current Directions in Psychological Science* 9 (1): 19–22.

———. 2000b. Sexual prejudice and gender: Do heterosexuals' attitudes toward lesbians and gay men differ? *Journal of Social Issues* 56 (2): 251–266.

Hill, S. 1998. The British dance music industry: A case study of independent cultural production. *British Journal of Sociology* 49: 234–251.

Holland, J., ed. 2001. *Ecstasy: The complete guide.* Rochester, N.Y.: Park Street Press.

Klitzman, R., H. Pope, and J. Hudson. 2000. MDMA abuse and high-risk sexual behaviors among 169 gay and bisexual men. *American Journal of Psychiatry* 157: 1162–1164.

Lewis, L., and M. Ross. 1995. *A select body: The gay dance party subculture and the HIV/AIDS pandemic.* London: Cassell.

Mattison, A. 2001. Circuit party attendance, club drug use, and unsafe sex in gay men. *Journal of Substance Abuse* 13: 119–126.

Mills, C. W. 1943. The professional ideology of social pathologists. *American Journal of Sociology* 49: 165–180.

Pfohl, S.. 1994. *Images of deviance and social control: A sociological history*, 2d edition. New York: McGraw Hill.

Reynolds, S. 1998. *Generation ecstasy: Into the world of techno and rave culture.* Boston: Little Brown.

Rofes, E. 1998. *Dry bones breathe: Gay men creating post-AIDS identities and cultures.* New York: Harrington Park Press.

Rotello, G. 1997. *Sexual ecology: AIDS and the destiny of gay men.* New York: Dutton.

Signorile, M. 1997. *Life outside: The Signorile report on gay men: Sex, drugs, muscles, and the passages of life.* New York: HarperPerennial Library.

Silcott, M. 1999. *Rave America: New school dancescapes.* Toronto: ECW Press.

Sullivan, A.. 1998. *Love undetectable: Notes on friendship, sex and survival.* New York: Alfred Knopf.

Thompson, K. 1998. *Moral panics.* New York: Routledge.

Thornton, S. 1996. *Club cultures: Music, media, and subcultural capital.* Hanover, N.H.: University Press of New England.

Vontz, A. 2002. The strange triumph of electronic music. *Salon.com.* http://salon.com/ent/feature/2002/06/19/electronic_music/

Yinger, M. 1982. *Countercultures: The promise and peril of a world turned up-side down.* New York: Free Press.

# CHAPTER 7

# Confesiones de Mujer

### The Catholic Church and Sacred Morality in the Sex Lives of Mexican Immigrant Women

GLORIA GONZÁLEZ-LÓPEZ

"The pope says that *el método natural* is the only way to prevent pregnancy but that is impossible!" vigorously stated Xóchitl, a thirty-four-year-old housewife who has lived in Los Angeles for more than nine years. Then, she continued, "As a woman, you have to look for different ways to avoid getting pregnant. So, the Church has to change, the pope has no idea of what a woman has to go through. Then, he is against abortion too! Can you imagine? I would have ten children by now!" Xóchitl proudly identified herself as a highly committed Catholic while recalling her personal experiences as a dynamic member of the Catholic organization *El Movimiento Familiar Cristiano* (the Christian Family Movement) in her native small town in Jalisco. Before migrating to Los Angeles, she also worked for many years as an active *cursillista,* teaching workshops organized by her local rural parish.

No doubt, the Catholic Church is a powerful source of sexual oppression and control over the sex lives of Mexican women. However, as illustrated by Xóchitl, contrary to a biased misrepresentation of Mexican women as *abnegadas* (self-sacrificing) and *sumisas* (submissive), Mexican women are far from having the monolithic female identity frequently portrayed in academic and popular literature. The Mexicanas I present in this essay challenge these stereotypes. Their narratives reflect how they may become active social agents who contest, resist, and redefine Catholic moral prescriptions from their own sexual experiences as women.

In this essay, I offer a feminist sociological perspective of how and why even highly devoted women such as Xóchitl may identify Catholic values with regard to female sexuality as unrealistic and highly antagonistic to central aspects of their daily life experiences and their social reality as heterosexual women. I examine the intersection of Catholic Church—religion—sacred morality—women's sexuality through the eyes and from the real sex life experiences of a group of Mexican immigrant women. I conduct my analyses based on individual interviews, asking in-depth, open-ended questions, conducted with forty self-identified heterosexual Mexican immigrant women living in the city of Los Angeles. I collected this data during the 1997–1998 academic year as part of my research work on Mexican immigrant women and their sex lives. I use pseudonyms to identify each of the informants' sexual narratives discussed in this essay.[1]

For this group of heterosexual Mexicanas educated in the Catholic faith, the interconnection between sex life and religion is experienced based on the following dynamics:

- Women not only become aware of the patriarchal nature of the Catholic Church as an institution but also perceive it as morally incompetent to regulate women's sexuality.

- Women who are aware of the gender oppression and contradictions promoted by regressive sexual moralities and ideologies do not automatically walk away from the Church nor stop exercising their faith, rituals, and religious practices.

- Mexican women's personal and individual heterosexual experiences as Catholic women acknowledges the existence of multiple Mexicana heterosexualities.

- And Mexican women, as a subordinate social group, mediate Catholic teachings on sexual morality based on their personal subjectivities emerging from their standpoint as women.

## Why Mexicanas and Sex?
## Why a Feminist Sociological Perspective?

I conduct sociology of sexualities research with Mexican immigrant women because of a group experience I had as part of my professional background as a psychotherapist. During my training as a marriage and family therapist in the early and mid-1990s, I led a Latina women's support group with eight adult immigrant women. This group was originally established in order to help women explore issues with regard to self-esteem, domestic violence, drug abuse, family life, and parenting skills, among other issues. All of those who met on a weekly basis in order to discuss these concerns as women gradually developed a deep bonding relationship with one another and with me as their group facilitator. And as they engaged in this process, they became highly vulnerable while revealing their most intimate feelings with regard to their emotional lives. Interestingly, however, I observed that the topic of sexuality had always remained unspoken of in their interpersonal exchanges. As I expressed my curiosity about their "sexual silence," women asked me if it was permissible to explore their sex lives during our meetings. That moment was only the beginning of a fascinating and endless journey of sexual exploration that revolved around these women's concerns with regard to virginity, orgasm and sexual satisfaction, masturbation, oral and anal sex, sexual fantasies, homosexuality (gay and lesbian), and sexual practices, among many sex-related topics that the women openly discussed. For most of these women, the group experience became an unfolding journey through which they discovered their personal feelings as they explored their most intimate sexual concerns. For me, this group's emotional adventures not only pointed to the topic of a doctoral dissertation that I defended later on in order to become a sociologist. These eight women also changed my professional fate. I learned from their first-person voices how and why female sexualities are connected to gender, racial, class, citizenship, and language limitations, among additional forces promoting social inequality. Their sex stories indicated the ways in which women may be sexually oppressed, but their testimonies also identified various avenues highlighting the possibilities in which they become active protagonists struggling for social justice and change. As part of this learning process, they helped me unleash my passion as I decided to become a researcher dedicated to studying Mexicans and sexuality as an act of intellectual activism.

This group process and my dissertation research with the additional group of forty immigrants that I discuss in this essay have offered me the opportunity to become "mentored" with regard to the complexities that define Mexicana sexualities. From both experiences, I developed a keen awareness of two aspects of conducting sex research with Mexicanas. First, I use a qualitative methodology to investigate sexuality because it is a complicated construct established, formulated, and transformed by, through, and within social practice (Gagnon and Simon, 1973; Gagnon 1977; Weeks 1985; Plummer 1995; Seidman 1994; Laumann and Gagnon 1995). By using a quantitative methodology (i.e., a fixed design) to conduct a sociological study of the heterosexualities of Mexicana immigrants, I would disregard the fluid nature underlying the social construction of human sexuality—a principle emphasized for decades in the field of sociology of sexualities. Thus, positivist assumptions (objectivity, social reality as a static process that can be measured and replicated, and the belief that we can best know the social world through distance and detachment) are difficult to sustain for a sociological study of Mexicana heterosexualities.

Second, from my research, I became committed to contesting the many distortions, stereotypes, and misconceptions that the literature across disciplines has promoted with regard to Mexican women. Even though for more than twenty years some Latina sociologists have examined the stereotyped images of Mexican American women, condemning them as "narrow and biased" (see Baca Zinn 1982), the literature frequently promotes images of women as passive actors that must fit static cultural molds that invariably oppress them. An example is the Madonna-whore paradigm consistently used in the Mexicana sexuality literature on both sides of the U.S.-Mexico border, in which the roles of good/bad *(buena/mala)* or virgin/whore *(la virgen/la puta)* determine a woman's sexual experiences and identities (e.g., Paz [1950] 1987; Guerrero Pavich 1986; Almaguer 1993; Alonso and Koreck 1993; Amuchástegui 2001). In that regard, some have asserted, "Latino women may be particularly prone to difficulties in acknowledging themselves as sexual beings" (Marín and Gómez 1997). A second example in the literature is the concept of *marianismo,* as illustrated in Travis and White(2000). In this anthology, the concept of *marianismo* is defined by Reid and Bing as a "concept based on the Catholic cult of the Virgin Mary, which dictates that when women become mothers, then and only then do they attain the status of Madonna, and in so doing they are expected to deny themselves in favor of their children and husbands" (p. 158). Interestingly, neither the Madonna-whore paradigm nor the morality prescriptions associating virginal images with a married woman's moral obligations were reported by any of the forty women I interviewed. Instead, I learned that even though gender inequality is promoted by the Church, the sexual and social realities of Mexicanas are shaped by women's complex gendered subjective interpretations taking place within the context of their everyday life experiences and circumstances. The actual sex lives of Mexicanas go far beyond cultural icons of virgins, Madonnas, and whores.

Thus, even though one cannot deny the oppressive nature of Catholic Church teachings with regard to women and sexuality, women are neither passive nor one-dimensional individuals who automatically adapt to these culturally and socially defined moral prescriptions shaping their sex lives in some ways. I argue instead that Mexicanas are sophisticated, multidimensional, and active social agents who react to these prescriptions in multiform and complicated ways. This essay is not only an assertive effort to put an end to the damaging effect of stereotypes and distorted misconceptions of Mexicanas and their sex lives. It also explores these female sexualities testimonies through Dorothy Smith's (1987) feminist sociological reflections of women's condition in society, as well as Lynne Segal's (1994) and Nancy J. Chodorow's (1995) views of female sexualities and gender identities. I hope that these testimonies give voice to the complexities of what it means to be female, Mexican, and Catholic within a patriarchal society that is more complex than monolithic images of cultural archetypes of Mexicana sexual identities. As a Mexican immigrant embracing progressive political ideologies, I hope their narratives may highlight avenues for social change and justice beyond stereotypes, prejudices, and unidirectional and simplistic Church-blaming discourses.

Lastly, ecclesiastical authorities have no absolute control over how religion and sexual morality are truly lived and experienced by Mexican women in their everyday sex lives. In this essay, I explore potential answers to the following questions: What Catholic religious teachings on sex and morality do Mexicanas bring as part of their sexuality baggage when they migrate to the United States? What do they report they do with it in their actual sex lives? To what extent does the Catholic Church influence Mexican women and their sex lives? Why or why not?

## "Carta al Papa": Letter to Pope John Paul II

In order to explore how the women in this study themselves perceive and judge the influence of the Catholic Church on their sexuality as Catholic women, I read the sexuality section of the "Carta al Papa" as part of my interviews.[2] Specific questions with regard to their opinions and reactions about the letter and the role of the Catholic Church on women's sexuality and their own sex lives were openly discussed. The women's personal reactions to the "Carta al Papa" are examined in this section. A paragraph of the "Carta al Papa" was read in Spanish to my informants. This is my English translation of the text:

It is about time that we, as a Church, recognize sexuality as holy and divine. It is about time that we assume sexuality as part of God's gratitude, and of those who mutually give themselves in freedom and generosity, not only to have children. It is about time to meditate and recognize that sexuality is holy and divine. It is about time that we, as Catholic women, recognize that God has granted us a body, which we should love and rescue because it is a transcendent part of us as persons and of our unity with God. It is urgent for the Vatican, bishops, and priests to act and think in a radically different manner, by allowing themselves to be questioned by the experiential world of women so they act according to the Plan of God. It is urgent for all of you to consider us as adult persons, capable of possessing our lives and our bodies so our options are trusted and respected, and having the right to intimacy, to sexuality, in a responsible manner and in harmony with the values of the Kingdom: in truth, in justice, in love, and in equality. Only in mutual respect, and with a recognition in plenitude of everybody's rights as persons, will we be able to contribute to a humanity with no limits and a "life in abundance" (John 10: 10).

The testimonies articulated by these women offer multiple interconnections between the social reality of Catholic Church as an institution and their representatives at all hierarchical levels (i.e., the pope, priests, nuns), Catholic religious faith, sexual morality, and what women raised in the Catholic faith *really do* with these interactions with regard to their sex lives. Their responses unmask the keen awareness developed by these women while being born and educated in predominantly Catholic families. Their responses expose the progressive mentality of these women: the overwhelming majority of the women in the study (80 percent) supported, praised, and joined the women who addressed progressive changes within the Catholic Church in the "Carta al Papa." What are the reasons behind such tremendous support for the idea of questioning and rebelling against traditional moralities with regard to women's sexuality? What are the causes responsible for such an enthusiastic encouragement of progressive changes within the Catholic Church? These are the most representative testimonies of this group of forty women.

## True Confessions: Beyond Cassocks and Penitence

"What these women said was right! The truth is that we, as women, are not free with regard to our bodies because the Church puts all these things inside our heads!" passionately stated Romelia, a community organizer. Then, she added in a sarcastic tone of voice, "And if the pope did not interfere that much, men would not be that *machistas*. Why? Because there would be equality, and if we had equality, there would not be a problem. Hey! What would happen to men if we had a female pope? [Laughs]." Romelia identified herself as a practicing Catholic and a faithful devotee of *la Virgen de Guadalupe*. A thirty-two-year-old married woman born and raised in Guadalajara, Romelia currently works as a part-time sales representative for a small company; she migrated to Los Angeles at the age of twenty-five.

Romelia's words best represent the most prevalent and consistent tone of these women's reactions to the text of the "Carta al Papa." These women passionately articulated their keen awareness with regard to gender inequality and the multiple interconnections between religion, culture, heterosexual relationships, and women's sexuality. Other women elaborated their sagacious gender awareness with regard to sexism, the Church, and women's rights to body ownership and control. In their stories, many of them used the terms *macho, machismo,* and *machista* in order to describe sexist beliefs and practices. In general, these women addressed two central themes as controversial.

The first theme began to be articulated by women such as Tomasita. She stated: "I trust priests and nuns, I respect them. However, I have met many who lead you through a different path, like those priests who abuse children. So, I think, how is a person who has done that type of thing going to talk with you about sexuality? How in the world are they going to tell you to preserve your virginity until you get married?" The provoking theme of sexual abuse of children by priests was one of the main reasons for Tomasita and some of the women in this study to repudiate the moral competence of the Church as an institution. Tomasita was a thirty-year-old separated woman and a full-time housewife who migrated from rural Jalisco at the age of twenty-one.

Similarly, Irasema, a Mexico City–born and -raised thirty-nine-year-old married woman who works as a seamstress, stated her disenchantment: "Well, all this is very controversial because they preach and teach you one thing and they do a different thing! Priests always . . . how can I say it? They were like an idol for me, the best, like a role model. But then, all the things that you learn about what priests do! If the Church looked at sex with more freedom and as something natural, it would be better."

Like Tomasita, Irasema denounced parallel moral inconsistencies on the Church's part and promoted progressive changes while expressing her confusion and moral disappointment. Both women addressed this controversial issue while questioning the moral authority of Church representatives over their sex lives as Catholic women. Both firmly stated the rationale behind their critical attitude in this regard. They denounced the aberrant nature of these practices while disapprovingly rejecting the Catholic Church.

Women had additional reasons to debate the legitimate moral value of the Church's teachings with regard to sexuality. Xóchitl, the highly involved Catholic I presented at the beginning of this essay, said: "An old priest, he ran away with his secretary and that was a thing in that small town, *olvídese!* [Forget it!] And then when I was thirteen or fourteen, I met a priest who spent his life rescuing women from the brothel. That was his job, and everybody in the town . . . ! You can imagine! It seems like he left the Church later on and got married." Women such as Xóchitl shared with me more than one story about *los amoríos* (love affairs) between priests and some of the women in her small town. Xóchitl described with great vitality and lucid detail the effect of this circumstance on her respect toward the Church as an institution failing in its obligation to set a good example of *moralidad y decencia.* As she recalled these stories for me, she condemned the inappropriate behavior of these priests. Then, she vigorously concluded: "So if they [priests] tell you to behave like this and like that, why do they do it? Why if they preach about all that, how come they are not honest? Don't you think?"

Other women similarly shared many interesting stories with great excitement while exploring in detail the reproduction of images of highly heterosexualized and hypersexualized priests. Beatriz, for instance, began to recall, "With *el padre* I visited many, many places! And when he arrived, we used to go out to have dinner or to dance or to have a drink. We also used to go to eat corn. We used to go to dance and the priests were so attractive! We said: *¡Qué Padre!* [A Mexican expression for 'great,' literally, 'What a father!']. [Laughs] Some of them . . . *¡Ay!* Well, I have to admit it, some of them were very handsome!" As Beatriz talked about her close personal relationships with some priests as a catechist working in her small town's parish, she recalled with a nostalgic tone of voice her experiences with her catechist friends while traveling from town to town, as part of their church-related activities.

As we continued with the interview, Beatriz clarified for me, "My mother was very ignorant because, according to her, since we were with the priest, we were safe, and well . . . I was happy!" She described how she enjoyed being a catechist while taking advantage of *la ingenuidad* (naïveté) of her mother in order to enjoy the personal freedom that otherwise would be difficult to obtain. For women like her, a disjuncture between the expected rigid and monastic lifestyles and real life practices of catechists, nuns, and priests may have create a space to explore personal agency, autonomy, and pleasure. Beyond this sense of freedom as a catechist, Beatriz told me, she understood and always practiced *respeto per-*

*sonal* toward the priests. "They should have the pope's permission!" Beatriz exclaimed, while calling for radical changes in the celibacy demanded of priests and explaining how *el padre* was exposed to the rejection of some people in her small town.

As Beatriz continued talking about her close relationship with the Church, she explained to me that even though she has attended Sunday mass since she was very young, she did not considered herself a *santurrona* (a "saintly" religious or morally conservative woman). Then, she referred to the clear personal boundaries she learned to establish while traveling with *el padre,* as she explained why this was not always the case for other women. Then, she stated: "There was a priest, . . . [pause] a friend of my very good friend . . . well, she had a child with that priest. And that is why I say that they do not practice what they preach. So, it is the same for them. Well, you find of all kinds, some of them comply with it but others do not." As she articulated her own understanding of the difficulty in complying with an idealized morality in real life, she expressed her own criticism of some priests' moral integrity. She said that one should be aware of the many moral contradictions within the Church.

Candelaria, a thirty-six-year-old married woman and a full-time housewife born and raised in a small town not far from the Jalisco coast, similarly talked to me about her old habit of attending Sunday mass. As she continued, she expressed her feelings of sadness while recounting in great detail her friend's story. She said, "I have a friend who had a child with a priest over there in my hometown, and he was lynched over there. And now the poor little boy has no father. And then, she does not tell him that his father was a priest so that he is not traumatized." As Candelaria finished her story, she concluded: "I think everybody has the right to enjoy sex. It would be better for priests to have wives and for nuns to have husbands." She talked about her knowledge of the moral contradictions within the Church and the corresponding need for the institution to change its regulations.

A fourth full-time housewife born and raised in a small town, thirty-seven-year-old Felicia, assertively stated with an ironic tone of voice, "In fact, I . . . , in my hometown, I met a priest who had some type of marital life, he had children! So, outside the church he was a normal man. But inside the church, he was a priest." She used the term *hipocresía* while describing many of the moral inconsistencies she has personally witnessed on the part of Church representatives.

Clearly, Xóchitl, Beatriz, Candelaria, and Felicia uncovered taboos in the sexual practices of highly heterosexualized and hypersexualized priests.

They always reacted with mixed emotions as they articulated enthusiastic narratives that gave life to their friends' and acquaintances' love affairs with priests in their small towns. As illustrated, some expressed compassion and understanding for their personal friends and the priests themselves while addressing the need for the Catholic Church to modify its sexual morality in order for heterosexual priests to enjoy healthy sexual and marital lives. Other women expressed a critical attitude, disapproving of these priests' behavior. All of them condemned these contradictions. All of them shared with expressive and colorful tones of voice their voyeuristic pleasure as they narrated their secret knowledge about what God's representatives on earth were disgracefully doing. Interestingly, the women who shared their testimonies on these issues were all from different small towns in Jalisco. Some of these towns where located within geographical or regional areas significantly distant from one another. Women from Mexico City did not reveal this type of story, which may be an indication that priests are more likely to be protected when they become invisible in bigger and safer geographical and social spaces. The social characteristics of large cities may allow women—and priests in this particular case—to be protected from rigid moralities and moral prosecution. These women and priests exemplify the social syndrome best known in Mexican popular culture as "*pueblo chico, infierno grande* [small town, big hell]."

In short, this first subgroup of women perceive the ecclesiastical organization as morally fractured and decayed while they question and condemn the ethical contradictions and hypocrisies they have observed within the system, including priests sexually abusing children and the reproduction of images of heterosexualized and hypersexualized priests (i.e., priests being married or having lovers).

Last, a forty-one-year-old married housewife born in rural Jalisco who migrated as an adolescent to Guadalajara, Deyanira, spoke for a group of women in this study: "I do not care about what *El Papa* has to say because he does not help you in any way, nothing from nothing. He does not help you economically or spiritually." Although not a majority, Deyanira and other women identified the actual ecclesiastical authorities while expressing their disapproval with regard to the Church's influence on a woman's sexuality. These women addressed some of the inconsistencies between the Catholic Church's highest hierarchy and the legitimacy of their morality teachings.

In sum, these women, as well as other informants, went beyond an explicit awareness of the patriarchal nature of the Church as an institution. Many of them expressed critical opinions while exploring controversial themes such as the Church's moral frailty and its moral double standard practices. Women addressing these issues perceived the ecclesiastical institution as a morally damaged and weakened organization. These women questioned the sexual morality that is linked to their own sexualities as Catholic women by challenging the conspicuous inconsistencies between morality ideals and real practices promoted by its authorities and representatives.

Did these women have these views before migrating? Most of them said they did. However, I conducted these interviews during the 1997–1998 academic year. And as I reflect on these data years later, I suggest that the crisis the Catholic Church is experiencing with regard to the scandal of pedophile priests may accentuate these and other immigrant women's perceptions of the Church as morally fragile and incompetent. In addition, popular culture expressions in both Mexico and U.S. Latino communities may further shape these women's views of the Church. The stories of the women I interviewed echo the images portrayed in the highly acclaimed Mexican movie *El crimen del padre Amaro* (*The Crime of Father Amaro,* 2002). Four priests are at the heart of this provocative movie, but the movie highlights Amelia and her mother, two devout Catholic women who have romantic and sexual relationships with two of the priests. When the movie was exhibited in the United States, it provoked controversy and heated discussion in primetime shows broadcasted by major Spanish-speaking television networks.

In this study, most of these women (39 of 40) were raised in the Catholic faith while growing up and living in Mexico; only one (Diamantina) was raised Protestant in Mexico. And of the 39 Catholic women, three converted to a Protestant denomination in the United States. Even though the conversion incidence is not striking, it is important to mention that two out of the three women who became Protestant (Belén and Fernanda) became more fundamentalist in their attitudes with regard to the sexual morality, especially while educating their daughters. Based on their religious values, both hope that their daughters will refrain from premarital sex. Interestingly, both women support the socially progressive changes proposed in "Carta al Papa." And Eréndira, the only single woman who became Protestant, in contrast reported a sexual morality transformation from conservative to liberal after her religious conversion.

In general, the overwhelming majority of women in the study are keenly aware of the patriarchal ideology and the morality contradictions practiced by the Catholic Church. As paradoxical as it may appear, they do not necessarily turn away from the Church nor do they stop practicing their religious beliefs, traditions, and observances. At the core of this process, they expose two complex patterns: Women *either* reconcile both sexuality matters and religious teachings by establishing a clearly polarized duality, *and/or* they exhibit personal agency through a subjective scrutiny of sexual morality teachings.

## The Church Is for the Spirit, Sex Is Separate

"*La iglesia es para el espíritu, el sexo es aparte* [The church is for the spirit, sex is separate]," said Patricia from Jalisco. A thirty-four-year-old married woman who works part-time as a nanny, Patricia expressed the words that best represent this perspective. Patricia, for instance, talked about her tradition of frequently attending Sunday mass, where she prays with respect and deep devotion. I asked her, "Do you think that the Church should tell women how to behave sexually?" She convincingly explained, "No, I think the Church should not tell us how . . . like that, the way you said it . . . to behave sexually. I think the Church should not tell us how to behave in matters of sex. When you go to mass, you go to pray; you go to ask for your personal needs. But sex is separate. Prayer is to take care of the spiritual, not of sex. Sex is separate."

Similarly, Rosalía, a forty-year-old married woman who has been working as a seamstress after migrating from Mexico City, stated: "Well, I say that it [sex] is separate, isn't it? We do not have to let ourselves be influenced by what the Church says about sex anymore." Like Patricia, she identified herself as a practicing Catholic. Rosalía clearly explained this duality between both sexual and religious aspects as a consequence of a historical evolution of the Church, modernity and social life, and her own life as a Catholic woman.

Other women such as Felicia were brief but clearly reacted by nodding her head while reacting to the paragraph of the "Carta al Papa": "Sex . . . well, I think that we do not have to involve God in those kinds of things because sex is something that is happening here in this world, on this earth, not in God's Kingdom."

Patricia, Rosalía, and Felicia established a clear division between sex and celestial affairs. For women like them, the Church is associated with practices promoting religious faith and spiritual growth; they establish a clear separation between the Church and religion, on the one hand, and sex and mundane affairs, on the other. These women established a clear-cut division, with sex and sexuality as aspects that belong to worldly matters involving the body and the flesh. For all of them, women's sexuality matters are personal, private, and intimate issues completely divorced from religious faith and spirituality concerns promoted by the Catholic Church. Some of them explained how religious they were, some of them said they attended mass regularly on Sundays but some said they did not, and some expressed with great pride their ardent devotion, respect, and love for *la Virgen de Guadalupe*. Beyond these differences, the common denominator among all of these women was an interesting belief: the Catholic Church is an institution that promotes faith and takes care of spiritual affairs and must not interfere with women's sexuality concerns or worldly issues directly connected to carnal, erotic, or sexual concerns.

This tendency to establish a clear-cut polarized division between religion-church-spirit, on the one hand, and sex-sexuality-body, on the other, is not an easy emotional endeavor. Soledad, a twenty-seven-year-old married woman from Mexico City who works part-time in a sweatshop, best exemplifies why this is a reality for some women. As she explained: "The pope objects to condom use and says it is bad. But if you have twenty children, the church is not going to give you money to support them and to give them a good education." For women like her, an inner struggle is unmasked as some of these women explained, with enraged tones of voice, the need for keeping both areas separate because the moral ideals promoted by the Church with regard to women's sexuality clash with central aspects of their daily-life personal experiences and their social reality as heterosexual women. Soledad's words best exemplify this discord between idealized moral expectations from the Church and a woman's need for personal agency, responsibility, and sexual autonomy. As we continued with the interview, she expanded on this issue: "Well, I think the Church should not say anything about sex. I think that all those issues about sexuality and birth control and abortion, and all that, is a personal matter, something about your personal life, and about your relationship between you and your partner."

In sum, this group of women are active agents yet members of a subordinate social group who in their marginalized identities must redefine the Catholic Church's responsibilities as those that involve exclusively and solely the promotion of faith and spiritual growth of its members. Even though it may create conflict and emotional stress, they split "sex/sexuality/the body" from "religion/the Church/the spirit" as distinct and autonomous concepts that belong in two different, divided, and mutually exclusive social spheres and/or personal dimensions in a woman's life.

Based on their social location and standpoint as women with sexualized bodies as well as personal and social realities, they clearly challenge the Catholic Church's involvement with sexuality matters or worldly concerns by becoming aware of its unrealistic sexual morality.

## Sexual Agency and Religion: The Woman Is the One Who Decides

As discussed at the beginning of this essay, Xóchitl, from a small town in Jalisco, talked to me about the excitement she experienced while attending *los cursillos de la iglesia* (courses periodically organized by the Church) when she was a teenager before she migrated to Los Angeles at age twenty-five. During the interview, behind her glowing expression and persistent curiosity, Xóchitl said she had a special interest in discussing issues connecting religion, the church, and women's sexuality because of her active participation in *El Movimiento Familiar Cristiano* and her personal experiences while living in a convent after a love disappointment. Xóchitl's zealous restlessness while discussing these issues became more evident while we explored her experience at *las pláticas prematrimoniales,* or premarital group presentations. Attending *las pláticas prematrimoniales* offered Xóchitl both the opportunity to comply with an official prerequisite to getting married by the Church and a clear social scenario to learn about the institution's sexuality teachings. "When you see that the information is good for you, you take it, if you see that is . . . well, old fashioned, you get rid of it, you do not pay attention to it," Xóchitl firmly stated as we explored what she did with all the information offered to her by *las amas de casa* (housewives) and *las parejas católicas* (Catholic couples) leading these presentations.

Xóchitl's words best represent my definition of *sexual agency* for purposes of this chapter. Agency in this sense refers to a woman's personal attitudes and behaviors aimed at contesting and redefining Catholic sexual morality while making individual decisions with regard to sexuality-related aspects of her life, including her reproductive health. Xóchitl also exhibited agency with regard to particular sexual practices. As we continued, Xóchitl explained to me the sexuality-related information she received from *las pláticas.* She described, for example, the mix of terror and curiosity she experienced as one of the presenters gave one of her lectures: "Anal sex, you cannot do it that way, it has happened that women get to the hospital dying with their intestines outside!" After Xóchitl overcame her own astonishment while describing her instructor's ideas on anal sex, I asked her: "When they tell you all this about anal sex, what do you do about it later on?" She replied, "Well, only if I experience it will I be able to know if it really happens or not. I tried to do it but it was something experimental. My husband and I understood that we could not do it and that was the end of it."

Clearly, Xóchitl exhibited personal agency and autonomy as she evaluated and explored the validity and reliability of the knowledge she received. Ultimately, she selected, accepted, or rejected the various sources of information she is exposed to while making personal decisions involving her sexual behavior. She claimed for herself the right to make decisions while meticulously discriminating, incorporating, and reconciling into her sex life only specific morality teachings based on their convenience or appropriateness according to her own personal lifestyle and social reality.

For instance, at some point during the interview, Xóchitl explained to me that even though she knew that virginity was a moral expectation demanded by the Catholic Church, she voluntarily decided to have sex before she got married and she said that she would not be concerned about her daughter experimenting with premarital sex. "They are too rigid . . . it cannot be that way!" she exclaimed. She told me that she was completely aware of the unrealistic nature of the Catholic Church's teachings on sexuality. As a way to conclude her opinion about all these issues, Xóchitl said: "Well, I think it is up to oneself, *uno es quien decide más que nadie* [oneself is the one who decides more than anybody else]."

As with the previous group of women, questioning one's loyalty to the teachings of the Catholic Church is not a simple process. While I was still drawn by my own curiosity, I commented, "You were a highly involved Catholic; did you ever question some of these priests or educators with regard to their teachings on sex?" Then she replied, "Yes! The priests would laugh; they only said '*¡Ah, tremenda muchacha!*' [What a young lady!]" As we finished our discussion on issues related to the Catholic Church and her sex life, I verbalized my last enigma. "It gets my attention that you were highly involved in the Church and at the same time you had your own progressive ideas about your sex life. How do you reconcile these two parts of your life?" She replied, "Well, you do not stop feeling guilty. I think that in the deepest part of my heart I have a little bit of guilt. But you have to take it out! You have to talk about it, even if you are invaded by these feelings of guilt and regret. Where would I end up if I did not do it?"

Xóchitl explained how she had played an active role by challenging the

Church's teachings; she continued explaining how priests ignored or avoided her progressive opinions.

As already discussed, the first group of women would recognize the contradictions as well as the chaotic disjuncture between the Catholic Church's sexual morality and their own sexual and social realities as women. For women like Xóchitl, reconciling a highly committed religious life with embracing personal agency in her sexual life is neither a smooth experience nor an overnight transformation. In addition, Xóchitl's personal inner struggle required her to pay a psychological cost in order to harmonize two important aspects of her life: on one hand, religious faith as a source of inner strength, and on the other, sexual autonomy and agency as important and intimate personal concerns for her as a woman.

Other women, not as highly committed to church activities as Xóchitl but embracing religiosity with the same faith and devotion, expressed parallel experiences. For example, Azalea, a forty-three-year-old married woman who eventually became an apartment manager after migrating from Mexico City, articulated in a gentle and warmhearted tone of voice: "I love the Catholic Church very much because they do not force us to do anything, there is freedom for everybody to do with our personal lives whatever we can. But we all know what is good and what is bad." As she organized her ideas to give an opinion about the "Carta al Papa," she said, "The pope and every single priest always tell you things. And that is O.K., but I think that it is better for each person to do whatever is convenient for that person. Right? I think that they interfere but each one of us possesses his/her life and we do what is good, not what is bad, according to ourselves."

Like Xóchitl, Azalea expressed her love and respect for the Catholic Church. Also like Xóchitl, she recognized the potential value found in some of the teachings offered by the Catholic Church and simultaneously identified the importance of granting agency to the individual to make personal decisions depending on her/his life circumstances.

I explored with Azalea concrete examples of her interesting ways to reconcile her deep devotion while attending Sunday mass on a weekly basis, her respect for what Church authorities have to say about sexual morality, and her flexibility to respect an individual's autonomy. She patiently explained the main reason why these three aspects of her personal religious life were not mutually exclusive: the Catholic Church is a highly permissive and informal institution. She recognized the possibility of confession as an outlet that makes everything possible. In addition, she emphasized the importance of redefining what is morally appropriate according to the individual's social and economic circumstances. As we discussed her opinion about reproductive health, she emphasized a woman's right to choose any contraceptive method including contraceptive pills and abortion, depending on her socioeconomic conditions or limitations. Elsewhere, I examine women's views of contraceptive use and abortion.[3]

Also from Mexico City, Irasema asserted: "I am Catholic because it was inculcated in my mind by my parents, but *yo tengo los pies en la tierra* [I have my feet on the ground]." Like Xóchitl and Azalea, Irasema also talked about the ways in which she reconciles her Catholic faith, a woman's need to be autonomous with regard to her reproductive health, and a woman's personal socioeconomic circumstances. Although she never lived in poverty, Irasema said that she is aware of the socioeconomic plight of the women she met while working at a garment shop in Mexico City. These women frequently got pregnant and had children *uno tras otro,* or year after year, because of a Catholic mandate she sarcastically recited for me: "*Yo voy a tener todos los hijos que Dios me mande* [I will have all the children God wants me to]." For Irasema, being realistic or keeping her feet on the ground did not translate into feelings of guilt or remorse. Based on her prochoice values, Irasema strongly supported a woman's need to make her own personal decisions, beyond religious mandates, about her sexual and reproductive health based on her personal and socioeconomic circumstances.

A fourth woman, also from Mexico City, joined this group of women. A forty-one-year-old domestic worker and a married woman, Yadira talked to me about her deep devotion as a *guadalupana* while showing me with great pride and respect some of her colorful and splendid lithographs of the Virgin of Guadalupe, the Virgin Mary, and other virginal images hanging on the walls of her home while we had an informal conversation before beginning our interview. "I am not completely religious because I am not completely involved in the Church. I believe in my virgins, in my Virgin of Guadalupe, in my God, and I attend Sunday mass," she later clarified for me with a euphoric and assertive tone in her voice after I asked her if she considered herself a religious person. As we engaged in our interview, we explored her opinion about the "Carta al Papa," which she celebrated with great joy. Yadira reacted to my reading of the passage with the following: "Well, yes, sex is a beautiful thing but the man is machista and things have to be done the way he says. But sex should be done on a mutual agreement; that is what makes it beautiful. The letter is not offensive, quite the opposite. As time and years pass by, the Catholic Church and human life have to evolve."

As paradoxical as it may appear, Yadira, a fascinating *guadalupana*, redefines for herself the meaning of religiosity while experiencing her faith and complying with each one of the established religious rituals and festivities. Simultaneously, she embraces a progressive mentality supporting continuous changes within the Catholic Church as part of modernity and social evolution. She expressed her religiosity while articulating a need to accommodate and integrate, while harmonizing her faith, religious practices, and progressive changes within the Church with regard to sexual morality. However, for Yadira, the process is complex to attune what seems irreconcilable. She elaborated during the interview with a gesture of concern as we explored some of her personal decisions with regard to her sexuality and reproductive health, "The Church does not authorize the use of contraceptive pills but I took them for a long time because . . . *¿cómo es que yo me iba a cuidar?* [How was I supposed to 'take care of myself,' in other words, 'prevent a pregnancy'?]." Intrigued by Yadira's struggle, I asked, "How do you do it? You follow your religious practices, and then you make your own decisions with regard to your sex life at the same time." She replied, "In part I feel fine, in part I do not feel fine. Because I know that I have done things against my religion but to some extent I feel relaxed because it is not possible to have many children if you do not have the economic means for it. Why bring children to this world if they are going to suffer?"

Besides describing for me her feelings of ambivalence and her personal struggle with Church mandates, Yadira confided to me the many times she felt guilty after she had premarital sexual relations and then after cohabiting for more than ten years. She told me how finally she made her confession not long ago and at some point felt more comfortable and at peace with God and with herself. Like Xóchitl as well as the first group of women, who establish a polarized duality to reconcile religion and sex, religious women like Yadira may experience an emotional struggle while integrating a desire to comply with these two important parts of her life and making important personal decisions.

In sum, the subjective experiences reported by this particular group of women become a collective experience if we observe how a subgroup of these women clearly exercise personal agency by selectively perceiving, judging, and incorporating or accommodating into their sex lives only specific information offered by the Catholic Church. In other words, these women meticulously discriminate and accept only the knowledge and values that would not interfere with their own personal lifestyles and value systems with regard to sexuality. Interestingly enough, women who were highly committed and involved in church activities in their places of origin displayed this type of pattern.


## Catholic Obedience: One Must Follow God's Mandates

"Well, I do not agree. I believe that in order to live in harmony *uno debe de seguir los mandatos de Dios* [one must follow God's mandates]," proclaimed Oralia with a serious facial expression, while stating severe disapproval of the "Carta al Papa." A thirty-nine-year-old married woman who currently works as a health educator after migrating from rural Jalisco, Oralia belongs to the minority of women (20 percent) who in the study questioned, objected to, and critiqued the text from the 'Carta al Papa." Her words best represent what the other few women in this group verbalized. These women considered it inappropriate and defended fundamentalist perspectives on women's sexuality and sexual morality that have been traditionally established and promoted by the Catholic Church. The vast majority of the women who objected to the paragraph that I read were from small towns in Jalisco, which may indicate a greater tendency for them to be exposed to fewer and more restrictive sexual discourses, and a higher pressure to conform in terms of sexual morality and Catholicism than those women educated in the capital of the state (Guadalajara) and/or from larger metropolitan areas.


## Analysis and Conclusion

These women's sexual lives within the context of their social condition as Catholics challenge the biased and prejudiced misrepresentation of Mexican women as *abnegadas* and *sumisas*. Mexican immigrant women do not automatically take and incorporate oppressive ideologies into their sexual lives, even those coming from the controlling and dominant Catholic Church. Instead, they may become active agents who contest, resist, and redefine in many creative ways such moral prescriptions from their own sexual experiences. What Mexican immigrant women report they do in their personal sex lives with regard to Catholic sexual morality is based on each woman's critical adaptations of these moral principles into her individual and unique experiences as a heterosexual woman. In this way, women socially construct emancipatory sexual moralities as they claim their right to control their own sexuality, including their reproductive rights. Sexually speaking, the uniqueness of each one of these women's personal and individual ways of experiencing their heterosexuality as Catholic women is consistent with the ways in which they experience their loss or preservation of premarital virginity and motherhood and sexuality.[4] That is, multiple female heterosexualities are constructed and systematically reproduced by, through, and within social practice. These dynamics resonate with the feminist theorist Lynne Segal's (1994) proposal to acknowledge the existence of multiple heterosexualities. Segal's invitation to recognize many heterosexualities while examining women's sexuality as a social and political issue (that is, considering each and every one of the social, cultural, and political forces that oppress women's sexuality) offers an enlightening alternative to explore the many possibilities for Mexican immigrant women to claim their rights to sexual autonomy, pleasure, and emancipatory sexual moralities. As Segal states: "There are different heterosexual experiences and different heterosexualities. We need to explore them, both to affirm those which are based on safety, trust, and affection (however brief or long-lasting), and which therefore empower women, and also to wonder (because it won't ever be easy) how to strengthen women to handle those which are not" (Segal 1994: 261).

In addition to recognizing multiple heterosexualities and Mexican women's sexuality within their social context, for Mexican immigrant women as a subordinate social group, Catholic teachings on sexual morality are dynamically mediated by their personal subjectivities emerging from their standpoint as women, that is, their individual judgment "within" in connection with their everyday and real-life sexual and social situations and/or circumstances. As illustrated by their sexual stories, these women do not automatically assimilate Catholic sexual moralities into their sex lives: they *either* question the Catholic Church representatives and their morally debilitated and/or ideologically inconsistent real-life practices, *and/or* they critically process, challenge, redefine, and accommodate sexual mores from various personal perspectives. Furthermore, women creatively use various mechanisms to soften and harmonize what may look irreconcilable at first sight. For these women, Catholic faith with its corresponding religious practices and sexual morality, on the one hand, and a woman's sex life and her real-life sexual practices, on the other, are not necessarily mutually exclusive. They are intimately interconnected by the many fluid paradoxes, contradictions, and nuances shaping these women's interpretations of religion and sex.

As illustrated by the personal experiences they highlighted in their testimonies, women have the potential to redefine the purpose of religion and faith in their lives while becoming aware of the disjuncture between ideal moral values and their authentic sexual and social realities as women. Women may reconcile a highly committed religious life while looking for possibilities for a self-governing sex life. However, women's decisions to transgress internalized Catholic prescriptions controlling their sexualities may exact an emotional cost such as feelings of guilt, ambivalence, and remorse. As part of this experience, a morally debilitated Church (e.g., priests abusing children, priests having children, etc.) may help them to cope with these feelings of inadequacy. In spite of the moral and psychological cost Catholic women may pay, it is still possible for them to have sexual agency while making concessions to preserve religious practices and beliefs.

These women's experiences of sexual agency happen within social and cultural contexts, but they also take place within these women's emotional worlds. The emotional state that accompanies each of these women's testimonies exemplifies Nancy J. Chodorow's (1995) notion of gender as both personal and cultural. As illustrated, these women perceive and contest the social meanings of a Catholic sexual morality, and as they engage in this process, they experience power relations emotionally. Shame, guilt, remorse, frustration, hope, concern, confusion, anxiety, excitement, and rage, among other emotions and feelings, accompanied and shaped these women's experiences of gender inequality. Thus, these women construct their meanings of a gendered sexual morality both socially and collectively, but also from their personal emotional uniqueness. They interpret the meanings attached to sexuality and the erotic based on their subjective interpretations of religion and faith.

The women in this study follow processes parallel to Jeanette Rodríguez's (1994) conceptualization of *religiosidad popular,* that is, how religion is truly lived and experienced by the majority of people.[5] Following a similar mechanism, the women in this study create a commonly self-defined emancipatory sexual morality, or *moral liberadora,* in many creative ways. Accordingly, they do not necessarily compromise their Catholic faith and religious practices. This *moral liberadora* emerges from what Dorothy Smith (1987) identifies as the "standpoint of women." For Smith, women's standpoint is defined as "[a] method that, at the outset of inquiry, creates the space for an absent subject, and an absent experience that is to be filled with the presence and spoken experience of actual women speaking of and in the actualities of their everyday worlds" (Smith 1987: 107).

This way, if we see Mexican women from their social location as a subordinate group and start from the standpoint of Mexican immigrant women's sexual experiences and everyday life experiences—as a subordinate social group, as Catholic, and as sexual beings—we will be able to make visible what was previously invisible. Accordingly, the dominant forms of sexual morality established by the Catholic Church rupture at the very point where a critical standpoint comes to surface: the experience of Mexican women raised in Catholic families as a standpoint from which being a woman, being sexual, and being Catholic can be known and understood *only* from "within." The rupture or disjuncture where the standpoint originates is closely associated with what Smith describes as "bifurcation of consciousness," a concept she uses to explain the subordinate status of women in society. For Smith, women—unlike men—experience a bifurcation of consciousness: women enter into a world ruled by and for men and at the same time go through a transition process to reposition themselves into their own location in society as a subordinate group, that is, as female and local. However, the local has not been the site for the development of systematic knowledge or rules governing society.

The similarities connecting these women's stories and their common patterns suggest a collective social struggle or bifurcation of consciousness shared by Mexican women as a subordinate social group. By creating new, more authentic and/or realistic sexual moralities (i.e., a *moral liberadora* for and by Mexican women), they may challenge the danger and risks of being sexually oppressed while still being able to practice their Catholic faith. Interestingly, the minority of women who do not experience a disjuncture or a need to reconstruct and create a liberating morality are obedient and faithfully comply with the sexual moralities promoted by the Catholic Church.

Most women in the study, however, clearly experience a bifurcation of consciousness: They were born and raised as members of the Catholic Church (an institution created and controlled by and for men) and were exposed to its rigid morality, and simultaneously, they experience a transition as they occupy their location and everyday life experiences as a subordinate group who has neither political nor economic power or control over such regulations. This bifurcation estranges Mexican women and keeps them voiceless. As illustrated, women who become aware of the disjuncture while looking at sex and religion from their standpoint break their silence. For heterosexual Mexican women raised in the Catholic faith who become aware of their bifurcation of consciousness, the disjuncture has multiple translations. It means challenging many moral contradictions and incongruities within the Church as an institution. It means redefining the Church, morality, and sexuality from a particular social location as women. It means praying the rosary while taking contraceptive pills and using condoms. It means making complex accommodations to reconcile religious faith and sex. It means belonging while being excluded. It means obeying while resisting. It means feeling guilt while contesting. It means going to mass and kneeling down in the morning and having sex while figuring out erotic pleasure at night. It means praying while being sinners.

## Notes

1. This essay represents a part of my dissertation work at the University of Southern California. My dissertation (González-López 2000), analyzes the impact of immigration on the sexual ideologies and behavior of forty women who identified themselves as heterosexual and who migrated from Mexico City (20) and Jalisco (20) to Los Angeles. The dissertation is based on interviews with women I recruited at various community-based agencies and elementary schools located in the Los Angeles inner-city area.

The lowest level of formal education for both groups was *educación primaria,* which is equivalent to completion of sixth grade; the highest level was a *licenciatura,* or a bachelor's degree. However, women from Jalisco were more likely to have a lower level of formal education (average = 7.1 years) than their Mexico City counterparts (average = 10.15 years). Accordingly, Jalisco women were less likely to have paid employment (9 out of 20) and more likely to be full-time homemakers (11 out of 20) than the Mexico City informants were. Most women from Mexico City reported having paid jobs (15 out of 20); a few of them reported that they were full-time homemakers (5 out of 20). Interestingly, women from Jalisco had permanently lived longer in the United States (average = 11.68 years) than the Mexico City group (average = 8.85 years). At the time of the interview, many participants were married (N = 27), and other women were cohabiting (N = 7). Other participants were legally divorced (N = 1) or separated after having been married (N = 2) or after cohabiting (N = 1). Only two of these women had never been married, neither of whom had any children. Thirty-nine out of the forty women were educated in families promoting the Catholic faith; only one was raised in a Protestant family. All of them were born and raised in a society strongly influenced throughout history by the Roman Catholic Church.

Financial and academic support made this project possible. I am profoundly grateful to the Social Science Research Council for the generous dissertation fellowship I received through its Sexuality Research Fellowship Program.

I want to express my gratitude to the forty women who trusted me with their personal lives and sexual stories. I hope my interpretations are an honest reflection of their personal experiences.

Segments of this essay are cited in my book (González-López 2005); see it for additional reflections on the Catholic Church and sexual morality in contemporary Mexico.

2. A group of actively involved women (religious nuns, catechists, and secular women) made the "Carta al Papa" public during the pope's visit to Mexico in 1990. As part of this letter, this group of Mexican Catholic women addressed their progressive ideology to the pope while examining their concerns as women with regard to sexuality matters. See de Barbieri (1990).

3. About 50 percent of the women in the study objected to abortion practices; 20 percent supported abortion or prochoice ideologies; 20 percent expressed ambivalent opinions about this issue; and 10 percent did not give an opinion about abortion. As discussed in this essay, the majority of the women in this study were more likely to promote and support progressive changes within the Church. However, a substantial number of them support an antiabortion ideology. What are the reasons for this seeming contradiction? Two groups within the antiabortion category represent this interesting paradox: (1) Women who simultaneously support progressive changes within the Catholic Church but perceive abortion as a socially regressive alternative for women. For them, a "modern" and "well-informed" woman should be able to take contraceptive pills or to have access to other potential contraceptive methods such as the rhythm or "natural family planning" method and condoms instead of choosing abortion. (2) Women who support progressive changes but who perceive abortion as a crime for reasons other than religious (e.g., women's subjective interpretations of pregnancy). Based on the first dynamic, a woman's personal decision to have an abortion transforms her publicly into a socially regressive woman living in the Dark Ages: an ignorant woman. Ultimately, the decision to have an abortion or not becomes a public affair subjected to the corresponding moral control of social institutions. As stated by Lucía Rayas (1998): "The feelings of guilt and indecency that surround abortion arise because the very fact of pregnancy attests to having exercised sexuality—a tremendous affront to institutions like the state, law, and religion which seek to control women's sexual lives." For examinations of this issue in Mexico and other Latin American countries, see Rayas (1998). For additional information on these forty women's views of abortion, please refer to my dissertation (González-López 2000).

4. Elsewhere, I examine these women's reasons to practice sexual abstinence before marriage, for example, women's fear of men's recriminations for their not being virgins at marriage and women's virginity as linked to an ethic of family honor and respect. See González-López (2003).

5. Jeanette Rodríguez (1994) explains how in the case of Mexican Americans, *religiosidad popular* is represented by the complexity of spontaneous expressions of faith, which have been celebrated by the people over a considerable period of time. The official hierarchy, in this case the Roman Catholic tradition, does not establish these expressions of religiosity. Rodriguez illustrates in her study how and why Mexican American women may perceive the image of the Virgin of Guadalupe as an empowering figure and not as a source of oppression.

# References

Almaguer, T. 1993. Chicano men: A cartography of homosexual identity and behavior. In *The lesbian and gay studies reader,* ed. B. Abelove, M. Barale, and D. Halperin. New York: Routledge.

Alonso, A. M., and M. T. Koreck. 1993. Silences: "Hispanics," AIDS, and sexual practices. In *The lesbian and gay studies reader,* ed. B. Abelove, M. Barale, and D. Halperin. New York: Routledge.

Amuchástegui, A. 2001. *Virginidad e iniciación sexual en México: Experiencias y significados.* Mexico City: EDAMEX.

Baca Zinn, M. 1982. Mexican-American women in the social sciences. *Signs* 8 (2): 259–272.

Chodorow, N. J. 1995. Gender as a personal and cultural construction. *Signs* 20 (3): 516–544.

de Barbieri, T. 1990. Carta al papa. *Debate Feminista* 1 (2) (September 1990): 357–361.

Gagnon, J. H. 1977. *Human sexualities.* Glenview, Ill.: Scott, Foresman and Company.

Gagnon, J. H., and W. Simon. 1973. *Sexual conduct: The social sources of human sexuality.* Chicago: Aldine Publishing.

González-López, G. 2000. Beyond the bed sheets, beyond the borders: Mexican immigrant women and their sex lives. Ph.D. diss., University of Southern California.

———. 2003. De madres a hijas: Gendered lessons on virginity across generations of Mexican immigrant women. In *Gender and U.S. migration: Contemporary trends,* ed. Pierrette Hondagneu-Sotelo. Berkeley and Los Angeles: University of California Press.

———. 2005. *Erotic journeys: Mexican immigrants and their sex lives.* Berkeley and Los Angeles: University of California Press.

Guerrero Pavich, E. 1986. A Chicana perspective on Mexican culture and sexuality. *Journal of Social Work and Human Sexuality* 4 (3): 47–65.

Laumann, E. O., and J. H. Gagnon. 1995. A sociological perspective on sexual action. In *Conceiving sexuality: Approaches to sex research in a postmodern world,* ed. R. G. Parker and J. H. Gagnon. New York: Routledge.

Marín, B. V., and C. A. Gómez. 1997. Latino culture and sex: Implications for HIV intervention. In *Psychological interventions and research with Latino populations,* ed. J. G. García and M. C. Zea. Boston: Allyn and Bacon.

Paz, O. [1950] 1987. *El laberinto de la soledad: Vida y pensamiento de México.* Mexico City: Fondo de Cultura Económica.

Plummer, K. 1995. *Telling sexual stories: Power, change, and social worlds.* London: Routledge.

Rayas, L. 1998. Criminalizing abortion: A crime against women. *Report on Sexual Politics* 31 (4) (January/February): 22–26.

Rodríguez, J. 1994. *Our lady of Guadalupe: Faith and empowerment among Mexican-American women.* Austin: University of Texas Press.

Segal, L. 1994. *Straight sex: Rethinking the politics of pleasure*. Berkeley and Los Angeles: University of California Press.

Seidman, S. 1994. *Contested knowledge: Social theory in the postmodern era*. Oxford: Blackwell.

Smith, D. 1987. *The everyday world as problematic: A feminist sociology*. Boston: Northeastern University Press.

Travis, C. B., and J. W. White, eds. 2000. *Sexuality, society, and feminism*. Washington, D.C.: American Psychological Association.

Weeks, J. 1985. *Sexuality and its discontents*. London: Routledge.

CHAPTER 8

# Disability and Sexuality

*Toward a Constructionist Focus on Access*
*and the Inclusion of Disabled People in the*
*Sexual Rights Movement*

RUSSELL P. SHUTTLEWORTH

Disabled people suffer significant social oppression in the United States and are stigmatized in many sociocultural contexts, perhaps none more so than within the contexts of dating and romance and in their attempts to negotiate sexual intimacy. Yet a critical constructionist approach to studying the intersection of disability and sexuality has been slow to emerge.[1] In the present essay, I first suggest some of the reasons for this neglect and argue that a key focus of this kind of research should be on the construction of access/obstruction to the sociocultural contexts in which desire is evoked and sexual negotiations become possible. I then discuss two of the primary obstacles that disabled men with whom I conducted anthropological research felt impeded their negotiating and establishing sexual intimacy with others—barriers that in effect construct them as undesirable and asexual in the U.S. cultural imaginary: (1) the cultural valuing of normative (nondisabled) functioning, and (2) hegemonic masculine expectations, dispositions, and embodied practices. I also make the case along the way for an engaged and participatory ethnographic approach. Finally, I will attempt to answer the question of what a constructionist focus on disabled people's sexual access brings to the sexuality studies table and its implications for an inclusive sexual rights agenda.

# Toward a Constructionist Focus on Access in Disability and Sexuality Research

Current thinking proposes that both disability and sexuality are socio-culturally constructed categories of experience. Although all societies notice and respond to some physical, cognitive, and/or behavioral differences, disability as a cultural category with its particular constellation of tragic, medical, and economic meanings is considered unique to societies influenced by certain Western European value-orientations that focus on the individual (Whyte and Ingstad 1995; Barnes 1996). Similarly, although sexual practices have always been part of the human equation, recent scholars in the human sciences have emphasized the cultural and historical specificity of sexuality and gender (for example, Foucault 1978; Vance 1991; Weeks 1986, 1995; Gagnon and Parker 1995; Halperin 1990). Jeffrey Weeks (1995: 33–34) puts the core constructionist principle as applied to sexuality thus: "we can only understand sexuality through understanding the cultural meanings which construct it." From this perspective, the intersection of disability and sexuality can be fruitfully viewed as a product of society, culture, and history.

Yet while constructionist scholarship on these categories has experienced exponential growth, research on their intersection has until recently been minimal. Despite occasional critiques every few years by disability studies scholars on the neglect of social, cultural, and political factors in disability and sexuality research, this area of study still tends to be dominated by medical-model thinking in which the meanings of the body are always seen in relation to functional norms and disability is fixed in a particular bodily impairment and its functional limitations (Hahn 1981; Waxman and Finger 1989; Waxman 1994; Gill 1989; Shakespeare, Gillespie-Sells, and Davies 1996). One significant reason for this neglect is that the disability rights movement has traditionally focused on what are perceived as more immediately pressing concerns, such as architectural and economic barriers (Shakespeare, Gillespie-Sells, and Davies 1996). Disability studies initially followed suit. In addition, the relatively new discipline also follows an historical trend in neglecting sexuality as a topic of study: sexuality research has suffered marginalization throughout the gamut of social sciences, which reflect certain moralistic attitudes toward sex that are prevalent in the society at large (di Mauro 1995).

Recently, however, disability studies has finally begun to seriously interrogate the impediments to sexual expression for disabled people as yet another example of a "disabling society" (see, for example, Shakespeare,

Gillespie-Sells, and Davies 1996; Shuttleworth and Mona 2000, 2002; Mona and Shuttleworth 2000; Shuttleworth 2000a, 2000b, 2001b, 2003a, 2005; Grossman, Shuttleworth, and Prinz 2004; Mona and Gardos 2000; Shakespeare 2003; Hamilton 2002; Wade 2002; O'Toole 2002; Shildrick 2004b; and Wilkerson 2002).[2] This idea, central to disability studies, is that impairment is not the cause of disability, as in the medical model, but rather disability is "a condition of a society in which people with impairments are discriminated against, segregated and denied full participatory citizenship. It is a shift away from 'disabled' being seen as a personal tragedy, to 'disabled' being a positive identity. And it is a shift from dependency and passivity, to the rights of disabled people to control decision-making processes that shape their lives" (Swain, French, and Cameron 2003: 1). Although there are differences of emphasis in the various sociopolitical models currently vying to supplant the medical model as the dominant disability paradigm and also between theories of disability such as materialist and postmodern perspectives, in all of these approaches disability is conceived as a sociocultural construction meant to oppress people with impairments; that is, those persons whose bodies, bodily movements, or behaviors fall outside the narrow aesthetic and/or functional range considered "normal" are subjected to stigmatization and disabling (exclusionary) practices.[3] Yet, despite increased critical constructionist attention to disability and sexuality in disability studies, implications of the notion of a "disabling society" have not been adequately conceptually fleshed out in terms of the sexuality of disabled people.

Important theoretical debates within gender and sexuality studies may have also inadvertently deterred a more constructionist research focus on disability and sexuality. Following the lead of Foucault (1978), feminists, and gay and lesbian studies, a significant amount of work has been concerned with the constitution of gender and sexual identities (see, for example, Stanton 1992; Stein 1992; Halperin 1990; and Butler 1990, 1997).[4] In much of this scholarship, achieving sexual intimacy with another in and of itself is not problematized as an issue to investigate. In short, the problem of accessing the interpersonal contexts in which desire is evoked and sexual negotiations become possible has not much structured theoretical debates within constructionist approaches to the study of sexuality. However, "sexual access" is perhaps the most significant area of concern for those disabled people who are more than mildly impaired.

Certainly, the issue of multiple oppression in which disability intersects with gender or sexual minority status complicates the theoretical landscape in the study of disability and sexuality. Contending with mul-

tiple oppressions based on a combination of disability and gender identity and/or sexual minority status can indeed be a formidable task. Important work is emerging that focuses on and theorizes these intersections (see, for example, Shakespeare 1998; Tremain 2000; Atkins and
Marston 1998; O'Toole 1996; Asch and Fine 1988; Morris 1996; Appleby
1994; Butler 1999; and McRuer and Wilkerson 2003).[5] This work must
of course continue, yet the key issue that disabled people face whether
they are gay or straight, women or men, is how to access the contexts of
dating and romantic relationships and negotiate sexual intimacy.

Although anthropologists' work on sexuality is often more subtly at-
tuned to "the ways different communities structure the possibilities of sexual interaction, thereby defining a given range of potential sexual partners and practices" (Parker, Barbosa, and Aggleton 2000: 7), they have
not much focused on interrogating the barriers to achieving sexual intimacy for certain minority members of a society. In terms of disabled
people specifically, anthropologists have often offered anecdotes on their
reduced dating, sexual, and marriage opportunities (see, for example,
Nicolaisen 1995; and Ablon 1984). There have even been a few papers written on aspects of disabled people's negotiation of intimacy and sexual relationships (see, for example, Wolf and Dukepoo 1969; Ablon 1996; and
Sentumbwe 1995). However, these works have been peripheral to the anthropologist's main ethnographic goals, and they also tend to underthe-
orize the articulation of beliefs and values, social structures, and gender
expectations with disabled people's intimacy and sexual restrictions and
opportunities. Several anthropological works on disability and sexuality
(and also on marriage negotiation) have appeared, however, that use more
innovative and critical constructionist approaches and bode well for the
future of this research specialty (see, for example, Block 2000; Guldin
2000; Kohrman 2000; and Shuttleworth 2000a, 2000b).

In terms of sexuality studies more recently, a broadening of the research
focus to highlight, as Gilbert Herdt (2001) puts it, "the study of social
inequality in the field of human sexuality" will, I think, bring the sexual
issues of oppressed minorities heretofore not well represented in sexuality studies research more clearly into view (also see the introduction to
this volume). The contributors to the present volume represent the most
concentrated effort in this expansion of the topical and theoretical vision
within human sexuality studies and the cultural critique of sociosexual
inequality in its multifarious manifestations. Parker's (1997: 31) paper calling for "a positive and empowering conception of sexual rights capable
of providing a point of departure for the work carried out across . . . di-

verse fields" also suggests inclusion. Inclusion of the intersection of disability and sexuality as a legitimate research topic in sexuality studies and as a legitimate concern of the larger sexual rights movement will, I think, push the envelope in constructionist theorizing on sexuality and indeed in how we approach the issue of sexual rights.

## The Concept of Sexual Access

On the whole, those persons who are more than mildly impaired experience significant restrictions in attempting to negotiate sexual relationships with others (Shuttleworth 2000a, 2000b; Shuttleworth and Mona 2002; Mona and Gardos 2000; Shakespeare, Gillespie-Sells, and Davies 1996). From 1996 to 1999, I conducted ethnographic research with fourteen men with cerebral palsy, and they mentioned a wide range of sociocultural issues that negatively affect their search for sexual intimacy. These issues include sociosexual isolation during their adolescent years, parents' negative or protective attitudes, a lack of sexual negotiation models for disabled people, unattainable ideals of desirability, social expectations of normative functioning, poor body image, and male gender role expectations, among other concerns (Shuttleworth 2000a, 2000b). These men generally perceive these issues as interrelated barriers. The cumulative effect of these barriers is to buttress the asexual representation of disabled people in the U.S. cultural imaginary and to severely restrict their access to contexts in which the negotiation of sexual relationships occurs.[6]

Accessibility is another cornerstone concept of the disability rights movement and its academic offshoot, disability studies, and is often used as the measure of a disabling society. That is, sociocultural contexts within a society are interrogated in terms of how accessible or not they are for disabled people. Adequate conceptualization of this idea is what, I believe, is missing from much of the new critical constructionist work on disability and sexuality (Shuttleworth 2003a, 2005). Of course, caution must be used in applying the not unfamiliar term *sexual access*. This notion as currently used by sociobiologists or evolutionary psychologists means access by males to sex with females (see, for example, Buss 1994). In gendered terms, sex is the resource that women have and men desire. Yet this masculinist and heterosexist understanding of access does not render the concept itself flawed but only the interpretational framework on which it is based.

The notion of sexual access as it is developing in the study of disability and sexuality is related to the disability rights movement's and disability studies' understanding of equality of access. However, because this concept's use in disability studies has been limited to easily demarcated contexts such as schools, workplaces, and the built environment, it has remained relatively untheorized. Truth be told, a rather legalistic and technical understanding of the term holds sway that does not appreciably alter even when programmatic access becomes the analytical target (see, for example, Burgstahler 1994). Embodied feelings, communicative processes, and the symbolic aspects of disability are generally not much taken into account. A narrow technical understanding of access is one reason that disability studies has been slow to interrogate sexuality as a cultural context and social field of possibility that is exclusionary for many disabled people.

A theoretically articulate understanding of the concept of access should incorporate an existential-phenomenological sense of access-obstruction as a continuum of our prereflective experience of the world-for-us (Shuttleworth 2000a, 2000b, 2001b, 2003a). That is, our felt sense responds to how accessible the objects of our intentions (things, social contexts, symbolic meanings, physical environments, etc.) are as different kinds of expansion or obstruction (Freund 1990; Buytendijk 1950; Fell 1977).[7] The felt obstruction of an intention is often the cue to the lived experience of a sociocultural exclusion.[8] Although personal characteristics always factor into the development and exercising of sexual agency, access to avenues of sexual expression and sexual negotiation are highly influenced by how well one embodies the cultural norms and expectations of personhood and desirability in a society. The barriers encountered by the men I conducted fieldwork with in one way or another all reveal their problematic relation to the embodiment of these norms and expectations.

Thus, the interrogation of sexual access for a particular minority group, in the present case disabled people, begins with an analysis of the felt sense continuum of access-obstruction to a society's avenues of sexual expression and sexual negotiation. Elucidating how felt sense is related to the relative accessibility of these avenues and how these avenues have been structured in accordance with a hierarchical ordering of bodies and persons and explicating the power relations and restrictions that are implied are the tasks of an access-centered approach. In actuality, this kind of approach would interrogate the entire spectrum of possible factors that might contribute to sexual exclusion including physical, aesthetic, historical, economic, psychological, political, symbolic, and social barriers. If one is, for example, communicatively impaired and has dysarthric speech or uses an augmentative communication device, then even if one occupies the physical space of a party or a nightclub, which are often meeting places for those interested in pursuing sexual relationships, one may be excluded from the social context of negotiating dates with most of the people there through one or more of a combination of relevant factors including the loud environment, poor lighting, body beautiful expectations, poor body image resulting from body beautiful expectations, normative functional evaluations (especially communicative norms), gender expectations, and negative cultural meanings of disability. For such a person, opportunities for sexual negotiation will often tend to elude their personal intentions.

Sexual access can also be measured in terms of sexual well-being. Sexual well-being is reliant on psychological, social, and cultural supports that sustain a positive sense of one's sexual self. Disabled people often report experiencing a lack of supports, whether in their families of origin, institutional contexts, or society at large, that acknowledge and nurture their sexuality and thus build their sexual self-esteem (Shuttleworth 2000a, 2000b; Mona and Gardos 2000; Shakespeare, Gillespie-Sells, and Davies 1996; Rousso 1993). Redeploying the concept of sexual access in interrogating felt sense, interpersonal relations, hierarchies of desirable bodies and persons, implied power relations, and the relative availability of social and cultural supports for sexual well-being will lead to new insights into disabled people's sexual issues and also act to politicize these issues (Shuttleworth 2003a, 2005; Shuttleworth and Mona 2002; Grossman, Shuttleworth, and Prinz 2004).

Paradoxically, a focus on accessibility and the cultural formations that attempt to sexually exclude people with particular types of bodies or behaviors and restrict certain embodied subjects from negotiating sexual intimacy may also lead to new insights and questions regarding the construction of sexual and gender identities. In fact, it is in relation to their restricted access to interpersonal contexts in which sexual negotiations become possible that the intersection of disability and gender appears most starkly to the disabled men with whom I talked as an issue to be reckoned with. A constructionist focus on sexual access/exclusion thus provided me with the theoretical entrée to these men's crisis of masculinity. For some men, the difficulties experienced in their sexual negotiations within the narrow parameters of hegemonic masculine standards impelled them to incorporate alternative gender dispositions and practices into their masculine repertoire. Of this expanded masculinity I will have more to say later in the essay.

# Participatory Ethnography
# in Disability and Sexuality Research

As mentioned, in the mid through late 1990s I conducted ethnographic research with fourteen men with cerebral palsy who live independently in the East San Francisco Bay Area, focusing on the interpersonal issues they face when searching for lovers. For the study I also interviewed seventeen relevant others on the subject of these men's sexual situation. The fourteen men who make up the primary sample were between the ages of eighteen and fifty-one when I began interviewing them. They all have some degree of mobility impairment: eleven men use wheelchairs, one man uses crutches, and two men limp when they walk. Eleven have speech impairments, and four of these use augmentative communicative devices such as an alphabet board or computer with speech output. Eight of the men were white; the rest represented a wide range of racial and ethnic backgrounds.[9] The snowball sample also turned up one gay man; one man who had experienced several brief "one nighters" with men but considered himself heterosexual; another man who was in a group marriage with a woman and a man but who always presented as more attracted to women; and eleven men who were attracted solely to women. Although the gay man did mention several issues in his search for sexual intimacy that differed from those mentioned by the straight men, he nevertheless revealed that there are also many similar access issues in gay sexual contexts and in straight contexts.[10]

My ethnographic work seeks to theoretically engage and also challenge the emerging critical constructionist movement in the study of disability and sexuality. I approach disability and sexuality by interrogating the cultural meanings that construct this intersection and the impediments to sexual expression, sexual negotiation, and sexual subjectivity for disabled people, and I also attend to the lived process of my informants' contention, negotiation, and resistance within an adverse context of disability and desirability (Shuttleworth 2000a, 2000b, 2001b, 2002, 2003a, 2004b). Further, I am also committed to a reflexive, participatory approach to ethnographic research (see Shuttleworth 2000a, 2001a, 2004c).

Traditionally, the anthropologist's immersion in a culture was temporary. Ethnographers usually returned from the field to write up their research in the relative comfort of their own society. Yet, this involves a cleavage of the ethnographer's experience and a separation from the exigencies, imperatives, and struggles of the particular group studied, no matter how many times the anthropologist returns to visit and renew friendships (see Clifford 1997; Gupta and Ferguson 1997; and Fabian 1983). Further, the anthropologist's participation in a particular society via the ethnographic method of participant-observation was often a contrived participation from the get-go, based on an adventurous whim, the lure of the exotic, or the availability of funds for certain research problems or for particular geographic/cultural areas. An anthropology based on serendipity and the experiential and interpretive gaps resulting from cleavage and separation perhaps fit with the objectivist tendency in the social science of the day. That is, in the age of objectivity, a certain lack of investment could perhaps be construed as an asset. Yet, increasingly anthropologists are calling for more politically committed and socially responsible ethnographic approaches beyond the limits of applied anthropology (see, for example, Berreman 1973; Paine 1985; Scheper-Hughes 1995; Kasnitz and Shuttleworth 1999; Shuttleworth 2000a, 2001a, 2004c; and Shuttleworth and Kasnitz 2004, forthcoming).

A move to participatory research, as discussed by Herdt (2001; also see the introduction to this volume), suggests some kind of vested interest in the group studied, whether that interest be similarity of identity (gender, sexual, ethnic, disability, etc.) or a prolonged intimate association with the research group or research issue that results in empathetic siding. Applying the term *participatory* to ethnography would particularly highlight this move in anthropology. Being a participatory ethnographer might also imply that one has other roles in the research community in addition to that of ethnographer. For the sake of transparency, the vested nature of participatory ethnography would necessitate a radical reflexivity concerning one's assumptions, roles, statuses, and allegiances within the research context and the relations that support and maintain this engaged participation (Shuttleworth 2000a, 2001a, 2004c).

The struggle for sexual liberation by diverse minorities necessitates a politically committed approach for those conducting ethnographic research with these groups; identification-based participation or, alternatively, empathetic siding with one's informants based on years of intimate association are more apt to foster social commitment than ethnographic practice based on serendipity and long periods of separation from the research population. Further, specific to a liberatory human sexuality studies, a crucial issue becomes not only how and in what ways we as researchers are positioned in relation to our informants, but especially what these positionings and relations can possibly reveal concerning any sociosexual inequalities experienced by our informants.

I came to my research with a deep understanding of disability issues honed from years of participation within disability culture, and as an ally in the struggle for disability rights. In fact, early experiences of going to the movies or some other function in the community with my disabled cousin and witnessing the stares of nondisabled people directed toward him (and thus indirectly at me) initially sensitized me to the stigma that disabled people often have to endure. This may have been one reason why I originally applied for a job in Berkeley as a personal assistant for young disabled men in the early 1980s. My job gave me an entrée into disability culture as lived in the East San Francisco Bay Area.

Over the years I have performed sundry personal care tasks for the men for whom I have worked, as well as provided assistance in the practical aspects of completing school assignments and in their communication with others in classes, meetings, and other public contexts. Thus I have an embodied knowledge of their practical daily needs, as well as an understanding of their interaction in a variety of interpersonal contexts in U.S. society. In this intimate role, I have also been privy to their thoughts and feelings on their pursuit of sexual relationships. I believe that the scope and depth of my involvement in the disability community and commitment to their struggles afforded me the opportunity to cultivate a unique, relational perspective from which to research and write about their sexual lives (Shuttleworth 2000a). Further, my familiarity with disabled people and their issues, especially men's sexual issues, over the course of many years instilled in me a deep investment in and commitment to conducting socially responsible research that can assist in sociocultural and sexual change.[11]

For several years, I lived and worked with one of the heterosexual men in the research, a close friend, Josh.[12] Perhaps the most participatory aspect of the research was accompanying this man to strip clubs as his personal assistant and assisting him in negotiating sexual encounters with sex workers. Josh uses an alphabet board and head-pointer, and people initially have trouble reading his board. Since I have known him so long, I can interpret for him very quickly and he often used me in this capacity. One of my primary tasks was accompanying him to his classes while he was going to college. I would essentially be his communicative vehicle during class. Visiting strip clubs with him and assisting him in acquiring sexual experiences through visits to sex workers were collaborations that I initially fretted over. I was very concerned about the ethics of my participation, anxious about whether my actions were inappropriate in the context of ethnographic fieldwork. In retrospect, and with the help of some recent writings about the ethnographer's sexuality in the field, I am now more critical of anthropology's long-standing taboo against the ethnographer participating in sexual experiences or interactions while in the field (Shuttleworth 2000a, 2001a, 2004c; Kulick 1995; Herdt 1999; Ashkenazi and Markowitz 1999; Lewin and Leap 1996).[13]

Assisting my informant in his quest for sexual experiences and sharing the heterosexual masculine gaze with him (a gaze that, I should add in my own case, is not unaware of the abuses of hegemonic masculinity and the assumptive nature of heteronormativity) certainly implicates me as a participant in his sexual interactions in the field. The anthropological silence concerning ethnographers' sexual experiences in the field in fact operates to reinforce our own society's moral evaluations regarding the appropriate contexts within which one may engage in or disclose one's sexual interactions. Yet, it was really only through participating in my informant's sexual dilemma, socially positioned as his friend and personal assistant, that I could begin to reflect on the degree to which sexuality is considered a reflexive personal project of the self in the United States and other Western societies (Giddens 1992), and also at least one of the reasons why sexual relationships that deviate from the ideal of self-sufficiency, such as sexual surrogacy and prostitution, which are utilized by some disabled people, are so stigmatized.

Sexuality as a reflexive project of the self relies on the rhetoric of autonomy and self-sufficiency. Those who fail to find a sexual partner in the sanctioned self-sufficient ways are thus open to negative judgment. Suffice it to say that this realization deepened my understanding of the sociocultural terrain that disabled people often encounter in their search for sexual intimacy in U.S. society—left to fend for themselves in a symbolic and structural realm of unequal opportunity, in which stigmatized alternatives are sometimes seen as one's only alternatives. As a facilitator of my main informant's quest for sexual experiences and as an almost round the clock discussant, I was able to capture an incredible array of his thoughts and feelings on this phase of his sexual life.[14] If I had simply been an ethnographer in the disability community for a year or two to conduct a study, and not in some sense a participant in disabled people's dilemmas, my reflections on ethics and subsequent understanding would likely never have emerged (Shuttleworth 2000a, 2001a, 2004c). A necessary concomitant of a socially responsible ethnography based on this kind of intimate participation, as alluded to earlier, taken in the context of the struggle for sexual liberation, is that I am compelled to lend my voice as an ally in calling for social and sexual rights for disabled people, as well as for other oppressed sexual minorities.

# The Construction of Asexuality

Despite the ascendance of a more democratic process within the "politics" of intimate relationships, what Giddens (1992) has called the pure relationship, the "politics" of partner selection in U.S. society, as discussed earlier, would try to exclude those exhibiting bodily, cognitive, and behavioral differences. In looking for a lover, one enters a domain of unequal opportunity. The interpersonal context of negotiating sexual intimacy thus poses a difficult challenge for many disabled people. Access here cannot rely on the rule of law or public policy. The San Francisco Bay Area, a bustling urban metropolis famous for its openness to difference, is home to a thriving disability community. To an extent not possible in other areas, disabled people can often escape the stares of nondisabled people. Yet, in their search for sexual love, the diversity of the Bay Area is no guarantee against adversity.

In the current essay, I want to focus on a couple of barriers that the men I talked with perceive as especially problematic in order to highlight the issue of access as it relates to disabled men living independently in the community. Later, in the context of sexual rights, I will raise some additional problems of access with which those disabled people who live in more restricted settings might have to contend.

## NORMATIVE FUNCTION AND HEGEMONIC MASCULINITY AS BARRIERS TO SEXUAL INTIMACY FOR DISABLED MEN IN THE UNITED STATES

The two issues that most often emerged in my discussions with the men with whom I conducted research were the difficulty that they experienced in meeting social expectations of normative functioning and control and male gender role expectations. In fact, normative function and hegemonic masculine expectations (as well as other factors) implicitly structure the contexts of desirability in U.S. society, stacking the deck against these men in their search for sexual intimacy.

### NORMATIVE FUNCTIONING

Michel Foucault's (1975, 1979) historical account of the emergence of normalization views sudden epistemological ruptures in particular institutional discourses related to medicine and the prison in the eighteenth and nineteenth centuries as providing the groundwork for our current emphasis on measurement, classification, and regulation. The disciplinary mechanisms of modern institutions, most notably hierarchical observation and normalizing judgment, made one subject to the evaluative gaze of both others and oneself. Normalizing judgment is especially relevant for disabled people in U.S. society. Norms, of course, inherently refer to a value system. As Canguilhelm (1989: 240) observes, "norms, whether in some implicit or explicit form, refer the real to values, express discriminations of qualities in conformity with the polar opposition of a positive and a negative." Normalizing judgment has become a typical modern cognitive style, classifying "people in terms of their relationship to a social norm" (Douard 1995: 154). For our purposes, it is understood to operate in one's making judgments about others in relation to a particular norm of bodily appearance or function but also as one subjects oneself to similar judgments.

In U.S. society then, normalization takes up, as one of its evaluative dimensions, the judgment of function (Shuttleworth 2000a). The social philosopher Cornelius Castoriadias (1987) notes that modern rationality is obsessed with the perfect lining up of aspects of any particular system in terms of its functional efficiency, but a functional efficiency stripped of an awareness of a raison d'être. It is because functionality has no intrinsic relation to ultimate ends, that Castoriadis sees it as the materialization of "the extreme autonomization of pure symbolism" (1987: 159). In other words, function itself has become fetishized. The fetishization of function illuminates the medical and rehabilitative emphases on cure and restoration, respectively, and indeed the cultural groundwork for our understanding of the notion of impairment itself. Expectations of efficient functioning and control are coded and structured in accordance with normative, that is, nondisabled, embodiment (Shuttleworth 2000a; Paterson and Hughes 1999). Proper alignment with these functionally oriented, embodied codes often underlie our perceptions and evaluations of others.[15] The transgression of these embodied codes within particular carnal contexts of meaning such as mobility or communication by disabled people and the combination and severity of transgressions can result in varying degrees of disjuncture for many nondisabled people and subsequent negative evaluation and symbolic associations conjured up from the U.S. cultural imaginary (Shuttleworth 2000a).

While bodily appearance in general is assumed as an important determinant of whether one is seen as sexually desirable in U.S. society, the functions and movements of the body have not been much interrogated in the construction of the sexual object. Yet, sexual desire and desirability as an embodied context of meaning are likely no less judged in terms of the functioning of the body than other contexts—a sexual aesthetics of bodily movement and functionality. This kind of functional evaluation may be especially relevant to disabled people's sexual situation. In fact, within the interpersonal context of trying to establish sexual relationships, the disabled men with whom I talked felt that others' perception of their lack of physical function and control constructed them as sexually undesirable.

David, who has a significant speech impairment and uses an electric wheelchair, told me, "We fly in the face of this society's emphasis on being in control of one's self." Dirk, who also has a speech impairment and uses a wheelchair, relates U.S. society's emphasis on function and control specifically to trying to negotiate sexual relationships:

> *Dirk:* One of the things that makes it difficult for many people to have a really intimate relationship with a person with a substantial disability is that on some level, the person with a disability is a child . . . developmentally, physically because they don't have this—they're operating physically on the—not as [a] person, as a being, as a physical being, they don't—they're operating on the level of a kid, of an eight-year-old, a five-year-old. If you can't go to the bathroom, if you can't feed yourself, if you're uncoordinated, if you're not graceful, those are all attributes of a little kid. Again, I don't think that people are necessarily aware of this stuff consciously but I think that there's a certain discomfort with the idea . . . of associating your intimate self with the intimate self with someone else who isn't where you're at.

Here, Dirk highlights the symbolic association he feels many nondisabled people make between limitations of physical functioning and control with being a child. Since children are generally not considered sexual beings in U.S. society, implicit in this association are two possible interpretations: (1) that disabled people with limited physical function are also asexual; or (2) that disabled people with limited physical function are not desirable as sexual objects because they are not seen as adults.

In their attempts to establish sexual intimacy with others, the majority of men felt that mobility was an issue. Notice how Jim, who has a significant limp, constructs his body image implicitly in comparison to normative mobility, which directly affects his attempts to establish intimate relationships:

> *Jim:* My body image comes directly in my face when I'm dealing in some kind of relationship with a woman. It comes up a lot, so much. Because

once again I put pressure on myself saying if I like a woman, I'd say how can she like me with my weird ass fucking body and the way I walk. I can go out and lecture and I can do whatever; I do that stuff really good, but when it comes to relationships, then that's the dark side of me.

The majority of men with speech impairments also felt that their non-normative speech or alternative mode of communicating acts as a barrier in negotiating sexual relationships. For example, listen to what Josh, who uses a head pointer and alphabet board, says:

*Josh:* It is like I'm trapped inside this body that doesn't work. . . .

*Russ:* Feeling trapped—how do you cope with that?

*Josh:* I really don't know. When I go to campus I see so many girls that I would try to talk to if I could.

*Russ:* And you don't think it would work to approach them with your board?

*Josh:* No. That is why I said it is like I'm trapped.

*Russ:* Not being able to speak to them?

*Josh:* Yes, it drives me nuts because I think I am a really nice person, but most people will never get to know that.

Another research participant, Bob, considers his difficult to understand speech and body difference in relation to body image as a major reason for his sexual rejection:

*Russ:* So, body image is still a struggle?

*Bob:* Always will be because of the way people look at you. I mean you want to be accepted . . . and being rejected by the mass majority is a major problem. You're rejected because you talk differently, because your body is in a strange position.

These men's difficulties in negotiating sexual intimacy, while on the one hand structured by others' negative responses to their differently functioning bodies, are also fueled by their own expectations of normative bodily functioning. As I have elucidated elsewhere (Shuttleworth 2000a, 2001b, 2002), it is by breaking their prereflective habitual expectation of rejection, conditioned by others' past negative responses and their own normative evaluation of themselves, that some of these men begin to cultivate a positive sexual self-image. Breaking the dispositional conditioning that they are bodily and functionally undesirable is thus one key aspect in the development of their sexual agency.

## HEGEMONIC MASCULINE EXPECTATIONS

Several disability studies scholars have noted the dilemmas that disabled men confront in the face of our society's hegemonic expectations of masculinity such as competitiveness, strength, control, endurance, and independence (Hahn 1989; Tepper 1999; Shakespeare 1999; Gerschick and Miller 1996; Valentine 1999). For the heterosexual men in this study, confronting the dilemma of how to be masculine when one is disabled most clearly emerges during their interpersonal attempts to negotiate sexual intimacy with others or when contemplating their sexual agency (Shuttleworth 2000a, 2000b, 2004b). Josh wonders, "It is funny because if a girl came up to me would I know what to do? Like I do not kiss very well. Or because my arms are down here [by his sides], I cannot very well try to hold her hand. So what the hell do I do? I think women like to be touched and hugged, and I cannot very well do that. It drives me nuts." An ex-girlfriend of one of the subjects revealed that she was dissuaded from continuing her relationship with him by the social pressures that cast him as an unattractive mate, one example being the comments of her friend, who kept asking her how could she stand being with a man who could not hold her in his arms.

In the following conversation, Ed reveals how masculinity, intimately tied to his own sense of embodiment, is also symbolically deployed in the potency represented by the functioning phallus in the larger cultural imaginary:

> *Ed:* Her and I dated for almost a year; she had a few girlfriends and she told me that they said, why are you with him? They thought I wasn't functional. Of course when we first started to get to know each other, she asked me, can I, can I? And I said, I can. And all of the sudden these girlfriends said all this, they didn't ask, can he? They just assumed, I can't. And her family was like, why? Why don't you find a real man?

> *Russ:* She said that's what they said to her?

> *Ed:* Yeah, no one's ever said that directly to me. That and I kind of feel like when I go out to the bars and some of these women feel that way. They just kind of don't want to, they want some action and I ain't going to give it to them.

> *Russ:* You see them as not taking you into account as . . . a man who could do that?

> *Ed:* Right, it's kind of the whole thing—sexually. . . . I would assume most women kind of want to be taken care of. . . . And I think that women see me in a chair and say, I can't do that. And all but one of the women

> that I have been with in a relationship, until we got to know each other, they have no trouble with that and they said, you can. I feel a little, if a woman gave me a chance, I could show her I can.

> *Russ:* If you feel they aren't giving you a chance, how do you feel about that?

> *Ed:* Frustrated.

According to Bourdieu (1977), men and women incorporate a gendered habitus involving gender-specific dispositions and bodily practices—culturally constructed feminine and masculine ways of being-in-the-world and of inhabiting, moving, and using the body. Although cultural research is beginning to take account of the construction of alternative masculinities and femininities (see, for example, Connell 1995; and Herdt 1993), in U.S. society hegemonic, narrowly construed, binary gender expectations are nevertheless assumed in most everyday social interactions and, depending on the context, can often restrict the expression of alternative gender identities and practices. Certain typical masculine expectations such as demonstrating initiative, competitiveness, self-control, assertiveness, and independence, incorporated as dispositions to varying degrees, also manifest in bodily comportment and corporeal and interpersonal negotiations and practices, and are crucial aspects of U.S. society's hegemonic masculinity. These expectations pervade our social being-with-each-other and are generally perceived as essential in business, sports, and dating, among other contexts, and symbolize male potency in the U.S. cultural imaginary. Noncompetitive, tentative, and disabled men are not generally located in our society's images of masculinity (Shuttleworth 2000a, 2000b, 2004b).

As can be seen from this discussion, men with cerebral palsy often cannot embody masculinity in some of these typical ways. Nondisabled people's assumptions about disabled men's sexual impotency often further construct disabled men as lacking masculinity and as asexual. One can thus see how hegemonic masculinity negatively influences these men's possibilities for negotiating sexual intimacy with others. Those men who continually measured themselves against rigid masculine expectations were more apt to remain immobilized or to socially withdraw when they fell short and/or were rejected as lovers. Those men, however, who did not view hegemonic masculinity as a total index of their desirability and who could draw on alternative gender dispositions and embodied practices, such as interdependence, prioritizing emotional intimacy, becoming friends first, and allowing the other to sometimes make the physical moves without feeling less of a man, could better stand rejection and remain open to the possibility of interpersonal connection and sexual intimacy, and, in fact, were able to cultivate significantly more successful sexual relationships than those who could not. Often linked with femininity in our society, such dispositions and practices thus take their place alongside those associated with hegemonic masculinity for these disabled subjects, effectively expanding their masculine repertoire (see Shuttleworth 2000a, 2000b, 2002, 2004b). For example, note Fred's insistence on emotional intimacy in a sexual relationship:

*Fred:*   I never wanted just sex.

*Russ:*   What do you want with sex?

*Fred:*   Intimacy.

*Russ:*   How do you define intimacy? What is it?

*Fred:*   Living with people in an intimate way.

*Russ:*   Close?

*Fred:*   Yes.

*Russ:*   What about emotions, do they come into it at all?

*Fred:*   That was why I did not try hookers.

Although Fred wants sex, he is very explicit about not wanting "just sex."

Contrary to researchers such as Gerschick and Miller (1996), who perceive the dilemma of disabled masculinity in abstract and idealistic terms (see Shuttleworth 2000a, 2004b), I see the construction and performance of gender as worked out in the hurly-burly of everyday life situations. For these disabled men, contending with particularly adverse social conditions and ongoing negative evaluations of their sexual worth, masculine identity becomes an issue precisely in trying to access the contexts that structure sexual negotiations with others (and to a lesser extent when trying to access other contexts defined by hegemonic masculinity). It is only in failing to measure up to typical masculine expectations when trying to access these social and sexual contexts that their masculinity becomes an issue of explicit concern. This is likely because hegemonic masculinity, like heteronormativity, is implicitly assumed.[16] Not measuring up, so to speak, sets in relief their distance from typical masculinity (Shuttleworth 2000a, 2000b, 2002, 2004b). Further, similar to these men's self-comparison to normative functionality, a psychic break with their habitual comparison to gender norms has to occur to widen their notions of gender and to garner some success in negotiating sexual intimacy with others.

Beyond the pragmatic recognition that expanding their masculine repertoire can result in increased sexual opportunities with others, several men explicitly realize the larger insight that gender is a constructed category of experience. Transcending their own sexual access issues, these men understand the cultural necessity to expand notions of gender beyond the narrow construction that dominates our society's understanding of this identity category. This is a promising sign for the development of a strong coalition between feminists, the gay, lesbian, bisexual, and transgender movement, and disabled people—a coalition that contests narrow and binary constructions of sexual and gender identity. Although some disabled women, disabled gay and lesbian scholars, and their allies necessarily point to gender and sexual minority oppressions and the need to expand our definitions of these identity categories (for example, Shakespeare 1998; Tremain 2000; Atkins and Marston 1998; O'Toole 1996; Asch and Fine 1988; Morris 1996; Appleby 1994; Butler 1999; McRuer and Wilkerson 2003), the recognition of a similar desire to expand our notions of gender identity that emerges from research with these primarily heterosexual men bodes well for the future growth of this coalition. Indeed, adding these disabled people's voices to those who struggle for gender and sexual diversity would be a significant step. Yet the converse recognition by feminists and sexual minorities, that of the constructedness of impairment and disability, especially as it relates to issues of sexual access/exclusion, should also be part of the building of this coalition and the sexual rights agenda that is currently emerging.

## Toward the Inclusion of Disabled People in the Sexual Rights Movement

Against the cultural assumption of their asexuality, the fact that many disabled people are currently claiming sexuality (Guldin 2000), and thus, I would argue, are inherently staking their claim not only to full personhood but also full subjectivity (Shuttleworth 2000a, 2000b, 2002), gives credence to constructionist arguments concerning the increasingly constitutive role for sex in terms of subjectivity and identity (for example, Foucault 1979; Halperin 1990; Weeks 1985).[17] The highlighting of oppression in the construction of gender and sexual identities by feminist researchers and gay and lesbian scholarship has added important intellectual weight to the feminist and gay and lesbian social movements, as well as assisted in positive changes in the circumstances of these groups in U.S. society. These discourses will inevitably have some bearing on any constructionist analysis of disability and sexuality (see Shuttleworth 2000a, 2000b, 2002, 2004b). And when the research focus becomes interrogating the processes and contexts that are conducive to the formation of disabled people's gender and sexual identities, they become directly relevant to an access perspective. That is, how accessible for disabled people are these identity formative processes and contexts?[18] Yet disability identity runs across genders and sexual orientations. Indeed, the sexual politics of disability is finally gaining momentum because many disabled people are now applying the major idea of the disability rights movement and disability studies to their sexual lives—that it is the social and cultural barriers that deny opportunity and access and sexually exclude them (Waxman and Finger 1989; Shakespeare, Gillespie-Sells, and Davies 1996; Shuttleworth 2000a, 2000b).

Given the need to investigate the construction of disability and sexuality in terms of access as well as identity, how does this alter the current discussion regarding sexual rights? Parker (1997: 35) states that "we will need to elaborate a clearly defined set of ethical principles, which might include sexual diversity, sexual decision-making autonomy and gender equality, as the objectives of sexual rights." Sexual decision-making autonomy is especially relevant to disabled people's concerns. This principle takes on added meaning in the context of disabled people's struggle for sexual access. Although the present essay has shown some of the sexual access issues for disabled men who live independently in the community, for those persons with developmental impairments who live in institutions, quasi-institutions such as group homes, or familial contexts, access to a sexual life is complicated by additional impediments. Institutional and familial barriers based on prevailing notions of personhood and sexuality are apt often to exclude these disabled people from making their own sexual decisions. A sexual rights agenda that includes the issues of both those disabled people living independently in the community and those residing in more structured settings needs to ask some tough questions. For example, does the disabled person living in a group home have the right to contract the sexual services of a sex surrogate or sex worker for home visits? If so, what are the barriers to accessing this sexual right? Does a disabled person with significant restrictions on bodily movement have the right to ask her/his personal assistant for help with masturbation or to help facilitate sex between him/her and another disabled person? Any movement for sexual rights that includes disabled people must at a minimum address the barriers to accessing the options for people who may not be able to achieve sexual expression and/or sexual intimacy with others through normative cultural avenues. Further, at what point are cognitively impaired adults who live either with their parents or in institutions deemed competent enough to make their own sexual decisions?[19]

If, as is the case with many disabled people living in more structured living situations, sexual access is socially restricted at every turn and one has minimal sociocultural support for expressing one's self sexually, forming sexual and gender identities (normative or not), and negotiating sexual relationships with others (Shuttleworth and Mona 2002; Hamilton 2002; Wade 2002), then to what degree can one even form a sense of one's self as a sexual agent or, for that matter, form a sexual or gender identity? Fausto-Sterling (2000: 122) asserts, "Without human sociality, human sexuality cannot develop." Yet does it make sense to talk about human sexuality within the context of a human sociality—that is, social relations within these more structured living situations—that lacks support for and access to sexual well-being and the possibility of sexual intimacy with others?

That sexuality studies and the larger sexual rights movement have not yet incorporated an understanding of sexual access issues into their research and rights agendas was brought home to me during the summer of 2001 at the first Summer Institute on Sexuality, Society, and Health at San Francisco State University. A female student who had just received her M.A. in rehabilitation counseling was taking an independent study with me on disability and sexuality. This student has a cognitively impaired son and has experience working with similar youths on sexuality-related issues. In another one of her classes (according to accounts, hers included), there was a pause in the discussion as everyone congratulated each other on the societal gains made in recent years regarding increased acceptance of sexual diversity and sexual minorities. In response, she piped up that many disabled people with developmental and/or cognitive impairments were still not able to make their own sexual decisions and that their sexual expression was severely restricted. She went on to describe their sexual situation. Reaction in the class was one of surprise followed by some positive discussion. Following the class, this student told me that she was approached by quite a few of her fellow students who wanted to know more and felt concerned that they had not even thought of the issue she had brought up. I contend that this issue was invisible to these students because they had never focused on the problem of sexual access/exclusion in their sexuality studies education as a theoretical frame or an empirical issue.[20]

# Notes

The research in this chapter was assisted by a doctoral fellowship from the Sexuality Research Fellowship Program of the Social Science Research Council with funds provided by the Ford Foundation. The writing of this chapter was assisted by the Ed Roberts Postdoctoral Fellowship in Disability Studies, University of California, Berkeley, funded by NIDRR the Department of Education #11133P020009. I want to thank Niels Teunis for important critical feedback on this essay. Feedback given by attendees at the 2001 American Anthropology Association session "Sexuality and Social Inequality" and by the other authors in this book who attended the workshop that followed several months later was also invaluable. I also appreciate the editorial suggestions made by Devva Kasnitz and Sue Schweik. I am indebted to Gilbert Herdt for his support of disability and sexuality as a critical research and educational focus in sexuality studies.

   1. By *constructionist,* I mean a broadly interpretive approach that aims at discovering the ways social reality and sociocultural phenomena are constructed, not strictly the school of thought influenced by post-structuralism that is sometimes identified as constructionist and is now dominant in feminist and sexuality studies and holds that categories of gender and sexuality such as masculine/feminine and hetero/homo derive from culture, although the broader formulation would include the latter analysis. In this sense, *constructionism* describes the ways sociocultural phenomena are created and institutionalized by human beings. For interpretive approaches generally, as Schwandt (1994: 118) notes, "The inquirer must elucidate the process of meaning construction and clarify what and how meanings are embodied in the language and actions of social actors." Studies that use the more circumscribed formulation of *constructionism* often incorporate a critical perspective and include an analysis of power relations, which derives from a liberatory impulse. However, a constructionist perspective, utilizing the broader understanding of the term, is not obliged to take a critical and transformative approach to research issues. By occasionally appending the term *critical* to *constructionist,* I wish to emphasize that discerning the politics and power relations involved regarding a particular research issue and advocating for social transformation are important aspects of the research task even when the focus is not strictly on categories of gender or sexuality.

   2. Evidence of this new more critical and political approach to the study of disability and sexuality was the international conference held at San Francisco State University, "Disability, Sexuality and Culture: Societal and Experiential Perspectives on Multiple Identities" (see Shuttleworth and Mona 2000; Mona and Shuttleworth 2000). There was a brief time in the late 1970s and early 1980s when it appeared that the study of disability and sexuality might move beyond a medical-model analysis (Shuttleworth 2003b). In fact, there was a disability and sexuality unit at the University of California, San Francisco. However, although this work was more sensitive to social issues, it primarily focused on peer counseling and education (Jacobson 2000); the political dimensions of disability and sexuality appear to have been minimally explored. And when the money dried up during

the early Reagan years, this unit had to close up shop. In the mid-1980s through the mid-1990s, there were a few lone voices that advocated putting disability and sexuality on political and research agendas. I am thinking of people such as Barbara Waxman (1994), a disabled activist, feminist, and scholar; Harlan Hahn (1981), the disabled political scientist; and Carol Gill (1989), a disabled psychologist. Scholars such as these railed against the lack of sociocultural and political analysis in the study of disability and sexuality. But their call was not seriously taken up until the mid-1990s. The publication of Tom Shakespeare, Kath Gillespie-Sells, and Dominic Davies's *Sexual Politics of Disability* in 1996 was a major turning point.

3. In English-language societies this would include transgressions of normative bodily appearance such as scarring from severe burns resulting in a social impairment, and also perceived transgressions of bodily, cognitive, or behavioral functions. Most disability studies scholars today recognize that impairment, like disability, is a sociocultural construction; that is, the medical, rehabilitative, and lay focus on functional limitations constructs our understanding of impairment as of particular significance for individuals. It is anthropologists, however, who are showing the cross-cultural variability of impairment through their empirical and/or theoretical work (see Marshall 1996; Burck 1999; Shuttleworth 2004a; and Shuttleworth and Kasnitz forthcoming). In fact, in other societies functional limitations may play less of a role in the constitution of impairment than those in which English language is predominant. Other physiological or psychological statuses, for example, humoral statuses such as a wet or dry body part (Burck 1999), may also result in the negative construction of an impairment, which if negatively followed through with an exclusionary social response then becomes a disability. Thus, even though aesthetics or functionality in the Western sense may not be involved, there may still be disabling social responses using a more critical meaning of *disability* (Shuttleworth 2004a; Shuttleworth and Kasnitz forthcoming).

4. Of course, there has been a great deal of research that has not specifically focused on gender or sexual identities, HIV/AIDS and reproductive health, for example. However, the research focus on gender and sexual identities has been the most visible both inside and outside the academy, perhaps because it has been consistently theoretically engaging and has within it the most potential for liberation.

5. A disturbing issue that is foregrounded in much of the work on disability and sexual identity and disability and sexual orientation is that gay/lesbian communities have been known to exclude disabled gays and lesbians and that the disability community is not immune from homophobia. This oppression directed at both gays/lesbians and disabled people, of course, reflects the larger society's prejudices; thus, disabled gays/lesbians experience multiple oppression from the larger society and oppression from each of these marginalized communities, which complicates analyses of their identity construction. Although access is sometimes discussed in these works, it is more generally about achieving access to each community; it is usually not specifically related to removing barriers to negotiating and establishing sexual intimacy with others.

6. This should not be taken to mean that disabled people are unilaterally seen as undesirable and face sexual exclusion at every turn. I second Shakespeare's (2003: 148) caution "not to replace a traditional account of disabled people as tragic

victims of bodily restrictions with a radical account of disabled people as inevitable victims of social oppression." Disabled people are not helpless victims of socio-sexual oppression and many do experience sexual love with others. Although I focus on barriers to sexual access in the current essay, I have also shown "disabled people resisting and exercising agency" (Shakespeare 2003: 148) in their sexual lives in a variety of ways (see Shuttleworth 2000a, 2000b, 2002, 2004b). However, one should also guard against the opposite tendency, that is, of painting too rosy a picture of the current sexual situation of disabled people. In fact, in English-language contexts people who are more than mildly impaired can often experience significant barriers to negotiating and establishing sexual relationships with others. Further, in a survey of the anthropological and disability literature, I found that in many societies in which disabled people realize most aspects of social personhood, sexual intimacy and/or marriage is often still very difficult to access (Shuttleworth 2004a). It is imperative that we develop ways of theoretically apprehending the political and power-relational, structural, symbolic, interpersonal, and psycho-emotional dimensions of the range of sexual difficulties that disabled people may confront.

7. The inclusion of core principles of phenomenology, that consciousness is intentional, and existential-phenomenological psychology, that our felt responses derive from basic feeling modes articulating with the fulfillment of our intentions, distinguishes the perspective taken here from a strict constructionist analysis, which views phenomenology as essentialistic. This nod to an intentional-felt sense foundation is an acknowledgment of the limits and indeed inherent reductionism of a purely constructionist argument.

8. In order for a felt obstruction of our intentions to be personally interpreted as a social exclusion, it would need to be defined and articulated as such within a society. In other words, to recognize social exclusion as not being able to access a building in which a city council meeting is being held, one has to connect the personal sense of obstruction to the social sense of exclusion for a group of which one is a representative member, given the right within our society that any person can attend city council meetings. It is much more difficult to verify exclusion in the interpersonal landscape of encounters and relations than in those situations that can be addressed in terms of political or legal rights (that is, whether the fact of one's obstruction from accessing interpersonal contexts and relations does in fact point to socially exclusive prejudices being used in personal evaluations). For example, many of the disabled men in the research I conducted told me that when they tried to move a relationship with an acquaintance or friend to a more sexual place, the other person would say they just wanted to be friends. Even though they often felt that their negatively construed impairment was the primary reason for the rejection, with the awkwardness of the desired other being their primary cue, they usually could not confirm this suspicion without a shadow of doubt. Yet, I would contend that the desired other's awkward response occurred far too frequently in these men's narratives to be a coincidence and that their hunches are often correct; that, as is often the case, oppressed minorities become hypersensitive to their negative evaluation during interpersonal encounters and relations (Goffman 1963). Thus, disabled subjects' felt sense of their sexual situa-

tion should be taken into account in our analyses. At the very least, this awkward interpersonal space needs to be opened up for interrogation.

9. In an effort to protect research participants' anonymity, I chose to minimally describe their physical appearances other than those physical differences that are important for this study. This is unfortunate but necessary, given the close-knit disability community in the San Francisco Bay Area. In previous work, for several reasons including enhancing anonymity in this intimate community, I also chose to report my sample as composed of a less differentiated racial/ethnic makeup. However, small differences in racial/ethnic identity proved to be important in drawing out several issues in the men's narratives, and so here I report the full list of research participants' racial/ethnic identities: eight Caucasians, two African American (parents born in the United States), one African American (parents from Jamaica), one Latino, one Chicano, and one Lebanese (immigrated when six months old).

10. It would be premature to speculate here on any differences in the specifics of interpersonal encounters and the barriers to sexual interactions mentioned by these men. There were simply too few men in this study who were not strictly heterosexual. There has also been minimal empirical research conducted on this issue. Future ethnographic work should be conducted that specifically explores the patterning of experience and barriers for those disabled men who practice alternative sexualities as different from those who follow a heteronormative path.

11. My relational perspective, of course, cannot substitute for the lived experience of sexual oppression that the men I worked for often endure.

12. All names are pseudonyms.

13. These works that began to appear in the mid-1990s take anthropology to task for the discipline's traditional silence around sexual interactions and relations in the field, which effectively functioned as a taboo. Perhaps the most significant reasons given for this silence include anthropology's early and mid-twentieth-century aspirations to the scientific objectivity of other sciences and also a similar aspiration toward professionalism in the discipline.

14. Josh is currently in a more normative phase. At age thirty-nine, he is in a long-term sexual relationship with a woman, and the couple recently became the parents of a baby boy.

15. By this I do not mean to imply that other societies do not perceive and evaluate people and the world in functional ways. But as Castoriadis (1987) argues so well, no other society (and here he is referring to societies with a Western European rationalistic orientation) has applied it so ruthlessly to so many of life's processes and domains.

16. As Jackson (2003: 77), echoing many current sexuality scholars, notes, "heterosexuals often do not know what they are; they do not need to know; they are simply 'normal.'" The same can be said of many men who incorporate hegemonic masculine dispositions and express themselves in typically masculine ways. Many sexuality scholars see heterosexuality and gender as mutually constituting with one or the other as the more primary organizing ideology (for example, Jackson 2003; Ingraham 1996). Given this perspective, it is not surprising that the crisis

of masculinity that these heterosexual disabled men experience is especially acute in their attempts at sexual negotiation.

17. In previous work (2000a, 2000b, 2001b, 2002, 2004b), I linked negotiating sexual intimacy within traditional avenues of sexual expression to the normative conception of sexual subjectivity (and thus, by implication, full subjectivity) and argued that this conception attempts to restrict disabled peoples' sexual access by perpetuating the construction of their asexuality. I also suggested that by resisting this negative construction of their sexuality, some disabled people open up to and discover new forms of creative sexuality and sexual practices, some of which do not include genital stimulation (Shuttleworth 2000a, 2002). Margrit Shildrick takes these issues up in an interesting postmodern analysis, using Butler and Deleuze and Guattari, among others, and attempts to theorize this creative sexuality in terms of disabled people's more explicit relation to a performative interconnectivity (for example, use of personal assistants, prosthetic devices) that "breaks with the putative emergence of a coherent sexual subject from practices of embodiment" and allows for transformative possibilities (Shildrick 2004a: 10). In a larger sense that moves beyond the focus on disabled people's sexuality, Shildrick is suggesting that "the performativity of [sexual] subjectivity could be radically transformed" for everyone if the western notion of the autonomous individual and integrated identity were opened up to allow for more flexibility (11). While I agree with much of Shildrick's analysis, I am a bit uneasy with the thorough dissipation of the notion of sexual relationality in her work that leads her to claim, "Skin on skin in the bedroom is no more privileged than the sensation of fine sand running through my toes, or the sweet taste of a juicy peach on my tongue" (8). I would suggest that without some limits, we run the risk of obscuring that human-to-human erotic—not necessarily genitally oriented and sometimes emotionally laden—relationality is, in fact, what is often prized by both normative and more creative sexualities.

18. Several years ago at a Society for Disability Studies Meeting, a disabled woman in her late fifties described for me the arduous process of learning to be feminine after she began residing outside of institutions in her midtwenties. She claimed that her institutional upbringing had afforded her minimal opportunity to form a gendered sense of herself. The fact is that our conceptual frameworks are woefully inadequate to apprehend the process of gender and sexual identity formation and diversification, especially as they intersect the category of disability (Grossman 2003). An access perspective holds significant potential to yield new insights regarding this intersection.

19. For an interesting discussion on sexual surrogacy services, see Shapiro (2002). See Mona (2003) and Tepper (2000) for articles that deal with personal assistant services and facilitated sex. See Wade (2002) for a history of policy issues relating to those persons with developmental cognitive impairments. See Hamilton (2002), and Fitzmaurice (2002) for articles that discuss professional practice, ethical, and family issues related to the sexuality of people with developmental cognitive impairments.

20. This is true for access as it relates to interpersonal sexual relations, and also

access to the processes and contexts that promote sexual and gender identity formation, which was only briefly mentioned in this essay. The latter bears further explanation since sexual and gender identity are central topics of concern in human sexuality studies. In short, the tendency in constructionist analyses of sexuality and gender to focus on the contingency of identity categories as socioculturally and historically produced is not oriented to the problem of an individual or group's relative access to the formative processes and contexts for these identity categories. Therefore, the struggle for access to sexual and gender identity formative processes and contexts by some significantly disabled people, especially those residing in structured living situations such as nursing homes or group homes, is easily overlooked by constructionist disability and sexuality studies scholars working on identity terrain (see, for example, Shakespeare 1998; Tremain 2000; Atkins and Marston 1998; O'Toole 1996; Asch and Fine 1988; Appleby 1994; Butler 1999; and McRuer and Wilkerson 2003). This body of work for the most part assumes an unproblematic access to the processes whereby and the contexts in which sexual and gender identities are negotiated and formed. Following constructionist logic, identities are negotiated and constituted in social and interpersonal spaces. For those forming alternative or transgressive sexual or gender identities, one defines oneself to a large extent against oppressive structures and relations that manifest in one's everyday life. Less conscious awareness is expended in forming hegemonic identities because these are assumed in the structures and relations of everyday life. Yet for either normative or alternative sexual or gender identities, access to the processes and contexts of negotiation and formation is taken for granted. An implicit assumption of "independent living" guides these analyses, and oppressive structures are viewed as relatively transparent in the interactive dynamics of everyday life. But what if interaction and communication are vastly constrained by the institutional aspects of more structured living environments? Post-structural influences further urge us to subvert the current binary sexuality and gender regimes for the sake of diversity. Thus, scholarly attention to the issue of accessing gender and sexual identity formation may appear irrelevant or perhaps even contrary to the goal of subversion, especially if one reads formation as development (see Grossman 2003). In today's progressive climate of inclusive sexual rights, there is still too little attention paid to the gender and sexuality identity issues of significantly disabled people. Yet there need not be a reliance on developmental models or a prescription of binary genders/sexualities if access to identity formative processes and contexts and not particular identities is acknowledged as a liberatory goal.

# References

Ablon, J. 1984. *Little people in America: The social dimensions of dwarfism.* New York: Praeger.

———. 1996. Gender response to neurofibromatosis 1. *Social Science and Medicine* 42: 99–109.

Appleby, Y. 1994. Out in the margins. *Disability and Society* 9 (1): 19–32.

Asch, A., and M. Fine. 1988. Introduction: Beyond pedestals. In *Women with disabilities: Essays in psychology, culture, and politics,* ed. M. Fine and A. Asch. Philadelphia: Temple University Press.

Ashkenazi, M., and F. Markowitz. 1999. Sexuality and prevarication in the praxis of anthropology. In *Sex, sexuality and the anthropologist,* ed. F. Markowitz and M. Ashkenazi. Urbana: University of Illinois Press.

Atkins, D., and C. Marston. 1998. Creating accessible queer community: Intersections and fractures with dis/ability praxis. Queer and dis/abled, theme issue. *Journal of Gay, Lesbian, and Bisexual Identity* 4 (1): 3–21.

Barnes, C. 1996. Theories of disability and the origins of oppression of disabled people in western society. In *Disability and society: Emerging issues and insights,* ed. L. Barton. New York: Longman.

Berreman, G. 1973. The social responsibility of the anthropologist. In *To see ourselves: Anthropology and modern social issues,* ed. T. Weaver. Glenview, Ill.: Scott, Foresman and Company.

Block, P. 2000. Sexuality, fertility and danger: Twentieth-century images of women with cognitive disabilities. *Sexuality and Disability* 18 (4): 239–254.

Bourdieu, P. 1977. *Outline to a theory of practice.* Cambridge: Cambridge University Press.

Burck, D. 1999. Incorporation of knowledge of social and cultural factors in the practice of rehabilitation projects. In *Disability in different cultures: Reflections on local concepts,* ed. B. Holzer, A. Vreede, and G. Weigt. Bielefeld, Germany: Transcript Verlag.

Burgstahler, S. 1994. Increasing the representation of people with disabilities in science, engineering and mathematics. *Information Technology and Disability* 1 (4). Online article posted at www.rit.edu/~easi/itdv01n4/article9.htm.

Buss, D. 1994. *The evolution of desire: Strategies of human mating.* New York: Basic Books.

Butler, J. 1990. *Gender trouble: Feminism and the subversion of identity.* New York: Routledge.

———. 1997. Performative acts and gender constitution: An essay in phenomenology and feminist theory. In *Writing on the body: Female embodiment and feminist theory,* ed. K. Conboy, N. Medina, and S. Stanbury. New York: Columbia University Press

Butler, R. 1999. Double the trouble or twice the fun? Disabled bodies in the gay community. In *Body spaces: Geographies of illness, impairment and disability,* ed. R. Butler and H. Parr. New York: Routledge.

Buytendijk, F. J. J. 1950. The phenomenological approach to the problem of feelings and emotions. In *Feelings and emotions: The Moosehead symposium in cooperation with the University of Chicago,* ed. M. L. Reymert. New York: McGraw Hill.

Canguilhem, G. 1989. *The normal and the pathological.* Trans. Carolyn Fawcett. New York: Zone Books.

Castoriadis, C. 1987. *The imaginary institution of society.* Trans. Kathleen Blamey. Cambridge, Mass.: MIT Press.

Clifford, J. 1997. Spatial practices: Fieldwork, travel, and the disciplining of anthropology. In *Anthropological locations: Boundaries and grounds of a field science,* ed. A. Gupta and J. Ferguson. Berkeley and Los Angeles: University of California Press.

Connell, R. 1995. *Masculinities.* Berkeley and Los Angeles: University of California Press.

di Mauro, D. 1995. *Sexuality research in the United States: An assessment of the social and behavioral sciences.* New York: Social Science Research Council.

Douard, J. 1995. Disability and the persistence of the "normal." In *Chronic illness: From experience to policy,* ed. S. K. Toombs, D. Barnard, and R. Carson. Bloomington: Indiana University Press.

Fabian, J. 1983. *Time and the other: How anthropology makes its object.* New York: Columbia University Press.

Fausto-Sterling, A. 2000. *Sexing the body: Gender politics and the construction of sexuality.* New York: Basic Books.

Fell, J. P. 1977. The phenomenological approach to emotion. In *Emotion,* by D. K. Candland, J. P. Fell, E. Keen, A. I. Leshner, R. M. Tarpy, and R. Plutchik. Monterey, Calif.: Brooks/Cole Publishing Company.

Fitzmaurice, S. 2002. Adventures in child-rearing: The sexual life of a child growing up with down syndrome. Symposium issue: Focus on sexual access for disabled people, ed. L. Mona and R. P. Shuttleworth. *Disability Studies Quarterly* 22 (3): 28–40.

Foucault, M. 1975. *The birth of the clinic: An archaeology of medical perception.* Trans. A. M. Sheridan Smith. New York: Vintage.

———. 1978. *The history of sexuality,* vol. 1, *An introduction.* Trans. R. Hurley. New York: Pantheon Books.

———. 1979. *Discipline and punish: The birth of the prison.* Trans. A. Sheridan. New York: Vintage.

Freund, P. E. S. 1990. The expressive body: A common ground for the sociology of emotions and health and illness. *Sociology of Health and Illness* 12: 452–477.

Gagnon, J., and R. Parker. 1995. Conceiving sexuality. In *Conceiving sexuality: Approaches to sex research in a postmodern world,* ed. R. G. Parker and J. H. Gagnon. New York: Routledge.

Gerschick, T. J., and A. S. Miller. 1996. Gender identities at the crossroads of masculinity and physical disability. In *Toward a new psychology of gender,* ed. M. M. Gergen and S. N. Davis. New York: Routledge.

Giddens, A. 1992. *The transformation of intimacy: Sexuality, love and eroticism in modern societies.* Stanford, Calif.: Stanford University Press.

Gill, C. 1989. Sexuality and disability research: Suffering from a case of the medical model. *Disability Studies Quarterly* 9 (3): 12–15.

Goffman, E. 1963. *Stigma: Notes on management of spoiled identity.* Englewood Cliffs, N.J.: Prentice Hall.

Guldin, A. 2000. Self-claiming sexuality: Mobility impaired people in American culture. *Sexuality and Disability* 18 (4): 233–238.

Gupta, A., and J. Ferguson. 1997. Discipline and practice: "The field" as site, method, and location in anthropology. In *Anthropological locations: Boundaries and grounds of a field science,* ed. A. Gupta and J. Ferguson. Berkeley and Los Angeles: University of California Press.

Grossman, B. 2003. Understanding disability and sexual identity development: Theory, method, and future directions. Paper presented at the First Disability Studies Association Conference, Lancaster, England (September).

Grossman, B., R. P. Shuttleworth, and P. Prinz. 2004. Locating sexuality in disability experience: Reflections from the United Kingdom Disability Association meeting. *Sexuality Research and Social Policy: Journal of the National Sexuality Research Council* 1 (2): 91–96.

Hahn, H. 1981. The social component of sexuality and disability: Some problems and proposals. *Sexuality and Disability* 4: 220–233.

———. 1989. Masculinity and disability. *Disability Studies Quarterly* 9 (3): 1–3.

Halperin, D. 1990. *One hundred years of homosexuality.* New York: Routledge.

Hamilton, C. 2002. Doing the wild thing: Supporting an ordinary sexual life for people with intellectual disabilities. Symposium issue: Focus on sexual access for disabled people, ed. L. Mona and R. P. Shuttleworth. *Disability Studies Quarterly* 22 (3): 40–59.

Herdt, G. 1993. *Third sex, third gender: Beyond sexual dimorphism in culture and history.* New York: Zone Books.

———. 1999. Sexing anthropology: Rethinking participant observation in sexual study. In *Culture, biology, and sexuality,* ed. D. Suggs and A. Miracle. Athens: University of Georgia Press.

———. 2001. Sexuality and social inequality: New approaches to participatory research and ethnography. Symposium abstract, American Anthropological Association Meeting, Washington, D.C. (December).

Ingraham, C. 1996. The heterosexual imaginary. In *Queer theory/sociology,* ed. S. Seidman. Oxford: Blackwell.

Jackson, S. 2003. Heterosexuality, heteronormativity and gender hierarchy: Some reflections on recent debates. In *Sexualities and society: A reader,* ed. J. Weeks, J. Holland, and M. Waites. Oxford: Polity Press.

Jacobson, D. 2000. The sexuality and disability unit: Applications for group training. Special conference issue 1, ed. L. Mona and R. P. Shuttleworth. *Sexuality and Disability* 18 (3): 175–178.

Kasnitz, D., and R. P. Shuttleworth. 1999. Engaging anthropology in disability studies. Position Paper 1 (1), World Institute on Disability.

Kohrman, M. 2000. Grooming Que Zi: Marriage exclusion and identity formation among disabled men in contemporary China. *American Ethnologist* 26: 890–909.

Kulick, D. 1995. Introduction: The sexual life of anthropologists: Erotic subjectivity and ethnographic work. In *Taboo: Sex, identity and erotic subjectivity in anthropological fieldwork,* ed. D. Kulick and M. Wilson. New York: Routledge.

Lewin, E., and W. Leap, eds. 1996. *Out in the field.* Urbana: University of Illinois Press.

Marshall, M. 1996. Problematizing impairment: Cultural competence in the Carolines. *Ethnology* 35 (4): 249–269.

McRuer, R., and A. Wilkerson. 2003. Introduction. Symposium issue: Desiring disability: Queer theory meets disability studies. *Journal of Lesbian and Gay Studies* 9 (1–2): 1–24.

Mona, L. 2003. Sexual options for people with disabilities: Using personal assistance services for sexual expression. *Women and Therapy* 26 (3/4): 211–220.

Mona, L., and S. Gardos. 2000. Disabled sexual partners. In *Psychological perspectives on human sexuality,* ed. L. T. Szuchman and F. Muscarella. New York: John Wiley and Sons.

Mona, L., and R. P. Shuttleworth. 2000. Introduction to the special issue (1). *Sexuality and Disability* 18 (3): 155–158.

Morris, J., ed. 1996. *Encounters with strangers: Feminism and disability.* London: Women's Press.

Nicolaisen, I. 1995. Persons and nonpersons: Disability and personhood among the Punan Bah of Central Borneo. In *Disability and culture,* ed. B. Ingstad and S. Whyte. Berkeley and Los Angeles: University of California Press.

O'Toole, C. 1996. Disabled lesbians: Challenging monocultural constructs. In *Women with physical disabilities: Achieving and maintaining health and well being,* ed. D. M. Krotoski, M. A. Nosek, and M. A. Turk. Baltimore: Paul H. Brookes Publishing.

———. 2002. Sex, disability and motherhood: Access to sexuality for disabled mothers. In Symposium issue: Focus on sexual access for disabled people, ed. L. Mona and R. P. Shuttleworth. *Disability Studies Quarterly* 22 (3): 80–101.

Paine, R., ed. 1985. *Advocacy and anthropology: First encounters.* St. Johns: Memorial University of Newfoundland, Institute of Social and Economic Research.

Parker, R. 1997. Sexual rights: Concepts and action. *Health and Human Rights* 2 (3): 31–37.

Parker, R., R. M. Barbosa, and P. Aggleton. 2000. Introduction: Framing the sexual subject. In *Framing the sexual subject: The politics of gender, sexuality, and power,* ed. R. Parker, R. M. Barbosa, and P. Aggleton. Berkeley and Los Angeles: University of California Press.

Paterson, K., and B. Hughes. 1999. Disability studies and phenomenology: The carnal politics of everyday life. *Disability and Society* 14 (5): 597–610.

Rousso, H. 1993. Special considerations in counseling clients with cerebral palsy. *Sexuality and Disability* 11 (1): 99–110.

Scheper-Hughes, N. 1995. The primacy of the ethical: Propositions for a militant anthropology. *Current Anthropology* 36: 409–420.

Schwandt, T. 1994. Constructivist, interpretivist approaches to human inquiry. In *Handbook of qualitative research,* ed. N. K. Denzin and Y. S. Lincoln. Thousand Oaks, Calif.: Sage.

Sentumbwe, N. 1995. Sighted lovers and blind husbands: Experiences of blind women in Uganda. In *Disability and culture,* ed. B. Ingstad and S. Whyte. Berkeley and Los Angeles: University of California Press.

Shakespeare, T. 1998. Out on the edge: The exclusion of disabled people from the British gay and lesbian community. *Disability Studies Quarterly* 18 (3): 169–174.

———. 1999. The sexual politics of disabled masculinity. *Sexuality and Disability* 17 (1): 53–64.

————. 2003. "I haven't seen that in the Kama Sutra": The sexual stories of disabled people. In *Sexualities and society: A reader,* ed. J. Weeks, J. Holland, and M. Waites. Cambridge: Polity Press.

Shakespeare, T., K. Gillespie-Sells, and D. Davies. 1996. *The sexual politics of disability: Untold desires.* New York: Cassell.

Shapiro, D. 2002. Incorporating sexual surrogacy into the Ontario direct funding program. In Symposium issue: Focus on sexual access for disabled people, ed. L. Mona and R. P. Shuttleworth. *Disability Studies Quarterly* 22 (3): 72–81.

Shildrick, M. 2004a. Queering performativity: Disability after Deleuze. *Scan: Journal of Media Arts Culture* 1 (3). Online, posted at http://scan.net.au/scan/journal/display.php?journal id=36.

————. 2004b. Silencing sexuality: The regulation of the disabled body. In *Sexualities: Personal lives and social policy,* ed. J. Carabine. Milton Keynes, United Kingdom: The Open University.

Shuttleworth, R. P. 2000a. The pursuit of sexual intimacy for men with cerebral palsy. Ph.D. diss., University of California, San Francisco and Berkeley.

————. 2000b. The search for sexual intimacy for men with cerebral palsy. *Sexuality and Disability* 18 (4): 263–282.

————. 2001a. Exploring multiple roles and allegiances in ethnographic process in disability culture. *Disability Studies Quarterly* 21 (3): 103–113.

————. 2001b. Symbolic contexts, embodied sensitivities and the lived experience of sexually relevant, interpersonal encounters for a man with severe cerebral palsy. In *Semiotics and dis/ability: Interrogating categories of difference,* ed. B. Swadener and L. Rogers. Albany, N.Y.: SUNY Press.

————. 2002. Defusing the adverse context of disability and desirability as a practice of the self for men with cerebral palsy. In *Disability and postmodernity,* ed. M. Corker and T. Shakespeare. London: Continuum.

————. 2003a. The case for a focus on sexual access in a critical approach to disability and sexuality research. Paper presented at the First Annual Disability Studies Association Conference, Lancaster, England (September). Posted on the Web at www.lancs.ac.uk/fss/apsocsci/events/ds_archive.htm#DSConf 2004Link.

————. 2003b. Disability and sexuality: From medical model to sexual rights. *American Sexuality* 1(1). Posted on the Web at http://nsrc.sfsu.edu/.

————. 2004a. Disability/difference. In *The encyclopedia of medical anthropology: Health and illness in the world's cultures,* ed. C. Ember and M. Ember. New York: Kluwer/Plenum.

————. 2004b. Disabled men—Expanding the masculine repertoire. In *Gender and disability studies,* ed. B. Hutchinson and B. Smith. New Brunswick, N.J.: Rutgers University Press.

————. 2004c. Multiple roles, statuses and allegiances: Exploring the ethnographic process in disability culture. In *Anthropologists in the field: Cases in participant observation,* ed. L. Hume and J. Mulcock. New York: Columbia University Press.

————. 2005. Sexual access. In *Encyclopedia of disability,* ed. G. Albrecht. Thousand Oaks, Calif.: Sage.

Shuttleworth, R. P., and D. Kasnitz. 2004. Stigma, community, and ethnography: Joan Ablon's contribution to the anthropology of impairment-disability. *Medical Anthropology Quarterly* 18 (2): 139–161.

———. Forthcoming. Introduction: Critically engaging disability studies and anthropological method and theory on impairment-disability. *Engaging anthropology and disability studies in mutual dialogue,* ed. D. Kasnitz and R. P. Shuttleworth, and C. Goldin. Research in Social Science and Disability, vol. 7. Williamsport, Conn.: Praeger.

Shuttleworth, R. P., and L. Mona. 2000. Introduction to the special issue (2). *Sexuality and Disability* 18 (4): 229–231.

———. 2002. Introduction: Toward a focus on sexual access in disability and sexuality advocacy and research. Symposium issue: Focus on sexual access for disabled people, ed. L. Mona and R. P. Shuttleworth. *Disability Studies Quarterly* 22 (3): 2–9.

Stanton, D., ed. 1992. *Discourses of sexuality: From Aristotle to AIDS.* Ann Arbor: University of Michigan Press.

Stein, E., ed. 1992. *Forms of desire: Sexual orientation and the social constructionist controversy.* New York: Routledge.

Swain, J., S. French, and C. Cameron. 2003. *Controversial issues in a disabling society.* Philadelphia: Open University Press.

Tepper, M. 1999. Letting go of restrictive notions of manhood: Male sexuality, disability and chronic illness. *Sexuality and Disability* 17 (1): 37–52.

———. 2000. Facilitated sex: The next frontier in sexuality? *New Mobility* 11 (84): 21–24.

Tremain, S. 2000. Queering disabled sexuality. *Sexuality and Disability* 18 (4): 291–300.

Valentine, G. 1999. What it means to be a man: The body, masculinities, disability. In *Mind and body spaces: Geographies of illness, impairment and disability,* ed. R. Butler and H. Parr. New York: Routledge.

Vance, C. 1991. Anthropology rediscovers sexuality: A theoretical comment. *Social Science and Medicine* 33: 875–884.

Wade, H. 2002. Discrimination, sexuality and people with significant disabilities: Issues of access and the right to sexual expression in the United States. Symposium issue: Focus on sexual access for disabled people, ed. L. Mona and R. P. Shuttleworth. *Disability Studies Quarterly* 22 (3): 9–27.

Waxman, B. 1994. It's time to politicize our sexual oppression. In *The ragged edge: The disability experience from the pages of the first fifteen years of the Disability Rag,* ed. B. Shaw. Louisville: Avocado Press.

Waxman, B., and A. Finger. 1989. The politics of sex and disability. *Disability Studies Quarterly* 9 (3): 1–5.

Weeks, J. 1986. *Sexuality and its discontents: Meanings, myths and modern sexualities.* London: Routledge and Kegan Paul.

———. 1995. History, desire, and identities. In *Conceiving sexuality: Approaches to sex research in a postmodern world,* ed. R. G. Parker and J. H. Gagnon. New York: Routledge.

Whyte, S., and B. Ingstad. 1995. Disability and culture: An overview. In *Disability and culture,* ed. B. Ingstad and S. Whyte. Berkeley and Los Angeles: University of California Press.

Wilkerson, A. 2002. Disability, sex radicalism, and political agency. *NWSA Journal* 14 (3): 33–57.

Wolf, C., and F. Dukepoo. 1969. Hopi Indians, inbreeding, and albinism. *Science* 164 (3875): 30–37.

# PART THREE

# Sexual Inequality and Sociality

Gays, lesbians, and bisexuals have a long history of organizing in the face of severe social oppression. However, organizing was mainly something done by those in the so-called productive years of their lives. One had to be an adult, first of all, to stake a claim in the sexual landscape as gay, lesbian, or bisexual. Second, those visible within organizations were able-bodied working men and women who had not yet retired. The two essays in this part address distinct ways in which young men and women and older men and women organize their lives socially and, in the case of the young ones, politically.

Older gays and lesbians have been virtually absent from the social science literature. In part, a cohort effect accounts for this. It is the baby boom generation that forged the first out LGBT generation in the country. Prior generations were not deeply involved in claiming a public place for themselves. The baby boom generation is therefore the first that could become older as open and out gay and lesbians. Brian de Vries and Patrick Hoctel describe ways in which this older generation has created friendship networks that are distinctively different from comparable networks among heterosexuals. Older gays and lesbian rely on their friends for emotional support to a far greater extent than their heterosexual counterparts. For the latter, emotional support is entirely derived from their immediate family. The need for friendship networks has been described in other LGBT studies, but the older generation of gays and lesbians has never been included in this field to this extent.

Adolescent gays, lesbians, and bisexuals have been the focus of study for a little longer, since the mid-1980s. The remarkable transformation in the organizational capacity of this generation described in this volume is this: In the 1980s, teens organized far away from anywhere where they were known. They removed their identities from their schools, their peers and their homes. This generation however is slowly creating a revolution, for they organize in the schools, in gay-straight alliances (GSAs), in plain view of their peers. This generation does not accept a hiding place, but fights for safety in schools where antigay harassment and violence has been the norm rather than the exception. These GSAs are therefore transforming entire school cultures.

# CHAPTER 9

# The Family-Friends of
# Older Gay Men and Lesbians

BRIAN DE VRIES AND PATRICK HOCTEL

The study of the lives of older gay men and lesbians has recently gained some popularity in gerontological thinking and research. These relatively "uncharted lives" (Siegel and Lowe 1995) are held to represent the unique juncture of history and biography (Mullan 1997). That is, these are individuals whose socialization experiences have been dramatically colored by having been "labeled as sick by doctors, immoral by clergy, unfit by the military, and a menace by the police" (Kochman 1997: 2). These individuals have survived AIDS, both as a disease and as a community-stigma, and are currently living lives as gay men and lesbians[1] with little historical experience or cultural expectations to guide them (Beeler et al. 1999).

Throughout these experiences of discrimination and stigmatization, the social relations of these individuals have figured prominently. Friends stand out in this regard—the people to whom individuals turned when they were doubted, questioned, or ostracized by their biological families and communities of origin. That is, gay men and lesbians found one another in secrecy (e.g., Chauncey 1994) and in protest (Berube 1990), as outcasts and security risks (D'Emilio 1983), and on prime-time television in a widening range of portrayals. They have cared for one another—creating communities as they have witnessed these same communities ravaged by disease.

The intimate nature of the relationships formed by lesbians and gay men in this historical and cultural context is the focus of the empirical efforts reported here. Amidst the defining of gay men and lesbians in *contrast* to family by governments, religious groups, social organizations, and even gays and lesbians themselves (e.g., Weinstock 2000), recent popular rhetoric places much emphasis on the "friends as family" and the "chosen families" of gay men and lesbians (e.g., Kimmel 1992; Weston 1991). This chapter is an attempt to uncover the subjective experience of friendship for older gay men and lesbians in the context of chosen family membership, the grounds for inclusion, and social perceptions of the concept.

To this end, this essay is organized as follows. Following a review of the relevant gerontological literature on the role of friends in the lives of older gay men and lesbians, we present a particular examination of the friend-family contrast. It is in this context that we describe the empirical study reported here: an in-depth interview study addressing the friendships and chosen families of twenty older gay men and lesbians. The results of the analyses conducted on these data are interpreted and discussed in the context of the heteronormative, family-centric bias of North America and the culture of friendship developed by gay men and lesbians.

## Friends and Older Gays and Lesbians

The gerontology literature makes frequent reference to social relations and social support, attesting to the pivotal role played by friends in the social, physical, and psychological health of individuals of all ages, and especially in later life (Antonucci and Akiyama 1987; de Vries 1996). The trend in this area, in part driven by quantitative measurement issues, has been to adopt somewhat of a commodity view of friendship focusing on the friends individuals *have* rather than on the friends individuals *are* (e.g., Davis and Todd 1985)—what Wright (1982) describes as a "side-by-side" rather than a "face-to-face" orientation.

Concomitantly, there has been a pronounced effort to assess characteristics of friendships such as frequency of contact and proximity—what we (Adams, Blieszner, and de Vries 2001) have referred to as proxy measures of friendship process, that is, those dimensions standing in for what researchers *really* intend to study: caring, supportive relationships of a relatively enduring nature. This research focus has resulted in frequently inadequate inferences about the nature and meaning of friendship, part of an unfortunate broader trend to take friends for granted—the failure to recognize the extent to which friends enable the smooth and orderly functioning of society (e.g., Paine 1974). Perhaps this is an extension of the pronatalist, profamily values that pervade North American culture and much of social science, the dramatic outcome of which is the placement of friends on the periphery of social order and public consciousness. More recent efforts have been directed at the ways in which friendships are *understood* by these same individuals whose lives are enhanced by their presence (Adams, Blieszner, and de Vries 2001; Matthews 1986), implicating strong effects on self-awareness, identity, and personal growth (de Vries 1996, 2001; de Vries and Johnson 2002).

Grossman, D'Augelli, and Hershberger (2000: 171) believe that the positive contributions of friends to individual well-being should be even more powerfully noted in the lives of older gay men and lesbians, given that friends and the support they provide "can serve a unique function in mitigating the impact of stigmatization." Nardi (1982: 86) has written that gay and lesbian friendships develop "out of a need to find role models and identity in an oppressive society. The friendship group for heterosexuals may be close and important, but it occurs as an option in the context of a heterosexually dominant society. However, the gay person must create, out of necessity, a meaningful friendship group to cope with threats to identity and self-esteem in a world of heterosexual work situations, traditional family systems, and stereotyped media images." The stigmatization of older gay men and lesbians is manifold, deriving from both outside and within the gay and lesbian communities, and is based not only on sexual orientation and age, but also on gender (for example, Kehoe [1986] describes lesbians as triply stigmatized) and the association of homosexuality with AIDS (Jacobson and Grossman 1996).

Little is known, however, about the role and meaning of friends in the lives of older gay men and lesbians. Much of the literature in this nascent area is colloquial and inferential and presented in compilations of personal narratives of older gay men and lesbians (e.g., Adelman 1986; Farnham and Marshall 1989; Vacha 1985). The few empirical attempts at examining friendship among gay men and lesbians, particularly in later life, include Nardi's (1999) study of gay men representing a broad age range, Dorfman et al.'s (1995) exploration of lesbians and gay men older than sixty, Quam and Whitford's (1992) study on gay men and lesbians older than fifty, and Beeler et al.'s (1999) study of mid- and later-life gay men and lesbians. In all of these varied efforts, the importance of friendship for the health and psychological well-being of older gay men and lesbians is dramatically underscored.

## Friends as Family

The research cited in the previous section frequently contrasts support from friends with support from family. Such a contrast is not uncommon in gerontological inquiries into social networks and social support; in fact, Johnson (1983: 120) has written that without "studying the two types of relationships in conjunction, the importance of either kinship or friendship can be overestimated or, on the contrary, overlooked." This distinction, however, has become blurred and ambiguous in the lives of older gay men and lesbians, as previously suggested. That is, heterosexual procreative families and gay and lesbian chosen families are not always mutually exclusive. Significant numbers of women and men of older cohorts have entered into heterosexual marriages prior to disclosing their homosexual identity. Following divorce, the heteronormative connections (with people related by blood and marriage) and the less culturally bound chosen family begin to overlap (Weston 1991).

Many popular accounts chronicle the "chosen families" of older gays and lesbians. Manasse and Swallow (1995), for example, in photographs and essays characterizing twenty-four gay families, report that friendships exist at the core: "The way a lot of gay men and lesbians come out in the world is very alienating. For many of us, building families of linkage and connection is very healing. It's important for us to feel that love and connection because it's the antithesis of the alienation of homophobia. It's important for us to say, 'This is the innermost circle'" (p. 153).

Dorrell (1991) also comments on the family "of comradery and caring" she helped to create around caregiving for an eighty-four-year-old, terminally ill lesbian named Benton. Dorrell (1991: 92) posits that "the support group was a family of choice for Benton—a diverse and scattered group, the opposite of a patriarchal structure." The presence of such families have been noted in empirical accounts as well; Beeler et al. (1999), for example, report that two-thirds of their sample of middle-aged and older gay men and lesbians held that they had a family of choice.

Such discussions of family of choice reveal the primacy of the family as an organizing construct. Its operation in the lives of gay men and lesbians, however, is complex (and perhaps structurally similar to popular discourse on the topic of "gay marriage"). That is, the adoption of the term *family* is both a form of conformity with mainstream heterosexual society (reifying the compromised position in which lesbian and gay friendships, and relationships, exist) *and* it is a form of resistance as it questions the traditional nature of heterosexual family and co-opts the term to represent something broader and more inclusive. Weinstock (2000) makes reference to this complexity in the pattern of friends as family she identified in her sample of midlife women: friends as substitute family members; friends as a challenge to the core structure of the family; and friends as in-laws. Similarly, Weston (1991) reports that many have fought the creation of the "chosen family," opposing its attempt to achieve heterosexual ideals and encourage oppression. Weinstock (2000) calls for further research to elaborate the extent, principles of inclusion, and rationale for the families created by gay men and lesbians.

## The Study

The study reported here is a descriptive effort to characterize these chosen families of older gay men and lesbians. We were interested in learning about the existence of these families of choice and their composition: How are these families represented and understood? How are the friends, around whom these families are structured, defined and distinguished? Also, we were interested in hearing if older lesbians and gay men thought that these friendships are consequently more important to gays and lesbians in general than they are to heterosexuals of comparable ages. The active verbs describing our interests are intentional and well-chosen; we wanted to give voice to a topic about which individuals infrequently spoke by those whose voices are infrequently heard. As Kochman (1997: 2) has identified in another context, "one of the greatest grievances . . . has been the way older gay men and lesbians have been relegated to a land where they are never seen or heard."

### SAMPLE DESCRIPTION

In-depth individual interviews were conducted with ten men and ten women, ranging in ages from 55 to 81 years of age; the average age of the sample was 66.9 years. The men and women of this sample were mostly long-term residents of the San Francisco Bay Area, averaging thirty-three years. Eighteen of the participants were Caucasian, one was African American, and one was Latino. All participants reported their health as either good or excellent and three-quarters of the sample had at least some college education. The majority of both the women and the men were partnered; six of the women had children, as did two of the men, and three of the women were grandmothers.

These individuals presented themselves to the authors of this essay upon hearing of the research project through community presentations. All identified themselves as gay or lesbian. Interviews were conducted at settings and times of mutual convenience, but most frequently in the homes of the respondents. These interviews ranged in time from thirty minutes to two hours, averaging approximately forty-five minutes.

The focus of these interviews was on the ways in which individuals construct, define, and find meaning in friends and friends-as-family. To this end, a series of open-ended questions was posed, to which verbatim responses were recorded as well as the extemporaneous comments offered by participants. Three questions are most pertinent to the topic of this presentation, although the interviews spanned a variety of related domains: Do you consider your friends to be your family? How do you define friend? Are friendships more important to gays and lesbians than they are to heterosexuals?[2] Responses to these questions were content analyzed.

## TEXT CODING

The questions addressing friend-family distinctions and the relative importance of friendship were coded using free-form, thematic content analysis procedures. The two authors reviewed all of the transcripts and established themes characterized in them. These themes were then articulated and applied during second and subsequent readings. There was unanimous agreement on the presence of these themes in these materials.

Responses to the questions about friendship definition were coded according to a scheme developed by Adams et al. (2000). In a review of the friendship literature, Parker and de Vries (1996) identified seventeen dimensions typically noted. These were then folded into a superordinate framework characterizing fundamental processes of friendship, as developed by Blieszner and Adams (1992). The composite is the scheme mentioned earlier, by which friendship definitions may be characterized by their behavioral (i.e., what individuals do with their friends), cognitive (i.e., what and how individuals think about their friends), affective (i.e., how individuals feel about their friends), and structural processes as well as by proxy characteristics, the latter two representing, respectively, group membership characteristics and indirect or "stand-in" features of friendship, as previously mentioned. The two authors of this essay independently coded all responses for the dimensions of friendship (and, by extension, the processes); intercoder agreement was 86 percent. Discrepancies were resolved through discussion, and the codes used for analyses reported here represent these final, negotiated values.

## DO YOU CONSIDER YOUR FRIENDS TO BE YOUR FAMILY?

All but one of the respondents considered their friends to be their family in some manner. The only dissenting voice was that of a lesbian who emphasized the role constraints of families, saying "with a friend, there isn't an obligation to rescue, whereas with a family member there is."

In general, respondents made frequent reference to the importance of choice in the creation of family. For example, one woman said that "a family is a circle of friends who love you. You can't choose your family, but you can choose your friends and make a family. Creating a family of friends is really a joy. The rewards are immense." Another woman wrote, "Well, I do consider them family, because I've chosen them as my family. You pick each other." It is noteworthy that the majority of respondents making such references were women. Weinstock (2000) has written about women's choices of families and suggests a category of lesbians who focus on friends as a challenge to the nuclear structure of the family, as a political challenge to the traditional family in which biological ties are privileged (Weston 1991). Perhaps such women are also represented here.

The nineteen affirmative responses assumed several categories (see figure 9.1). Six people, four women and two men, answered simply, saying that "Our friends are like a family to us." In a partial elaboration, several respondents spoke of how these friends fulfill roles and perform activities in each other's lives that otherwise would be fulfilled and performed by kin: "I think we know that we can depend on each other for the kinds of things that families do." One woman, for example, spoke of how other women in her social network "have my file, instructions for when I'm ill and dying." Frequently, the two "families" knew each other, as one man noted: "With a lot of them, they know my family, also. . . . We are involved with each other's families."

Other responses were qualified in different ways. Three participants, two women and one man, felt that their friends were like family yet different. They searched for ways to describe these relationships, using terms such as *alternative* and *extended*. "I consider them like an alternative family," or "I do consider my friends as family but not in the same way as my blood family; it's like my second family." Another respondent reported that he prefers the term "*extended family:* I put them in a different cate-

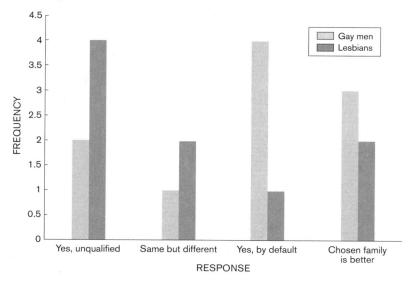

Figure 9.1. "Do you consider your friends your family?"

gory than my blood relatives. It's a different relationship; I do consider my friends an extended family."

Five people, four men and one woman, viewed their friends as family by default. "They're all I have left," or "I see my friends as my family, because I don't have any connections with my birth family." Similar in some ways to the simple affirmative category described earlier, several respondents also claimed, in this context, that their chosen families would be there for them when the need arose: "If I were impaired in any way, they are the ones who would take care of me, and I them." One woman commented that "a lot of times, people's families aren't around—that's just the way society is." Her friends filled the void left by her absent family. The preponderance of men engaging this theme as a description of their chosen families is remarkable, perhaps suggesting abandonment by biological kin (initiated by either party) in greater proportion than is the case for lesbians. Such a finding and such an interpretation merit further exploration.

Finally, five respondents, three men and two women, saw their friends as greater than or superior to their family. They expressed sentiments such as "I feel closer to them than to my own family," as reported by one woman. Several respondents framed these comments around issues of acceptance, as in the case of the following woman: "I can rely on my friends, depend on them . . . there's a level of acceptance I get from them." Another woman wrote that "to my family of choice, I am a whole person. My friends see the whole me, my homosexuality as an integrated part of who I am as a person. I was invisible to my biological family." One man commented that "they [friends] provide the sustenance that you ordinarily would want a family to provide. They give me validation."

Weinstock (2000) identifies a category of chosen families as "friends as substitute family member," similar to that proposed by Weston (1991). This theme may well be better represented by the multiple definitions cited earlier. That is, substitute family may arise in parallel, in extension or as an alternative, by default, or as superior. Recognizing the many paths may lead to a more comprehensive conceptualization of these families. In general, however, what emerges from this discussion is evidence of the efforts of older gay men and lesbians to find a legitimate place for their friends in the (family-dominated) context and language of North American society.

## The Definition of Friends for Older Gay Men and Lesbians

The prominent role of friends, at least as evidenced by their achieved family status in the lives of these respondents, leads naturally to questions of their definition. That is, how are these "family-friends" defined? Participants were asked what *friend* means to them and "what makes someone a friend?" The responses to these questions were coded in ways that describe behavioral processes of friendship, cognitive processes, affective processes, structural characteristics, and proxy measures of process.

The behavioral processes reflect dimensions of self-disclosure, sociability, assistance, and shared activities. Examples of each of these follow.

*Self-Disclosure*

A true, close friend is someone you can confide in, use as a mentor. (female, age 64)

You can talk to them and tell them what's going on. (male, age 72)

*Sociability*

You share both good times and bad times with. (male, age 77)

You share your life with them in various ways. (female, age 71)

*Assistance*

A person you can count on for emotional support and activities. (female, age 67)

Someone who will give you advice and help. (male, age 68)

*Shared Activities*

Someone willing to cooperate in doing things, such as going out to the theater or going out to eat. (male, age 81)

We do activities together. (female, age 67)

The cognitive processes reflect dimensions of loyalty or commitment, trust, shared interests and values, acceptance, empathy, and appreciation or respect. Examples of this process are:

*Loyalty/commitment*

A friend will always be there for you—in good times and in bad. (male, age 77)

A friend sticks with you through thick and thin. (female, age 55)

*Trust*

Someone with whom I have a trusting relationship. (female, age 58)

Someone I've bonded with, I trust and support. (male, age 61)

*Shared Interests/Values*

I guess a certain mutuality of interests. (male, age 71)

There is a commonality of interests. (female, age 65)

*Acceptance*

People who accept who I am, because I am an eccentric person. (female, age 57)

Someone who is nonjudgmental and who will accept you for who you are. (male, age 77)

*Empathy*

What makes a friend is someone that returns my concerns. (male, age 70)

A friend is someone that when you are experiencing some kind of loss of yourself, you call them up on the phone and they remind you who you are. (female, age 64)

*Appreciation/Respect*

Friend is a relationship of mutual respect for differences. (female, age 72)

The experience of friendship is feeling valued. (male, age 63)

Care and compatibility were the two affective dimensions that respondents mentioned.

*Care*

There is some mutual understanding that we like each other. (female, age 67)

Someone who I am emotionally close to. (female, age 58)

*Compatibility*

We do activities together. (female, age 67)

Someone you would just like to be with and talk about almost anything. (male, age 77)

Solidarity (i.e., cohesion) and homogeneity were the two structural characteristics named as part of the respondents' definitions of friendship. These were rarely mentioned; in fact, solidarity was mentioned by only one participant, a woman (age 68) who spoke of "commonality of experience." Homogeneity was mentioned twice, in one case by a 64-year-old woman who spoke of friends being of "a certain age."

Proxy indicators of interactional processes were similarly rare and included length of acquaintance, frequency of contact, and duration of contacts; evidence of this latter dimension was not found in these data. An example of length of acquaintance was offered by a 67-year-old female, who said that "I've known them long enough that we've built a relationship." An example of frequency of contact was offered by a 63-year-old male, who said that a friend is someone with whom they socialize "on some sort of regular basis."

Overall, in order of decreasing frequency, the women and men of this sample defined friendship in terms of at least one cognitive process (95 percent), affective process (70 percent), behavioral process (65 percent), structural characteristic (15 percent) and/or proxy measure (30 percent). In previous research with a heterosexual sample of more than one hundred individuals ranging in age from 55 to 92 (e.g., Adams et al. 2000, percentages embedded in table 9.1), the comparable figures for each of these processes were 70 percent for cognitive processes, 40 percent for

TABLE 9.1. Elements of Friendship Definitions

| Element of Definition | Frequency/Percent | Percent (Adams et al.) |
|---|---|---|
| *Behavioral Processes* | *13/65* | *76.9* |
| Self-disclosure | 5/25 | 47.9 |
| Sociability | 6/30 | 39.3 |
| Assistance | 4/20 | 23.9 |
| Shared activities | 6/30 | 20.5 |
| *Cognitive Processes* | *19/95* | *70.1* |
| Loyalty/commitment | 8/40 | 36.8 |
| Trust | 13/65 | 24.8 |
| Shared interests/values | 12/60 | 22.2 |
| Acceptance | 7/35 | 12.8 |
| Empathy | 8/40 | 11.1 |
| Appreciation/respect | 4/20 | 5.1 |
| *Affective Processes* | *14/70* | *40.2* |
| Care | 8/40 | 20.5 |
| Compatibility | 10/50 | 23.1 |
| *Structural Characteristics* | *3/15* | *29.9* |
| Solidarity | 1/5 | 29.1 |
| Homogeneity | 2/10 | 4.3 |
| *Proxy Measures of Process* | *6/30* | *23.9* |
| Frequency of contact | 4/20 | 13.7 |
| Length of acquaintance | 3/15 | 11.1 |
| Duration of contacts | 0/0 | 1.7 |

affective processes, 77 percent for behavioral processes, 29 percent for structural characteristics, and 24 percent for proxy measures. In sum, the friendships of the gay men and lesbians of this sample may be described as more cognitive and affective in focus, less behavioral and structural, and about as likely to be based on proxy measures as those of heterosexuals.

It is interesting to note that this pattern of results characterizing the responses of gay men and lesbians in implicit contrast with comparably aged heterosexuals was also reported in the results characterizing the responses of older Canadians in comparison with those of older Americans

(Adams et al. 2000). That is, Canadians were significantly more likely to define friends along cognitive and affective processes, whereas Americans were more likely to define friends along behavioral, structural, and proxy measures of friendship process.

The results of these transnational analyses were interpreted along the lines of a cultural critique. Assuming the risk of overstating these data, the idea of this critique is that in relative contrast to the individualism and independence of Americans, Canadians may be seen as somewhat more communal and interdependent, with the welfare of others implicating the welfare of the self (and hence a focus on affective and cognitive processes). A more local cultural critique was also offered; that is, the Canadian sample was recruited from a comparatively recently settled, large West Coast city, whereas the American sample came from a more established Eastern city of moderate size. Perhaps these regional, geographic, and historical differences manifest, in the case of the American city, in a social organization influenced by tradition, greater structure, and more established norms governing social interaction (and hence a focus on behavioral, structural, and proxy processes). In either case, the role of culture is implicated in some form in the definition and meaning of *friend*.

In the same way, the more specific culture of the friendship for older lesbians and gay men is implicated in the analyses and results given earlier. These results suggest a depth of analysis of and reflection on friends in ways that differ from the previous research on presumably heterosexual older (American) adults. The importance of friends as self-referents as well as the importance of having a community may be reflected in the high percentage of lesbians and gay men describing friends in cognitive terms, particularly in the realms of trust and shared interests/values. Feeling welcomed and included in this community and within a circle of friends may account for the higher frequency of affective terms. In both of these cases, these are issues that are less commonly assumed (and found) in the accounts of friends among heterosexuals, for whom family fulfills these roles. That behavioral processes were less frequently mentioned may be interpreted along these same lines: it is less what people do together and more how they feel and think about one another that matters (i.e., the safe haven of friendship). In general, a greater number of coded dimensions were engaged in the description of friends (5.1 for this sample, compared to 3.4 for the heterosexual sample), further suggestive of friendship as a richer construct in the lives of gays and lesbians.

Looking at specific dimensions revealed several interesting (statistically significant, $\chi^2$) gender differences, necessarily qualified by the small samples used for such analyses. Lesbians were more likely than gay men to include trust as a dimension of friendship; women were also more likely to include shared activities, compatibility, and care. Having trusting, compatible individuals with whom one may share life and life experiences appear to be particularly salient values for lesbians. Gay men were more likely to include acceptance and empathy; that is, gay men appeared to value the secure base and compassion of their friendships. Previous research with samples of older heterosexual women and men has supported some of these patterns and not others.

In sum, these definitions suggest a cultural specificity to the ways in which gay men and lesbian consider their friends and the potential role that these friends may play in their lives. That is, the friends of older gay men and lesbians are defined in ways that one might expect would be applied to kin among heterosexual adults. This reinforces the high frequency with which these respondents identified their friends as their family and begs the question of their perceived place in their lives.

## Do You Believe That Friendships Are More Important to Gays and Lesbians Than to Heterosexuals?

Given the relatively distinctive approach to friendship on the part of these older gay men and lesbians, it is interesting to examine whether or not these individuals believe friendships are more important in the lives of gay men and lesbians than in the lives of heterosexuals. A slight majority of the respondents (twelve) believed this to be the case. As before, a range of responses is implicit in this dichotomy.

Two respondents, one man and one woman, commented that friends are more important, but qualified their responses with reference to sexuality as a potential impediment to the friendships of gays and lesbians. For example, the gay man commented that "there is often so much sex and history involved" in gay friendships and this has to be addressed in order for friendships to flourish. He added that "once this hurdle was surmounted, gay friendships were stronger as a result." This was similarly referenced by the lesbian, who commented on "this sexual innuendo, those feelings" in gay and lesbian friendships.[3]

The vast majority of those responding affirmatively to this question raised issues about families of choice in their comments. The basic tenet in all of these remarks is that friendships are more important to gay men and lesbians because their friends, for various reasons, become their family. Inherent in this idea is that gays and lesbians need each other more than heterosexuals do, because the support that a family of origin might ordinarily supply is somehow absent. For example, one man said that "that's our community, too. We don't have all the given support that the 'straight' community provides, so we need to stand by each other even more so." Another man added that "my brother and sister-in-law have children and grandchildren, which I don't have. It keeps their lives full. My friends fulfill all of that kind of need, that whole space that my brother's kids fill for him. Gay people *have* to make their friends their family. If my brother and sister-in-law's friends fell away, they'd still have their family. If my friends fell away, I would have nothing." Yet another reported that "I think for gay people—many of whom are disowned by their families because of their sexual orientation—their friendships are stronger." One woman made the cohort-specific connection in her response: "So many of us have lost our original families—particularly older people, because of our sexuality. We need each other in a way that heterosexuals don't. We've led a life of nobody being there."

In a related, but stronger, formation, several respondents spoke of how friends were instrumental to their very existence. For example, one man said, "I probably couldn't have gotten through my life without them. If it wasn't for my friends, I wouldn't be here." One woman commented, "because for many gays and lesbians, we're a despised minority. I make the analogy with being a Jew. You need to connect with your own to survive. I think it is because we need each other." Another woman mentioned that "when you get older, friendship warms your heart. It makes you want to live. . . . I could always live without a lover, but I couldn't live without friends."

The sexuality and sexual tension qualifying the initial responses to this question, mentioned earlier, were similarly engaged by some of those who felt that the friendships of gay men and lesbians were not more important than were friendships of heterosexuals. For example, one woman noted that among "groups of heterosexual women friends I've seen [some are] more open and supportive because there's not this sexual thing. They know their roles."

A couple of respondents expressed the view that although friendships were probably more important to gays and lesbians in the past, this was not the case any longer: "a good friendship is a good friendship." For example, one woman commented that "once upon a time, that might have been true for lesbians and gays before it was so easy to be out—when you had to have that certain thing with people to be protected," but "today," added another woman, "I think people are more understanding, more knowing. I can see in the past where that would have been true when people couldn't come out. There wasn't the movement to support them. Today you can be out and open and who you are. Our presence has caused them to open up to other ways of being with people. We give people permission to be who they are."

The remaining respondents felt that "gayness has nothing to do with it as far as I can see," as stated by one man. Others believed that "friendships are important to everyone, though I'm not sure everyone realizes that." Another man agreed, commenting "I don't think there's a line. . . . Straights need their friends, too. It's not an either/or as far as I can see."

The concept of chosen family was once again engaged as individuals weighed the relative importance of friends and family. For many, friends were more important, even essential, to gay men and lesbians because they became family. For others, the sexual tension reported to exist between friends qualified their importance relative to heterosexuals: the roles were blurred. Still others provided testimonials to friends independent of sexual orientation, further confirming their central function in the lives of individuals.

## Summary and Concluding Thoughts

The foregoing paragraphs offer some insight into the social and relational worlds of gay men and lesbians in the third age. From the analyses of friendship, for example, are accounts of the largely cognitive features that define the relationship. Friendships are given their meaning, by lesbians and gay men, in terms that suggest relationships of authenticity; they suggest relationships that enable individuals to feel "heard" and understood; they suggest relationships on which individuals may depend. Many of these same terms have been employed by attachment theorists to describe the nature of family ties between individuals who shape and nurture one another. These friendships are based on affective ties—the expressions of care that support these cognitive claims.

Lesbians and gay men use these cognitive and affective processes more frequently than do heterosexual women and men of similar ages; moreover they define friends using a larger number of constructs. Together, these findings may reflect a deeper level of information processing, further supported by the finding that all but one of the interview respondents considered their friends to be their families—as an alternative, as similar to but different, by default, or as superior to biological family.

This range of frameworks by which chosen families are characterized and the subtle gender differences in their endorsement are provocative findings worthy of further pursuit. Weinstock (2000) explored women's conceptualization of chosen families, some of which are replicated here. The politics of families of choice were decidedly missing from these accounts. This might be attributable to the sample; alternatively, notwithstanding the political statement that a chosen family makes, the *experience* of such families may not be political, but social and emotional instead. These results suggest a further complexity of the concept and ultimately call for further investigation.

Needing these family-friends in a variety of ways was also a factor in suggesting that friends are more important to homosexuals than heterosexuals. Reference was made in this context to the age of participants in the sample as well as their cohort experience. Respondents thought that in later life, friends are increasingly important since "so many of us have lost our original families." Without commenting on the absence of families, other respondents similarly felt that friends were important, and credited the cohort of older persons of facilitating a culture that allows individuals to achieve significant friendships: "Our presence has caused them to open up to other ways of being with people. We give people permission to be who they are."

Gays and lesbians who today are in their later years have led largely uncharted lives of increasing interest to gay and lesbian scholars and gerontologists. Their experiences of living open lives has been as a result of and has resulted in pervasive social movements and influences. These include many of the public declarations of pride and group membership well known in North American communities; these also include redefining terms and reshaping concepts, of which friends and family are included. Addressing the lives of these older men and women addresses these evolving norms and social experiences.

Certainly, friends figure prominently in the social worlds of older gay men and lesbians. But is this a prominence and level of processing unlike that in the lives of heterosexuals of comparable ages? Perhaps; but apart from the process-by-process comparison given earlier, the comparison is more implicit than explicit, given that questions about the relative valuing of family and friends were not asked (and tend not to be asked) of the heterosexual sample. And these are the sorts of questions that tend not to be asked in social and family gerontological studies. The heteronormative and family-centric bias of North American social gerontology and the associated absence of a language to adequately characterize friends hinders our ability to fully understand their role and impact at all junctures of the life course.

In this way, the study of gay and lesbian aging issues not only contributes to our understanding of the lives of older gays and lesbians, it contributes to our understanding of aging more generally through the ways in which we question, conceptualize, and interpret our research (de Vries and Blando 2004). A gay and lesbian gerontology on its own is both rich and limiting, as is an exclusively heteronormative gerontology. Friendship is a case in point.

## Notes

The authors wish to thank David Megathlin for his assistance in the preparation of this manuscript.

1. The terms *gay* and *lesbian* are used interchangeably with *homosexual* in this essay, although the authors recognize that these terms have political and cohort-sensitive references and may not be used interchangeably by the individuals whose relationships are described here.

2. These are representative questions. Frequently, the interview took the form of a conversation, and as such, additional questions were posed and the responses to these questions are included in the coding described here.

3. Indeed, in the course of the interviews, the majority of respondents (five gay men and nine lesbians) reported that they are currently friends with individuals with whom they had previously been romantically involved. One woman quoted a theory that she said was often repeated in the gay and lesbian community that lesbians (unlike gay men in this context) "never truly break up, they just become friends with a history."

## References

Adams, R., R. Blieszner, and B. de Vries. 2000. Definitions of friendship in the third age: Age, gender, and study location effects. *Journal of Aging Studies* 14 (1): 117–133.

Adelman, M., ed., 1986. *Lesbian passages: True stories told by women over 40.* Los Angeles: Alyson.

Antonucci, T. C., and H. Akiyama. 1987. Social networks in adult life and a preliminary examination of the convoy model. *Gerontologist* 42: 519–527.

Beeler, J. A., T. D. Rawls, G. Herdt, and B. J. Cohler. 1999. The needs of older les-

bians and gay men in Chicago. *Journal of Gay and Lesbian Social Services* 9 (1):
31–49.

Berube, A. 1990. *Coming out under fire: The history of gay men and women in World War Two.* New York: Free Press.

Blieszner, R., and R. G. Adams. 1992. *Adult friendship.* Newbury Park, Calif.: Sage.

Chauncey, G. 1994. *Gay New York: Urban culture, and the making of the gay male world, 1890–1940.* New York: Basic Books.

Davis, K. E., and M. J. Todd. 1985. Assessing friendship: Prototypes, paradigm cases, and relationship descriptions. In *Understanding personal relationships: An interdisciplinary approach,* ed. S. Duck and D. Perlman. Newbury Park, Calif.: Sage.

D'Emilio, J. 1983. *Sexual politics, sexual communities: The making of a homosexual minority in the United States.* Chicago: University of Chicago Press.

de Vries, B. 1996. The understanding of friendship: An adult life course perspective. In *Handbook of emotion, adult development, and aging,* ed. C. Magai and S. McFadden. New York: Academic Press.

———. 2001. Grief: Intimacy's reflection. *Generations* 25: 75–80. Adaptation published in *Family Focus.*

de Vries, B., and J. A. Blando. 2004. The study of gay and lesbian lives: Lessons for social gerontology. In *Gay and lesbian aging: Research and future directions,* ed. G. Herdt and B. de Vries. New York: Springer.

de Vries, B., and C. L. Johnson. 2002. Multidimensional reactions to the death of a friend in the later years. *Advances in Life-Course Research* 7: 299–324.

Dorfman, R., K. Walters, P. Burke, L. Hardin, T. Karanik, J. Raphael, and E. Silverstein. 1995. Old, sad and alone: The myth of the aging homosexual. *Journal of Geronotological Social Work* 24 (1/2): 29–44.

Dorrell, B. 1991. Being there: A support network of lesbian women. In *Gay midlife and maturity,* ed. J. A. Lee. Binghamton, N.Y.: Harrington Park Press.

Farnham, M., and P. Marshall, eds. 1989. *Walking after midnight: Gay men's life stories.* New York: Routledge.

Grossman, A. H., A. R. D'Augelli, and S. L. Hershberger. 2000. Social support networks of lesbian, gay, and bisexual adults 60 years of age and older. *Journal of Gerontology* 55B (3): 171–179.

Jacobson, S., and A. H. Grossman. 1996. Older lesbians and gay men: Old myths, new images, and future directions. In *The lives of lesbians, gays, and bisexuals: Children to adults,* ed. R. C. Savin-Williams and K. Cohen. Forth Worth, Tex.: Harcourt, Brace.

Johnson, C. L. 1983. Fairweather friends and rainy day kin: An anthropological analysis of old age friendships in the United States. *Urban Anthropology* 12: 103–123.

Kehoe, M. 1986. Lesbians over 65: A triply invisible minority. *Journal of Homosexuality* 13 (3/4): 139–152.

Kimmel, D. C. 1992. The families of older gay men and lesbians. *Generations* 17 (3): 37–38.

Kochman, A. 1997. Gay and lesbian elderly: Historical overview and implications for social work practice. In *Social services for senior gay men and lesbians,* ed. J. Quam. New York: Haworth Press.

Manasse, G., and J. Swallow, eds. 1995. *Making love visible: In celebration of gay and lesbian families.* Freedom, Calif.: Crossing Press.

Matthews, S. H. 1986. *Friendships through the life course.* Newbury Park, Calif.: Sage.

Mullan, J. T. 1997. "Bereavement and the life course: Some views from AIDS and Alzheimer's caregivers." Symposium conducted at the meeting of the Gerontological Society of America, Cincinnati, Ohio (November).

Nardi, P. M. 1982. Alcohol treatment and the non-traditional "family" structures of gays and lesbians. *Journal of Alcohol and Drug Education* 27 (2): 83–89.

———. 1999. *Gay men's friendships: Invincible communities.* Chicago: University of Chicago Press.

Paine, R. 1974. Anthropological approaches to friendship. In *The social compact: Selected dimensions of friendship,* ed. E. Leyton. St. John's: Memorial University of Newfoundland.

Parker, S., and B. de Vries. 1993. Patterns of friendship for women and men in same and cross-sex relationships. *Journal of Social and Personal Relationships* 10: 617–626.

Quam, J. K., and G. S. Whitford. 1992. Adaptation and age-related expectations of older gay and lesbian adults. *Gerontologist* 32: 367–374.

Siegel, S., and E. Lowe. 1995. *Uncharted lives: Understanding the life passages of gay men.* New York: Plume.

Vacha, K. 1985. *Quiet fire: Memoirs of older gay men.* Trumansburg, N.Y.: Crossing Press.

Weinstock, J. S. 2000. Lesbian friendships at midlife: Patterns and possibilities for the 21st century. *Journal of Gay and Lesbian Social Services* 11 (2/3): 1–32.

Weston, K. 1991. *Families we choose: Lesbians, gays, kinship.* New York: Columbia University Press.

Wright, P. J. 1982. Men's friendships, women's friendships and the alleged inferiority of the latter. *Sex Roles* 8: 1–20.

# CHAPTER 10

# Sexual Inequality, Youth Empowerment, and the GSA

## *A Community Study in California*

GILBERT HERDT, STEPHEN T. RUSSELL,
JEFFREY SWEAT, AND MICHELLE MARZULLO

"Sexuality" as a cultural notion has gradually expanded since the 1960s to include a broad spectrum of identities, rights, and communities that has enlarged the meaning of "diversity" in neoliberal democracy. The LGBTQ movement has played a large role in this change, of course, but not without twists and turns that have followed the inclusion of bisexuals, then transgenders, and, more recently, queer people. More than a generation ago, these issues were focused almost exclusively on adults, with gay and lesbian adults disconnected from youths and fearful of being involved more closely because of persistent false accusations of sexual influence (Herdt 1997b; Sedgwick 1991). But by the beginning of the 1980s, and then in conjunction with the AIDS epidemic, queer youths and youth groups began to "come out" and live openly as self-identified gays and lesbians (Herdt 1989), though rarely in high school (Herdt and Boxer 1993).

Coming out during adolescence typically excluded the schools; indeed, only later did advocates move to encompass sexuality as a larger social empowerment for youth (Fine 1988; Moran 2000; Szalaha 2001). Meanwhile, Americans continued to view sexuality as a "problem" to be "fixed" in young people's lives: continuing debates on "raging hormones" and "abstinence-only" programs, as well as popular films (Eberwein 1999) that depict youths as "nothing but" sex machines, all miss the point of how young people increasingly view sexual inequality as a prompt for social engagement. However, as adolescent specialists have long known, issues surrounding the social expression of sexual inequality among young people are highly compelling for this age group. Indeed, by the beginning of the 1990s, these social changes led youths to become involved in efforts at reform and social justice in the cultural spaces of the greatest import in their lives—the high school. The most significant of all these social changes was the emergence of gay-straight alliances (GSAs) in the United States. This essay argues that GSAs are a unique example of the youth empowerment movement because they involve challenges to sexual inequality that are critical and urgent as influences on adolescents' lives: education and heterosexuality (see Russell 2002).

This essay examines the emergence of youth empowerment through the GSA of teachers, administrators, students, and students' families and friends in California. We focus on the cultural meanings and social practices of activists and youths who are currently living out the struggle for equality, tolerance, and diversity in their schools, communities, friendship networks, and families. The setting is Northern California, and although there are distinctive features of this region, the same struggles through GSAs could be studied elsewhere in the United States. Through a cultural lens we study GSAs and the motivations of their members' involvement, including the way that youths experience gender and sexual conformity to gendered regulations in the high school setting, as well as the intersection of ethnic/racial identities with the sexual identities in a GSA context. Although our data are backgrounded by anthropological fieldwork and interviews, this essay is primarily concerned with three in-depth focus groups. We brought together these groups in the autumn of 2001 and the early months of 2002. The initial group was composed of full-time staff of GSA Networks and a community-based nonprofit organization located in California. The subsequent groups were with youth members of local GSAs and GSA Network staff.

## The History of a New Social Movement

Beginning in the early 1990s, GSAs became increasingly visible in the landscape of American high schools. Born from the struggle for sexual equality and social justice and the need for "safe space" that respected sexual diversity, GSAs gained recognition in Boston and kindred areas of the East Coast. The brainchild of a dynamic teacher who had observed gay bashing and homophobia and its terrible effects on student morale, GSAs quickly began to gain national support. The impetus first came from heterosexual teachers and administrators. Later the impetus came from students, their friends, and their families—all of whom were familiar with the pattern of "faggot" jokes, harassment, innuendo, and, in some instances, open violence in schools—who were otherwise tolerant. The drive to create a "safe space" for sexual diversity had begun to broaden the base of support for sexual diversity. A decade later, in spite of progress in many areas, as Perrotti and Westheimer (2001) have noted in a popular account of this movement, homophobia remains one of the last acceptable social prejudices within the institutions of the United States. Laura Szalaha (2001) has demonstrated in her groundbreaking study in Massachusetts, however, that once a GSA is established in a school, the pattern of sexual inequality is increasingly contested by a pioneering generation of young people and their teachers in the schools.

It is estimated by the Gay, Lesbian, and Straight Education Network (GLSEN) that more than a thousand GSAs now exist around the United States. GSAs have multiple goals—to promote tolerance and diversity, and to work against the forces of homophobia, sexual inequality, and gay bashing in secondary and middle schools. GSAs are, in this sense, a social movement—a new historical and cultural formation that provides the means for what we shall call youth empowerment at the grassroots level. Movements in support of gay and lesbian youths and their needs began to take form in the early 1980s (cf. Herdt and Boxer 1993; Herdt 1997a), but these "coming out" groups were created and operated independent of schools. In fact, it was impossible for these groups to operate inside the schools because of community opposition or internal resistance from students.

Of course, since the time of G. Stanley Hall at the close of the nineteenth century, the invention of adolescence as a sexual period has gone hand in hand with the emergence of public schools as an arena for social control of adolescent sexuality. Adolescence has long been a time of sexual contestation and debate in the United States (Mead 1928). American high schools have long been an arena for social experiments also—a place for education innovation and cultural change in the ways to be a citizen. Today, GSAs represent a new age in a movement of youth empowerment, and a nascent social movement as these efforts at sexual inequality have moved inside the schools. There has been no anthropological or sociological study of GSAs in a community context thus far, and none that we know of in California.

Students and staff at a small private school in Massachusetts founded the first GSA in 1989. In its early years, the GSA movement reached only a few schools in the immediate vicinity through social networks. However, following the report of the Governor's Commission on Gay and

Lesbian Youth in 1992, GSAs became widespread in Massachusetts and beyond. The national GSA movement has since been propelled by the New York community-based organization GLSEN. Founded by Kevin Jennings, a high school teacher who became an activist, GLSEN achieved prominence quickly. Massachusetts in particular, through its Safe Schools Program for gay and lesbian students, pioneered the establishment of socially progressive policies and laws that have enabled the creation of numerous GSAs (Perrotti and Westheimer 2001; Szalaha 2001). Moreover, a series of landmark cases has focused public attention on injustice and homophobic violence directed toward LGBTQ youths, resulting in new legislation that protects sexual diversity in the classroom—a change that has also occurred in California since 2002. During this same time—the years of the Clinton administration—social challenges surrounding gays in the military, increasing controversy over "same-sex marriage" laws, and the infamous Matthew Shepard murder in Wyoming all had the cumulative effect of lifting public approval of homosexuality in the opinion polls, an unprecedented change in such a short period of time (Herek 2004).

The Safe Schools Project in Massachusetts has been the focus of a recent book, *When the drama club is not enough* (Perrotti and Westheimer 2001). The work is a wonderful compendium of testimonies, strategies, test cases, and resources for helping LGBTQ youth and adults cope with and challenge sexual inequality in the schools. The authors speak directly to youths and the adults who support them in making the changes necessary to have safe schools—families, teachers, administrators, and community leaders. They show that youths who once "felt different" and were able to find "safety" in the drama or art club or were excluded and isolated in general, even being forced out of the schools by harassment, have been able to find a new context for support and friendship. Involvement in GSAs, which has enabled these changes, has clearly changed the lives of these youths. Their stories tell of how they have been transformed from feeling like scared, lonely "social failures or outcasts" to being brave, connected, and socially successful. Likewise, teachers and administrators have found the courage to speak openly in support of these youths or to "come out" themselves—either as self-identified gay, lesbian, bisexual, or transgender adults, or as their heterosexual allies. Thus, the book helps with clues about how to create a school environment wherein all youth feel safe and respected.

As social scientists, we have applied some of these clues to an innovative community-based ethnographic study that attempts to systematically understand the relationship between the formation of GSAs and the empowerment of youths who find their way into these organizations. We will examine only a small number of the narratives of the activists and adult advisors who work with them in an expanding circle of what we will call youth empowerment. We draw on a series of focus groups that were held in Northern California with members of the (California) GSA Network of youth activists, as well as with the GSA Network staff. Our aim was to explore and understand the meaning of GSAs in the daily lives of these people. We also were concerned to see how these people put empowerment into practice—an issue to which we shall return in the conclusion.

## GSA and Youth Empowerment: A Community Study

A "youth movement" is emerging in the contemporary United States. As in the civil rights movements that preceded it, in which African Americans, women, and adult gay men and lesbians challenged dominant cultural and power structures that systematically marginalized them (D'Emilio and Freeman 1988), young people themselves are among the most vocal and visible leaders in the movement for youth empowerment. Environmental rights activists also claim young adherents, but GSAs are based in schools—first.

In communities across the United States, the language of youth problem prevention is shifting to include attention to positive youth development (National Research Council, Institute of Medicine 2002). Youths are becoming active members of their communities—not only at school, but also in government, in their faith communities, in the programs that serve them, and as activists who are taking the lead in addressing the relevant issues in their lives (Camino 2000; Youniss, McLellan, and Yates 1999). GSAs provide a unique example of how this youth empowerment movement has challenged the institutions that are central to the social shape of adolescent lives: education and heterosexuality (see Russell 2002).

Early in their histories, GSAs established what was to become the key focus of these organizations: the empowerment of youths through work toward social change. A club announcement placed in the school newspaper in 1989 where the first GSA was formed read as follows:

We call ourselves the Gay/Straight Alliance because we are all working together to make Phillips Academy as safe and as comfortable a place to be gay, lesbian, or bisexual as it is to be heterosexual. We are all working to end homophobia as a step toward furthering the appreciation of the diversity on this campus and a stance against an oppression, which prohibits individuals from being the whole human beings that they are. (Quoted in Mallon 1998: 42)

This announcement was prescient in how it underlined two of the three main functions of GSAs—to provide safe space and to promote activism (education is not explicit, but is presumably one way of making school a safer place for LGBTQ students).

California is a special cultural context of multiculturalism, especially its LGBTQ support, and its schools provide a social climate for the creation of GSAs different from that of other parts of the United States. The state has a long history of socially, racially, and politically progressive mainstream voters. Although negative political reactions to GSAs have emerged in certain areas, especially Central California and areas of Southern California, the state has a positive record of change in the area of gay and lesbian rights, including the adoption of partner benefits by the State of California. In particular, a California law (AB 537) provides a pivotal initiative for ensuring that schools move to create diverse and safe spaces for all youth, including LGBTQ youths, who will now have a higher profile than before. Openly elected gay and lesbian politicians have played a key role in these legal and social initiatives, but at the grassroots level it is GSA Network of California that has done the most critical work.

It was not always so. GSA Network in California had its beginnings in student activism. GSAs play a number of roles in the lives of students and schools; some provide counseling and support for LGBTQ youths, while others serve mainly as a social or recreational alternative to typical high school activities and organizations. However, many GSAs focus their attention on advocacy and activism, with the goals of improving the school climate and thereby supporting individual students. Carolyn Laub tells the story of how she was inspired to create a GSA network following a request for support in training teachers. Later, a variety of efforts began to coalesce around support, such as student trips to Sacramento in 1996 and 1997 to lobby for a school nondiscrimination policy to include sexual orientation. Then, in 1997 a group of about forty students began to meet locally. They learned about a young person at East High School in Salt Lake City, Utah, who was struggling to form a GSA at her school. The students in California began talking about having GSAs at their own schools. The idea was generated for "a network of students learning from each other about gay-straight alliances so they don't have to reinvent the wheel as they set out to try to create student clubs in the face of incredible resistance . . . administrators trying to prevent them from starting the club, or resistance from other students, or parent groups" (interview with Carolyn Laub).

The founder began creating a formal network, and, by the fall of 1998, GSA Network was an officially sponsored project of the Tides Center, a nonprofit umbrella organization in the San Francisco Bay Area. At the time of our study, GSA Network had grown from a single staff member in San Francisco to include six full- or part-time staff with offices covering three California regions: Northern (San Francisco), Central (Fresno), and Southern (Los Angeles). The network conducts needs assessments of existing GSAs, and works with regional youth councils to conduct local, regional, and statewide training workshops and conferences to support intensive leadership, activism, community organizing and skills building, and arts empowerment. Notably, GSA Network became a central mobilizing force in the passage of California's Assembly Bill 537 in 2000, which links the school nondiscrimination code to the hate crimes statute of the penal code, thereby including sexual orientation and gender (defined to include the concept of gender identity) among protected categories within the policies of the state Department of Education.

What kinds of motivations lead people to become GSA activists? The stories that these community organizers share are of a vision of a world of inequalities, and a felt need to change this and promote social justice. For example, one of our informants, Diana, a woman in her late forties who has been active in the Central Valley area of California for some years, revealed how she had first been alerted to the needs of LGBTQ youth through a church telephone hotline:

The call came one afternoon from a social worker—a fifteen-year-old Latino boy who was gay [called in]; he had tried to commit suicide. [The social worker revealed that] she really had no choice but to return him to his home, but before she did, she would like someone to come and talk with him at the church where I was on staff. It was an open congregation, and so she was aware of who we are. The boy was from a Catholic family with a very domineering parent who had consistently tried to exorcise demons out of him and was really very emotionally abusive to him. And so I called my friend Tony, and he and I went to talk with this young man. We made a plan so that he would call and check in with us over a period of days, and we'd link him up with community organizations that would support him. We tried to give him some affirmation for a reality he saw that he didn't want to deal with. . . . And when we left, we told the social worker what we had done, and she said, "Do you think you could come and do training for our whole staff?" And Tony and I kind of just stopped and looked at each other, and our mouths kind of hung open because that was the first time we had understood the incredible need in that town for support for these young people.

The fact is that there are social workers who have no training whatsoever, and she said there are four or more young boys just like this one a month who were there for the same reason. And so I kept a relationship with this boy and also then broadened my contacts and continued to meet more and more young people, students, who were really kind of lost in that hostile environment without much support. And so Tony and I went to GSA day to talk about how we could effect some kind of positive change.

This example illustrates the critical role played by concerned adults in fostering support for what in many communities has become a youth-led movement. All too often, even today, stories such as these reveal that not only students of GSAs become empowered to create social change; the adults in their lives feel compelled and become empowered to help address sexual inequality to promote social justice.

## Narrative of Empowerment: Youth and Gender

How does empowerment for LGBTQ youths and their youth and adult allies come about in school settings that are typically defined by heterosexism? From our conversations with these students and adult supporters, we suggest that schools become a site for new forms of agency and activism. Social workers report on harassment and violence directed toward LGBTQ youths (Mallon 1998) when young people begin to challenge the gendered and racialized scripts for sexuality that are prevalent in the dominant youth (and adult) culture. Under the banner of tolerance and acceptance of sexual diversity, youths both explicitly and implicitly challenge the strict gender and racial/ethnic regulations that plague schools—a shared project vital to the future of diversity and social justice.

Are there gendered trajectories into a GSA? In other words, do young men and women have different reasons and sexual lifepaths (Herdt 1997b) that compel their involvement? In this preliminary exploration we cannot answer this question with finality, but we have some evidence that it is typical for girls to become straight allies for their gay male friends—a common configuration of many GSAs. Staff members of GSA Network are careful not to generalize about the membership of GSAs. Advocates recognize how local differences preserve cultural diversity within and across the clubs. However, founder and executive director Carolyn Laub describes the "classic GSA [as] the gay guy and all his straight female friends." This configuration occurs often enough to create the perception by some that this is *the* main form of GSA (see also Perrotti and West-heimer 2001). The gender and sexual influences and various social pressures that might lead to this outcome remain to be seen, yet they clearly provide a structural shape to many GSAs in schools. Further study is necessary to determine both the actual frequency of the "straight female–gay male friend" phenomenon in GSAs and the factors contributing to it.

Although there are no hard and fast data on the gender and sexual orientation makeup of GSAs, our fieldwork suggests that there are barriers to involvement in a GSA that stem, in part, from the stereotype that it is a "gay" club. The common belief by nonmembers in high schools is that GSAs must be "lesbian or gay" and this creates a stigma, a force of marginalization that is real and formidable. Clearly, homophobia in the high school is a prime factor here—especially the phobia of heterosexual or "straight" males, who may go to extremes to avoid being labeled queer (Elia 1993/94; Mallon 1998; Pettet 2003). Moreover, the ever-present fears of so-called closeted youths, who are at most risk if they were to be outed, cannot be discounted, especially in more conservative ethnic, religious, and cultural settings (Herdt and Boxer 1993). Those who face the potentially highest risk of harm should they be "discovered" (either accurately or inaccurately) are "straight" males and, today, transgender youths. By contrast, GSA membership is comparatively less risky for three other categories of youth: (1) LGBTQ youth who are already out to almost everyone; (2) youth who are often judged or misidentified as LGBTQ (regardless of their own felt sexual identity) because of their perceived gender behavior or their resistance to typical gender roles; and (3) straight females who, simply because of their sexual orientation, are regarded as more heteronormal and gender typical, and are less likely than straight males to be suspected of having divergent sexualities.

GSA members from the San Francisco Bay Area and the Central Valley also say that male youths who are labeled as "effeminate" or gay have the most difficulty at school because of harassment by other boys. As one GSA member put it bluntly, "It's more difficult at my school to be a queer male." One young woman spoke of the heightened level and frequency of violence faced by gay male youths compared to lesbians. Still another young woman gave a more detailed explanation:

I've seen a lot of ignorance, mostly on the part of male people at school, students at school. . . . Males are so discriminatory toward gay men because they feel threatened. They think that a gay person is going to hit on them, and they feel threatened by that. They want to keep their, you know, manhood. They want to keep that strong, powerful image, and [if] they say that they're not afraid to be hit on,

it brings their sexuality into question and takes that image away from them. . . .
I think that's a huge issue of why guys are so much more afraid to come out in a
school setting.

Hypermasculine heterosexuality—expressed more often by boys than by
girls—involves homophobic remarks that denigrate gay or effeminate
males. It is used to prove gender conformity and sexual typicality. Hyper-
masculinity is clearly a strategy used by boys (including some closeted
homosexual males) to achieve acceptance into tough, macho circles, an
elevated social status among peers (Van der Meer 2004). Such an observation is surely in keeping with Goffman's (1964) rules of discredit and
stigma in status hierarchies, which denote the assertion of aggressive selfhood when identity is threatened.

In other words, the higher they are, the harder they fall. Those with
the highest social status and privilege among the student body in high
schools along the axes of gender and sexuality—namely straight (or successfully closeted) boys—have the most to lose from being discredited by
their membership in a GSA. They must stay clear of the "gay club" stereotype of the GSA, they feel, given the commonplace belief in guilt by association with "queers." Given these perceptions, it is not surprising to
encounter many GSAs composed entirely of young men who either are
totally socially "out" and/or are overtly feminine in their social behavior
and their straight female friends.

Diana (a GSA Network Central Valley community organizer) provides
an important insight into a reverse mechanism for straight young women's
involvement in GSAs. She has observed the ways in which young heterosexual women's roles as straight allies involve being both nurturing
and divergent. "There are a lot of girls that I think really want to distinguish themselves in doing something that is meaningful and powerful. . . .
They're very, very alternative in the way they present, and they're very
nurturing at the same time. It's almost like they are going to defy and say,
'I'm going to be nurturing and I'm going to be alternative,' and this is a
very meaningful way to do that." Playing a straight ally role means embodying qualities of nurturance, serving to bolster the status of young
women in terms of their feminine gender role in accordance with the normative criteria of the dominant system of gender. Yet, their friendship and
association with queer youths sets them apart from other peers. Obviously, the same does not hold true for heterosexual youths, since nurturing
is not a trait they are socialized into or rewarded for, rather the reverse.
Conversely, this more "female" gender role characteristic is stereotypically
attributed to gay men. What role does social justice play in this process?

Before we can answer this question, it is necessary to address the issue of gender nonconformity in GSAs.

## The Role of Gender Nonconformity

The study of queer youths has long been associated with gender nonconformity or resistance typical of gender roles (Herdt and Boxer 1996; D'Augelli 1991; Herdt 2000). Aside from the configuration of membership in GSAs and the different pressures on youths based on their perceived anatomy, gender presentation, and sexual identity, gender conformity continues to play a large role in GSAs. Gender nonconformity here means performing or doing gender differently. In the biographies of some GSA members, gender conformity plays a key role in understanding the formation of these student groups and their meaning for the members. Social scientists have long known that gender played a huge role in the high school and its socializing role for American youth (Moran 2000). However, today the meaning of being "queer" has social, not simply sexual, meanings, particularly as "bisexuality" has become more common and more "cool" for some youths (Herdt 2000). Social regulation of gender nonconformity is heterosexism, homophobia, and transphobia—variations of gendered roles and sexual behaviors expected of typical sexual prejudice (Herek 2004)—and it involves both individual and collective factors in U.S. society. Homophobia and harassment based on gender nonconformity are central features of the histories told by many young people who become involved in GSAs. These experiences span the spectrum of sexual identities, it is true, yet they seem most punishing for individuals whose sexual and gender divergence draws attention from their peer group.

The policing of gender norms and the experience of this control by the targets of such harassment are dominant themes in the varied developmental paths leading into GSAs. Alternatively, the desire to help nurture or support these gender "rebels" is provoked in part by social justice. It is clear that the impetus for much of the harassment faced by gender nonconforming youths is linked to stereotypes, particularly of the effeminate gay male but also of the masculine lesbian, images that foster hatred and injustice.

Let us consider the stories of three young people, Jake, Melissa, and Cathy, who illustrate the common ground of gender-based harassment across sexual identity lines. Jake, a straight white male youth in the Central Valley who founded the GSA at his school, relates both a personal story and an observation of another person harassed based on *perceived* sexual orientation. Such perceptions are most often drawn not from overt signs of sexuality, but instead are an application of stereotypes linking perceived gender atypicality with LGBTQ orientations. Jake was verbally taunted with accusations that he was a "faggot" by his classmates, despite his self-identified straight sexual identity. He speaks of another student at his school who had suffered, with drastic consequences, from similar harassment based on perceived sexual orientation:

Shortly before I started GSA, in my junior year, there was a student that committed suicide at [my] high school. . . . I witnessed him being harassed at school, and it was nonstop for him. And whether he was gay, transgender, or not, the fact that people perceived him so and picked on him for that really hurt me inside. And I, I just didn't want that to happen anymore. So I started a GSA to give people support.

Jake spoke of his own biography and this more extreme story of a peer's suicide as being interconnected, and driven by social justice, in the sense of how he was motivated to start a GSA. Moreover, the two events are related in another sense: they both imply that gender policing is an overt manifestation of deeply embedded systems of social oppression based on gender and sexuality inequality.

Perhaps an even clearer illustration of this comes from Melissa, a Latina youth, also from the Central Valley, who is trying to start a GSA. She reflects on these interconnections in her own story of harassment:

When I was in sixth grade, this girl, because I was always, like, more a tomboy then, called me "lesbian" for like two days straight and I got tired of it, told my teacher, and he said, "I'm not in charge of this." So I went to the principal. And the girl ended up getting a reprimand. And I realized the power I had. I was, like, "wow," I didn't think anything would actually happen. And then after that, the girl hit me on the head with a frozen water bottle, which didn't feel good, and she was again punished and despite the fact that I'm straight, I, it was just a terrible event to have been, like, persecuted like that. And that's just being a straight person, I mean I can't even begin to understand how . . . transgendered and bisexuals can take that.

We would argue that Melissa *can* imagine how LGBTQ youths feel. This is her sense of social justice. It is this harassment, based on her own gender nonconformity that provides her with an experiential basis for empathy with LGBTQ youths and the desire to correct the injustice. This empathy, in turn, underlies her political commitment to fight against the constraints placed on everyone by an oppressive sex-gender system.

It is notable that straight allies get harassed too. For example, Joanie has spoken of the importance of perceived sexuality. She argues that some straight allies, even before their involvement in a GSA, were "perceived to be gay, and like you know, they get all the crap, and they get called fag . . . so they are eager to say, 'What can we do to stop it?'" Emilie Eagin, the Northern California community organizer for GSA Network, states similarly that some youths who are "perceived to be queer or perceived to be trans . . . get involved." Allies are not always simply supporters of LGBTQ "others" in order to change conditions for those oppressed groups. Allies sometimes experience homophobia directly when others police their heterosexual gender presentation, or when sexual inequality wrongs someone very close to them.

These largely gender-based expectations and instances of harassment are, of course, not limited to straight youths. Cathy, a seventeen-year-old lesbian who self-identifies as butch (masculine in demeanor, clothing, and hairstyle), narrates a series of experiences that motivated her to start a GSA at her own high school: "I was ostracized. . . . I was a victim of hate crimes, physical assault, and one sexual assault, and I had property stolen, I've had property defaced . . . by students . . . and a lot of verbal harassment. I had my tires slashed last year while I was parked at school." The hatred driving these attacks most likely has much to do with Cathy's nonnormative gender presentation as well as her identification as lesbian. According to C. C. Sapp, GSA Network's Southern California community organizer, "In my personal experience, the challenge has been actually going back to gender and making the connection to gender. . . . [W]hen I came out to my friends, they were relatively open about my sexuality, but the one thing they said to me was 'don't cut your hair.' Because it was okay that you were lesbian, but don't change your gender presentation!"

Perhaps peer support is possible to extend, or easier to extend, when the difference between self and friend is greater (straight woman, gay man); perhaps invidious comparisons threaten such support. At any rate, gender and sexuality, as normative systems and structures of inequality, intersect so completely in such accounts that they are inextricable. We have seen that social oppression based on gender norms affects straight and LGBTQ youth. As such it can supply a way to unify GSA members across the spectrum of sexual identity differences.

GSA Network staff members often speak with passion and at length about the social injustice of gender and sexual inequality and the ways in which a more complex understanding of these issues is emerging in social consciousness. They observe that this is one of the driving forces behind both LGBTQ participation and straight ally involvement in the GSA movement.

> We have a gender binary system in our society that is incredibly oppressive to people, to *everyone*. . . . Coming out [as queer] really made me think about gender a lot more and how we get these messages about gender, and how people fit into this binary system in the first place. To me sexual liberation has everything to do with gender liberation. (Interview with Carolyn Laub)

> There's an analysis of homophobia that goes back to gender. . . . People [are] becoming aware of how homophobia can affect the folks who identify as straight or who don't have a queer identity but see that homophobia is tied to these kinds of expectations of masculinity and femininity and that . . . can feed a personal investment to see this force in society "that affects my life too and I don't like it, and I don't want to resign myself to that system." (Interview with Emilie Eagan)

Since this system of sexual inequality affects straight and LGBTQ youths, and because anyone can become politically engaged to alter it, gender and heteronormativity as objects of activism unify youths across the spectrum of sexual identities and divergent sexualities.

There are other ways in which such unity—not identity—is emphasized in the GSA movement. One GSA member defined an *ally* as a person who approaches interactions with the attitude that "your sexual orientation, your gender, has nothing to do with this." Clearly, social justice saturates the political ideologies expressed by many members, either directly or indirectly. GSAs, in this sense, are utopian experiments that provide a context in which gender and sexual orientation *do not* matter because, in the views of its members, they *should not* matter. Certainly, GSA members are critical of how gender nonconformity and/or sexual orientation preclude some people from being full citizens. Another GSA member described how the open and accepted diversity of gender expressions (both normative and non-normative) in the club also acts to unify people: "There's a woman who is more masculine and here's a man who is more feminine next to a woman who is feminine, and a man who is masculine, and they're working together cooperatively toward a common goal. And I think that way it breaks down barriers. It allows you to see that they are all good people."

## Ethnicity and Sexuality in GSAs

The link between gender and sexual inequality is present in the minds of GSA students. But connections to ethnicity, race, and color are less obvious to youths in the Central Valley, who perceived less ethnic diversity in their schools or communities, and thus only little connection between issues of race and issues of sexuality in their GSAs. Central California seems also to have shown more resistance to GSAs than elsewhere in California. Of course it must be remembered that for many Americans, ethnicity and race remain more contested, and less consensual, as sources of social contestations compared to heterosexism, in spite of decades of the civil rights movement in the United States (Cohen 1999; Díaz 1998). However, youths in Northern California, and staff of GSA Network, observed that these two forms of social inequality operate hand in hand. Race and ethnic identity experiences were discussed through examples of nonwhite students feeling unwelcome in GSAs. They spoke about the "whiteness" of GSAs. Nonwhite students generally felt less welcome or plainly did not want to participate in predominantly white GSAs. They have the sense that it is not a place for them, especially when a GSA is within a diverse school environment composed of diverse groupings, including ethnicity. This idea is clearly stated by Cece, a young woman of color and a GSA Network community organizer, in Southern California:

There are, you know, lots of different reasons why people don't get involved [in GSAs], and one of them is racially, like one of the things that we found [in research conducted by GSA Network] . . . is that predominantly GSAs are not reflective of their environment, the school climate. Predominantly GSAs are white, and young queer people of color don't feel as comfortable going to those GSAs for a variety of reasons. One of which is that the idea of queerness is very often linked with something that is white or thought of as a "white thing" and a white issue, and/or GSAs don't allow the space for people to deal with both their race and their sexuality.

Indeed, the connection between queerness, gayness, and whiteness speaks clearly of a deeply embedded form of double prejudice. Andre, a copresident of a GSA in Northern California and a gay African American male, has found a way out of the tensions outlined by CeCe by expanding the diversity in his GSA. He has managed to get a diverse group of people to run the GSA and to attend GSA meetings to break the stereotype that GSAs and the LGBTQ movement in general are only for whites. It has not been easy. Andre expresses his sense of the tentative and emergent quality of his group: "Walking by the meetings and seeing real people . . . they tell me they see me, Andre, standing there like at the top, like, all the kids are listening, and they're like all different types and all different backgrounds and experiences. It's hard, it's cool." Further work is needed to understand the role of whiteness in organizing GSAs. People of color may be marginalized in the process and may not feel empowered to belong. However, these two narratives suggest that the inclusion of people of color immediately changes the perception of diversity: GSA stands for the whole of society.

We sense that the move toward social justice is so powerful that ethnic diversity will become increasingly important to GSAs. Indeed, having a GSA that is not reflective of the ethnic population of a student's school is perceived to be a real problem by white students in GSAs, as well as by nonwhite students interested in them. As Byron, a GSA leader in Northern California, puts it: "Sometimes it does bother me because I'll go and I'll think, 'Wow, you know, we really are reaching out to all groups as much as we should. But then I think there's a huge cultural, just like, it's like a huge cultural no-no to be gay, you know, in the Asian community and the Eastern Indian . . . and so it's . . . hard." Again, the role of ethnicity in sexual inequality here is vital, as the strong, traditional barriers of heteronormativity in some ethnic and religious groups militate against youths of sexually diverse identities being open. Other youths may realize that each ethnic group has its own history and social pressures. Being "out" is not acceptable to them. The factors of status hierarchy are relevant here as well, since nonwhite youths may be in double jeopardy of lowering their social status by being nonwhite and being gay or lesbian as well. That is problematical.

We were struck by how central issues of ethnicity and color appeared to inflect sexual inequality more broadly among Northern California youths, while they were seemingly invisible to those in the Central Valley. Why? No doubt this regional difference is related to these distinct social settings. Although the Central Valley is not devoid of ethnic diversity, by any means, the fact that students perceive the valley to be "white" is an indication of the self-segregation that characterizes the communities and schools in that region. Long ago, the novels of John Steinbeck implicitly reflected this bleak aspect of Central California life. All of the youths from Northern California with whom we spoke, except one, attended schools in the urban or suburban areas adjacent to the San Francisco Bay Area. Their opportunities for exposure to diverse cultural messages is much greater, and their schools are, indeed, more diverse ethnically. Northern Californians pride themselves not only on their diversity but also on their celebration of multiculturalism. These experiences are simply more central to their lives at school and in their communities. Nevertheless, gendered expectations and regulations play a key role in these communities — and, of course, in GSAs. Although not all youths in the Central Valley were from agricultural communities, the Central Valley of California may still be characterized in part by a conservative and agrarian milieu. Likewise, the cities and large urban areas share with Northern California a greater commitment to the mission of neoliberal democracy, especially in their public schools. That social justice menu is reflected in the stories of the GSAs.

## Conclusion

Sexual inequality has emerged as a pivotal part of youth empowerment movements in the United States. In this essay we have examined links between youth empowerment and the social experiment of GSAs in two community high schools in California. The emergence of struggles for social justice and sexual equality in the high school is a long-term structural change, perhaps fueled by the AIDS movement in the 1980s and on, and the emergence of sexuality as a human right in rights-based discourses in the 1990s (Herdt 1997b; Petchesky 2002). GSAs' discourse and social action are focused on gender and sexual inequality related to the struggle for social justice among queer youths and their straight allies.

Of course the spectrum of cultural differences in dealing with sexuality and gender inequality in the United States is vast and complex, and it is only beginning to be studied, as this book has repeatedly shown. Again, the high school is a central battleground for these struggles (Irvine 2002). GSAs are beginning to surmount heterosexism, homophobia, and the ethnic and gender stereotypes in ways that other cultural movements in America have not, at least initially, addressed (cf. Levine, Nardi, and Gagnon 1997). We think that these transformations suggest not only the unfinished nature of the GSA as a kind of social movement in the schools, but the structural barriers that continue to obstruct all forms of social democracy in multicultural society.

Those who have worked in the arena of sexuality education and the schools know only too well of the issues confronting LGBTQ youths and gender nonconforming peers—and although much progress has been made, stigma and violence, especially against transgender youths, are all too common. Gay bashing remains a very real threat in the public schools, and the tragedy of the Columbine High School disaster, whose perpetrators were often bullied and treated as "fags," demonstrates the point. Thus, homophobia, bullying, marginalization, and sexual stigma are critical factors in a series of national incidents, including the Matthew Shepard murder (Herdt and Van der Meer 2003), and these provide a link in helping to reconceptualize the meaning of diversity in the schools. In the twenty-first century, human rights and sexual rights are a new frontier for thinking about diversity and intolerance, and GSAs are a key example of an organization helping to create a new master narrative for thinking about difference.

Sexual orientation and gender nonconformity matter greatly in the social life of the high school today, and GSAs in California have helped to ameliorate the situation. GSAs are spaces that provide a place for same-gender friendships and interest and ways of reflecting on diversity. Having a place to turn to is freeing for these youths. Young people who seek to overcome inequality and injustice in sexuality are also seeking a means of empowering themselves, of becoming more agentic—more the agents of their own desires (Fine 1988)—than ever before. The GSA is thus a historic means to achieve self-discovery and social change by virtue of its central attack on sexual inequality in the schools. Experience suggests that the effect is taking hold in a broader generation of more tolerant young people in the United States.

## Note

The research reported on in this chapter was made possible by a grant from the Gwyn-Follis Foundation. The authors wish to thank GSA Network and Carolyn Laub in particular for their help and support in this project, and for Carolyn's very helpful and incisive feedback on this essay.

## References

Camino, L. 2000. Youth-adult partnerships: Entering new territory in community work and research. *Applied Developmental Science* 4: 11–20.

Cohen, C. 1999. *The boundaries of blackness.* Chicago: University of Chicago Press.

D'Augelli, A. 1991. Lesbians and gay men on campus: Visibility, empowerment, and educational leadership. *Peabody Journal of Education* 66: 124–162.

D'Emilio, J., and E. Freedman. 1988. *Intimate matters.* New York: Harper & Row.

Díaz, R. 1998. *Latino gay men and HIV.* New York: Routledge.

Eberwein, R. 1999. *Sex ed: Film, video and the framework of desire.* New York: Routledge.

Elia, J. 1993/94. Homophobia in the high school: A problem in need of a solution. *High School* 77: 177–185.

Fine, M. 1988. The missing discourse of desire. *Harvard Educational Review* 2: 29–53.

Goffman, E. 1964. *Stigma.* Inglewood Cliffs, N.J.: Prentice-Hall.

Herdt, G., ed. 1989. *Gay and lesbian youth.* New York: Harrington Park.

———. 1997a. "Intergenerational relations and AIDS in the formation of gay culture in the United States." In *In Changing Times: Gay men and lesbians encounter HIV/AIDS,* ed. M. Levine, P. M. Nardi, and J. H. Gagnon. Chicago: University of Chicago Press.

———. 1997b. *Same sex, different cultures.* New York: Westview.

———. 2000. Social change, sexual diversity, and tolerance for bisexuality in the United States. In *Gay, lesbian and bisexual youth: Research and intervention,* ed. A. D'Augelli and C. Patterson. New York: Oxford University Press.

Herdt, G., and A. Boxer. 1993. *Children of horizons.* Boston: Beacon.

———. 1996. Afterword. In paperback edition of *Children of Horizons.* Boston: Beacon.

Herdt, G., and T. Van der Meer. 2003. Introduction. In Homophobia: A special issue, ed. G. Herdt and T. Van der Meer. *Culture, Health and Sexuality* 5: 99–101.

Herek, G. M. 2004. Beyond "homophobia": Thinking about sexual prejudice and stigma in the twenty-first century. *Sexuality Research and Social Policy* 1: 6–24.

Irvine, J. 2002. *Talk about sex.* Berkeley and Los Angeles: University of California Press.

Levine, M., P. M. Nardi, and J. H. Gagnon, eds. 1997. *In changing times: Gay men and lesbians encounter HIV/AIDS.* Chicago: University of Chicago Press.

Mallon, G. P. 1998. *We don't exactly get the welcome wagon.* New York: Columbia University Press.

Mead, M. 1928. *Coming of age in Samoa.* New York: Marrow.

Moran, J. 2000. *Teaching sex: The shaping of adolescence in the 20th century.* Cambridge, Mass.: Harvard University Press.

National Research Council, Institute of Medicine. 2002. *Community programs to youth development.* Washington, D.C.: National Academy Press.

Perrotti, J., and K. Westheimer. 2001. *When the drama club is not enough.* Boston: Beacon.

Petchesky, R. P. 2002. Sexual rights: Inventing a concept, mapping an international practice. In *Framing the sexual subject,* ed. R. Parker, R. Barbosa, and P. Aggleton. Berkeley and Los Angeles: University of California Press.

Pettet, C. 2003. Homophobia and harassment in school-aged populations. *American Sexuality Magazine* 1 (2).

Russell, S. T. 2002. Queer in America: Citizenship for sexual minority youth. *Applied Developmental Science* 6: 258–262.

Sedgwick, E. K. 1991. How to bring your kids up gay: The war on effeminate boys. *Social Context* 2: 19–27.

Szalaha, L. 2001. The sexual diversity climate of Massachusetts' secondary schools and the success of the Safe Schools Program for gay and lesbian students. Ph.D. diss., Harvard University.

Van der Meer, T. 2004. Premodern origins of modern homosexuality and masculinity. *Sexuality Research and Social Policy* 1 (2): 77–90.

Youniss, J., J. A. McLellan, and M. Yates. 1999. Religion, community service, and identity in American youth. *Journal of Adolescence* 22: 243–253.

# Contributors

SONYA GRANT ARREOLA, Ph.D., M.P.H., is a psychologist and epidemiologist in the HIV Research Section of the San Francisco Department of Public Health. She also works with the Center for AIDS Prevention Studies at the University of California, San Francisco, investigating the role of childhood sexual abuse in risky sexual behaviors in adulthood among Latino gay men. She received the Best Research Award from the National Organization against Male Sexual Victimization in 2001.

HÉCTOR CARRILLO, Dr.P.H., is an assistant professor at the Center for AIDS Prevention Studies of the University of California, San Francisco. His book, *The Night Is Young: Sexuality in Mexico in the Time of AIDS* (University of Chicago Press), received the 2002 Ruth Benedict Prize of the American Anthropological Association. His current work focuses on the intersections among migration, sexuality, and health.

CHRISTOPHER CARRINGTON is an assistant professor of sociology and of the Program for Human Sexuality Studies at San Francisco State University. He received his Ph.D. from the University of Massachusetts at Amherst in sociology. An ethnographer and sexuality scholar, he has studied and written extensively on lesbian and gay relationships and gay male sexual culture in the United States. He is the author of the critically acclaimed book *No place like home: Relationships and family life among lesbians and gay men,* a work focused on work-family issues within long-term lesbian and gay relationships, published by the University of Chicago Press.

BRIAN DE VRIES, Ph.D., is a professor of gerontology at San Francisco State University and a Fellow of the Gerontological Society of America. He is associate editor of the *International Journal of Aging and Human Development.* He has edited four books, including *Gay and lesbian aging: Research and future directions,* coedited with G. Herdt (Springer, 2004), and has authored or coauthored sixty journal manuscripts, book chapters, and other reports on narrative concepts in later life including life review, social relationships in later life, and end of life issues including bereavement.

RAFAEL M. DÍAZ is the director of the César E. Chávez Institute and a professor of ethnic studies at San Francisco State University. He is the author of multiple journal articles, book chapters, and monographs, including the book *Latino gay men and HIV: Culture, sexuality, and risk behavior* (Routledge, 1998), a leading guiding framework for the development of HIV prevention interventions with gay men of color, and *Social discrimination and health outcomes: The case of Latino gay men and HIV* (NGLTF, 2001), a policy monograph released by the Policy Institute of the National Gay and Lesbian Task Force.

JESSICA FIELDS, Ph.D. (sociology, University of North Carolina at Chapel Hill), is an assistant professor of sociology at San Francisco State University. In her research, teaching, and activism, Fields focuses on both the liberatory potential of sexuality education and the risks that sexuality education will reinforce racial, gender, and sexual inequalities. Her work has appeared in *Symbolic Interaction* and *Sexuality Research and Social Policy;* another piece is forthcoming in *Social Problems.*

GLORIA GONZÁLEZ-LÓPEZ, Ph.D., is an assistant professor of sociology at the University of Texas at Austin. She has conducted and published sexuality research with Mexican immigrant women and men. She has worked as a psychotherapist, teacher, and sex educator at community-based agencies serving Latino immigrant families in Texas and California.

GILBERT HERDT is professor and director of human sexuality studies and the director of the National Sexuality Resource Center at San Francisco State University. A cultural anthropologist who has pioneered the anthropological study of sexuality among the Sambia of Papua New Guinea and in the United States, Herdt is the author and editor of more than thirty books and one hundred journal articles and chapters. A Fulbright, National Institute of Mental Health, and Guggenheim Fellow, Herdt has taught at Stanford University and the University of Chicago. He is editor of *Sexuality Research and Social Policy: Journal of the NSRC.*

PATRICK HOCTEL received his M.A. in gerontology at San Francisco State University. He has been active on the board of openhouse, a nonprofit association in San Francisco whose goal it is to develop and support housing for older LGBT adults. Patrick Hoctel works for the city of San Francisco, and previously held a position in the Department of Aging and Adult Services.

MICHELLE MARZULLO received her M.A. in human sexuality studies from San Francisco State University. She is currently a graduate student in the Department of Anthropology at American University.

RICHARD PARKER is professor and chair of the Department of Sociomedical Sciences and director of the Center for Gender, Sexuality and Health in the Mailman School of Public Health at Columbia University in New York City. He is the author or editor of a wide range of publications, including *Beneath the equa-*

*tor: Cultures of desire, male homosexuality and emerging gay communities in Brazil* (Routledge, 1999). He is also the editor-in-chief of the journal *Global Public Health.*

STEPHEN T. RUSSELL is an associate professor in the John and Doris Norton School of Family and Consumer Sciences, University of Arizona. His Ph.D. is in sociology from Duke University (1994). He has been a William T. Grand Foundation Scholar (2001–2006) and a Distinguished Visiting Professor of Human Sexuality Studies at San Francisco State University. His research focuses on adolescent ethnicity, sexual behavior, and sexual identities.

RUSSELL P. SHUTTLEWORTH is a visiting scholar at the Institute of Urban and Regional Planning, University of California, Berkeley. His recent published work on disability, gender, and sexuality includes "Sexual access," in the *Encyclopedia of disability* (2005), "Disabled masculinity: Expanding the masculine repertoire," in the edited volume *Gendering disability* (2004), and "Defusing the adverse context of disability and desirability as a practice of the self for men with cerebral palsy," in the volume *Disability/Postmodernity: Embodying disability theory* (2002). Dr. Shuttleworth teaches an innovative course, Critical Perspectives in Disability and Sexuality, at San Francisco State University. In the academic year 2002–2003, he was a prestigious Ed Robert's Fellow in Disability Studies at the University of California, Berkeley.

CHUNGHEE SARAH SOH is an associate professor of anthropology at San Francisco State University and the author of *The Chosen Women in Korean Politics: An Anthropological Study* (Praeger, 1991) and *Women in Korean Politics* (Westview, 1993). Her current research, which won a grant from the John D. and Catherine T. MacArthur Foundation, is concerned with the "comfort women" issue. Her most recent publication on the subject is "Aspiring to craft modern gendered selves: 'Comfort women' and chŏngsindae in late colonial Korea," *Critical Asian Studies* 36 (2) (2004): 175–198.

JEFFREY SWEAT is a sociologist who completed his doctoral thesis (University of California, Davis) on identity and activism within gay-straight alliances. He is currently a postdoctoral fellow in the AIDS Research Training Program at UCLA, where he is working on a study of the organizational factors that facilitate or hinder the early detection of HIV and an intervention study for homeless drug-abusing youths. His primary interests are identity, social interaction, sexualities, HIV/AIDS, and gender. His work focuses on the broad themes of social justice issues for youth and the social construction of self.

NIELS TEUNIS is an assistant professor in human sexuality studies and a research associate at the Center for Research on Gender and Sexuality at San Francisco State University. He conducts research on racism in the gay male community. In the context of his research, he produces plays that support the fight against racism. His work has appeared in *AIDS Education and Prevention,* the *Journal of Gay, Lesbian, and Bisexual Identities,* and *AIDS and Behavior.*

# Index

abortion, Mexican immigrant women's view of, 164, 171n3

abstinence-only policy: sexuality education conforming to, 66–67, 68, 78–79; of U.S. government, 5, 8–9

academy: American sexual inequality reproduced by, 10–12; change in views of, of sexuality, 14–15; social movements' influence on, 12, 13–14; social policy as concern of, 18–21

access. *See* sexual access

Adam, B., 12

Adams, R., 218

Adolescents, expanded view of sexuality of, 233–34. *See also* gay-straight alliances (GSAs); sexuality education

African American family, Moynihan report on, 11

age, of participatory ethnographer, 72

agency. *See* sexual agency

Aggleton, P., 3, 6, 12, 15

AIDS. *See* HIV/AIDS

AIDS Conference, Fourteenth International (Barcelona), 50–51

AIDS crisis: sexuality research spurred by, 15; slow response of academics to, 4; as social movement, 13–14

Altman, D., 12, 110

American Psychiatric Association, homosexuality declassified by, 12, 14

American Psychological Association, 14

Arreola, Sonya Grant, 23

Ayala, G., 59

Barbosa, R. M., 6, 12, 15

Beeler, J. A., 215, 216

blaming the victim, in antigay violence incidents, 8

Blieszner, R., 218

Bourdieu, P., 190

Boys, attitudes and behaviors of, in sexuality education class, 75–77, 79. *See also* childhood sexual abuse; gay-straight alliances (GSAs)

Browning, Frank, 134

Cairo conference (1994), 5, 12

Calderone, Mary, 4

Calderone, Victor, 124

California: Circuit events in, 123–24, 129–30, 132; GSAs in, 238–40, 241–42, 247–49; study of Latino gay men's sexuality in, 40–48

Call to Action to Promote Sexual Health and Responsible Sexual Behavior, Surgeon General's, 5, 8–9

Canguilhelm, G., 186

Carrillo, Héctor, 18, 23

Carrington, Christopher, 23

"Carta al Papa," 152–53, 154, 157, 158, 159, 166, 171n2

Castoriadis, Cornelius, 186, 198n15

Catholic Church: impact on sexuality of Mexican women, 148–49, 151, 152–53, 166–70; obedience to beliefs of, 166; patriarchal and morality contradictions of, 153–59; polarized division between sexuality and, 159–61; sexual agency and, 161–66, 168, 171n3

Centers for Disease Control (CDC), 15, 50–51

childhood sexual abuse: defined, 38–39; Latino gay men's accounts of, 44–46; risk for HIV infection and, 37–38; risky sexual situations and, 39–40, 46, 47; voluntary sexual initiation vs., 43–44

chlamydia, among surviving Korean comfort women, 91–92

Chodorow, Nancy J., 152, 168

Cho Yun-ok, 90

the Circuit, 123–45; description of party of, 123–24; as form of cultural self-assertion and rebellion, 129–30, 143–44; fundraising at events of, 129; gays' views of, 133–36, 145; heterosexuals witnessing, 129–30, 145; HIV/AIDS and, 124, 137, 140–43; as homoempathic environment, 138–39; homoeroticism of, 144–45; methodology for ethnographically researching, 130–33; negative appraisals of, 125, 130, 135–37; participants in, 128–29; prevalence of events of, 125, 135; rave scene compared to, 127–28, 129; reasons for considering perspective of participants in, 125–26; social science literature on, 137–38; as subculture, 126–27

comfort women, 86–103; class-action lawsuit by surviving, 89–90; defined, 86; factors determining impact of sexual enslavement on, 87, 99; han complex of, 86–87, 101n1; han narratives of, 86, 87, 94–97; impoverished background of, 90, 99, 102n6; instances of, throughout history, 102nn3–5; Japanese military's system of, 86, 88–89; marriage and childbirth among surviving, 87, 90–92, 97–99, 102n2, 102n14; recruitment of, 99, 103n17; relationship between infertility and enslavement period of, 97–99, 100

community-based organizations (CBOs), 13–14

conservative Christians, abstinence-only sex ed advocated by, 78–79

constructionist approach, critical, 174, 195n1

Crehan, K., 21–22

*El crimen del padre Amaro* (*The Crime of Father Amaro*), 158

culture: challenging, of sexuality inequality, 21–25; subaltern, 21–22. *See also* sexual culture; subculture

D'Augelli, A. R., 215

Davies, Dominic, 196n2

DeMille, Agnes, 123

Devereux, G., 13

de Vries, B., 218

Díaz, Rafael M., 6, 16, 23, 59

disabilities, gay men with, 174–200; gay/lesbian community's discrimination against, 196n5; hegemonic masculine expectations as problem for, 180, 189–92, 198n16; including, in sexual rights movement, 178, 192–94, 199nn18–19; lack of research on sexuality of, 181, 198n10; normative functioning as problem for, 185–88, 198n15; sexual access for, 176, 177, 178–80, 194, 196n6, 197nn7, 8, 199n20

disability and sexuality: critical constructionist approach to, 174, 195n1; evolution of research on, 175–78, 195n2, 196nn3, 5; participatory ethnographic approach to studying, 181–84, 198nn9, 11

disabling society, 175–76

Dorfman, R., 215

Dorrell, B., 216

Duggin, L., 9

Eagan, Emilie, 245, 246

ecstasy (MDMA), 124, 133, 142, 143

empowerment: HIV prevention work emphasizing, 112–13; youth, GSAs as element of, 235, 237–40, 249–50

Erikson, E. H., 96

ethnicity: fetishization based on, 42, 46; in GSAs, 246–49

family: friends as, for older gay men and lesbians, 216–17, 229; hiding HIV serostatus from, 60–61; study of, of older gay men and lesbians, 217–21, 230n2; study of African American, 11

Farmer, Paul, 3, 6, 16

Fausto-Sterling, A., 194

feminism: as ahead of academy, 12; critical, of participatory ethnographer, 72; and information given in sexuality education classes, 66, 81; methodologies of, as advocating change, 21

Fields, Jessica, 8

Fortenberry, J. D., 52

Foucault, Michel, 14, 176, 185

Fourth World Women's Conference (Beijing, 1995), 12

Frank, Thomas, 9

Freire, Paulo, 1, 17–18, 22

friends: hiding HIV serostatus from, 60–61; made at Circuit events, 145

friends of older gay men and lesbians: as "chosen families," 216–17, 229; concluding thoughts on, 228–30; definitions of, 221–26; importance of, 226–28, 229, 230n3; study of, 217–21, 230n2

functioning, normative, as problem for people with disabilities, 185–88, 186n15

Gagnon, John, 10

gamma hydroxybutyrate (GHB), 127, 132, 133

Gay, Lesbian, and Straight Education Network (GLSEN), 235, 236

gay/bisexual men: study of HIV/AIDS stigmatization among, 52–53; unaware of their HIV serostatus, 36, 50–51; violence against, 2, 7–8, 236, 249. See also disabilities, gay men with; Latino gay men; older gay men and lesbians

gay/lesbian community, discrimination against people with disabilities by, 196n5

gay/lesbian studies, 14–15

gay liberation movement, 12

Gay Men's Health Crisis (New York), 14

gay-straight alliances (GSAs), 233–50; characteristics of students involved in, 240–42; community-based ethnographic study of, 236–40; as element of youth empowerment, 235, 237–40, 249–50; ethnicity in, 246–49; gender nonconformity by members of, 243–46; origin and growth of, 234–37

Geertz, C., 12, 21

gender: attitudes and behaviors toward sexual knowledge as varying by, 75–77; of participatory ethnographer, 72; research on sexual identities and, 176, 196n4

gender equality, HIV prevention work and, 109, 113–14

gender nonconformity, by GSA members, 243–46

Gerschick, T. J., 191

GHB (gamma hydroxybutyrate), 127, 132, 133

Giddens, A., 185

Gill, Carol, 196n2

Gillespie-Sells, Kath, 196n2

girls: attitudes and behaviors of, in sexuality education class, 75–77; meaning of sexual knowledge for, 82–83; parents' concerns about, in sexuality education classes, 78–81. See also gay-straight alliances (GSAs)

Goffman, E., 242

González-López, Gloria, 6, 24

Gramsci, Antonio, 21

Grossman, A. H., 215

GSA Network, 239

GSAs. See gay-straight alliances (GSAs)

Hahn, Harlan, 196n2

Hall, G. Stanley, 235

Halperin, David, 8, 14

han: causes of, for surviving Korean comfort women, 94, 100; defined (translated), 86–87, 93, 101n11; Korean conceptualization of, 92–94, 100–101, 103n18

han narratives: data for study of comfort women supplied by, 86, 87; examples of, 94–97; variation in, 94

Harmony Project, 132

Hebdige, D., 126–27

Henderson, Russell, 8

Henson, Maria Rosa, 97

Herdt, Gilbert, 7, 13, 177, 182

Herek, G. M., 3, 52, 62

Hershberger, S. L., 215

heteronormativity: activism against, by GSAs, 246, 248; assumption of, and men with disabilities, 184, 191; the Circuit as escape from, 130; theoretical construct of, 14, 22 high schools, as battleground for sexual inequality, 8–9. *See also* gay-straight alliances (GSAs); sexuality education

*The History of Sexuality* (Foucault), 14

HIV/AIDS: the Circuit and, 124, 137, 140–43; ecstasy (MDMA) and, 133; risk of, among Latino gay men in U.S., 36–37, 46; risk of, childhood sexual abuse and, 37–38; structural violence and, 6

HIV/AIDS stigmatization, 50–64; among Latino gay/bisexual men, 56–58, 60–64; decrease in, 51–52; defined, 54, 62; as deterrent to finding out HIV serostatus, 51; as internalized oppression, 54–55, 64; lack of research on, among gay/bisexual men, 52–53. *See also* Nuestras Voces (Our Voices) study

HIV optimism, 51, 64

HIV prevention work, 109–20; addressing sexual/gender inequality in, 113–14; common strategies in progressive, 109; empowerment emphasized in, 112–13; ethnographic study of sexuality and, in Guadalajara, Mexico, 109–10, 114–19; history of, in Mexico, 110–13, 120n6; information dissemination emphasized in, 111, 120n2; skills taught in, 112, 120nn3, 6

HIV serostatus: hidden from family and friends, 60–61; HIV/AIDS stigmatization as deterrent for finding out, 51, 52; lack of awareness of, 36, 50–51; revealing, to potential lover, 57

HIV testing, avoidance of, 36, 52

homophobia: as barrier to involvement in GSAs, 241, 243, 245; in disability community, 196n5; as form of oppression of Latino gay men, 53, 54, 55, 61, 64; GSAs as effort to counter, 234–35, 237, 246, 249; as real-world process of inequality, 2; science challenging, 4; as structural violence, 2, 3

homosexuality: acceptance of, by family of choice, 221; AIDS as spurring study of, 15; American Psychiatric Association's declassification of, 12, 14; public opinion on, 15–16, 236; as sinful and illegal, 71–72

human rights, sexuality as, 4–5, 12. *See also* sexual rights movement

International Conference on Population and Development (Cairo, 1994), 5, 12

Irvine, Janice, 9, 15

Jackson, S., 198n16

Japan, comfort system of military of, 86, 88–89

Jennings, Kevin, 236

Johnson, C. L., 216

Kang Yong-kwŏn, 90

Kim Dae Jung, 100

Kim Hak-sun, 89, 93, 94–96, 97, 100

Kim Kayoko, 98

Kim Kwi-ok, 102n5

Kim Sun-dŏk, 98, 102n15

Kim Yŏl-kyu, 93

Kinsey, Alfred, 4, 16

Kochman, A., 217

Korea, military comfort system of, 88, 102n5. *See also* comfort women

Krieger, N., 3, 11

Lancaster, R. N., 10

Latino gay men, 35–48; childhood sexual abuse of, 37–38, 39–40, 46; intention-behavior incongruence in sexual activities of, 53–54; researcher's experience working with, 35–36; risk of HIV among, in U.S., 36–37, 46. *See also* Latino gay men's sexuality study; Nuestras Voces (Our Voices) study

Latino gay men's sexuality study, 40–48; childhood sexual abuse described in, 44–46; conclusions from, 46–47; methodology for, 40–41; need for actions revealed by, 48; need for further research beyond, 47–48; sexual initiation discussed in, 43–44; sexual silence revealed by, 41–43

Laub, Carolyn, 238–39, 240, 246

Laumann, E. O., 15

*Lawrence v. Texas,* 6

Lee, Jae Hoon, 93

lesbians: participatory ethnographer's silence about, 71–72; triple stigmatization of, 215. *See also* older gay men and lesbians

Lewis, L., 137

*Life Outside* (Signorile), 135

*Love Undetectable* (Sullivan), 135

MacKinnon, Catharine, 8
Magnitude Party (San Francisco), 129
Malluwa, M., 3
Manasse, G., 216
Marsh, Julian, 139
Martin, C. E., 16
Masculinity, hegemonic expectations of, 180, 189–92, 198n16. *See also* heteronormativity
Massachusetts, GSAs in, 235–36
Mattison, A., 127
McKinney, Aaron, 8
MDMA (ecstasy), 124, 133, 142, 143
Mexican immigrant women, 148–71; bifurcation of consciousness of, 169–70; "Carta al Papa" and, 152–53, 154, 157, 158, 159, 164, 166, 171n2; Catholic Church's impact on sexuality of, 148–49, 151, 152–53, 166–70; multiple heterosexualities of, 167, 171n4; obedience to Catholic Church, 166; opinions about contradictions of Catholic Church, 153–59; separation between sexuality and religion adopted by, 159–61; sexual agency of, and religion, 161–66, 168, 171n3; sociological study of sexuality of, 148–51, 170n1; stereotypes and misconceptions about, 151–52
Mexico: ethnographic study of HIV prevention work and sexuality in, 109–10, 114–19; history of HIV prevention work in, 110–13, 120n6
Miller, A. S., 191
Mills, C. Wright, 126
Morning Party (Fire Island, NY), 128, 135, 139
Moynihan Report, 11
Mun P'il-gi, 92

Nardi, P.M., 215
New Right, 9
norms: of functioning, and people with disabilities, 185–88, 186n15; need to target, regarding homosexuality among Latinos, 48. *See also* heteronormativity
North Carolina: study of sexuality education in, 67–83; Teach Abstinence until Marriage (TAUM) legislation in, 66, 68
"Notes on the Cock Fight" (Geertz), 12

Nuestras Voces (Our Voices) study, 55–64; findings from focus group of, 55–58; findings from quantitative survey of, 58–62; HIV/AIDS stigmatization revealed by, 62–63; hypotheses on rates of HIV/AIDS stigmatization revealed by, 63–64

O'Hanley, Peter, 91
older gay men and lesbians, 213–30; academic interest in, 213–14; "chosen families" of, 216–17, 229; friends as defined by, 221–26; gerontology literature on friends and, 214–15; importance of friendships to, 226–28, 229, 230n3; study of friends of, 217–21, 230n2; thoughts on friendships of, 228–30
oppression. *See* social oppression

Pak Ok-nyŏn, 91, 99, 100, 103n16
Parker, R., 3, 6, 12, 15, 20, 177, 193
Parker, S., 218
*Pedagogy of the Oppressed* (Freire), 1
Perrotti, J., 235
persons with AIDS (PWAs), fear of, 52
Petchesky, R., 3, 12
Pew Trust, 9
Pines Party (Fire Island, NY), 129, 135
Pomeroy, B., 16
positionality: defined, 12–13, 25n2; of ethnographer studying surviving comfort women, 88; of ethnographer studying the Circuit, 130–33; as influence on analysis of sexual inequality, 7, 16–18, 22; lack of change in, 16; of participatory ethnographer studying sexuality education, 70–73
postmodernism, sexuality as viewed by, 14, 15
poverty: as background of Korean comfort women, 90, 99, 102n6; as oppression experienced by Latino gay men, 53, 54; studies of culture of, in Mexico, 11
prostitution, military-operated systems of, 88–89, 102nn3–5. *See also* comfort women
public opinion: change in, on sexuality, 9–10, 15–16; on comprehensive sexuality education, 9; on homosexuality, 15–16, 236

Quam, J. K., 215
queer theory, sexual inequality untouched
    by, 14, 15, 18

race: as category for study of human varia-
    tion, 11; of participatory ethnogra-
    pher, 72
racism: as form of oppression of Latino
    gay men, 53, 54; as form of structural
    violence, 2, 3
rave scene, the Circuit compared to, 127–
    28, 129
Rayas, Lucía, 171n4
recreational drugs: at Circuit events, 127,
    135; ecstasy (MDMA), 124, 133, 142,
    143; gamma hydroxybutyrate (GHB),
    127, 132, 133; made illegal, 133
*religiosidad popular,* 168, 171n5
research methodologies, 23. *See also specific
    studies*
Rich, Adrienne, 13
Rio de Janeiro conference (2000) on
    sexuality and social change, 20
Rodríguez, Jeanette, 168, 171n5
Ross, M., 137
Rotello, Gabriel, 135
Ruff-O'Herne, Jan, 97, 98, 102n14

Safe Schools Project (Massachusetts),
    236
safe sex: at Circuit events, 142, 144; infor-
    mation about, given in HIV preven-
    tion work, 110, 111; sexual liberaliza-
    tion as promoting, 109, 112, 120;
    sexual silence as barrier to, 41–42
Sapp, C. C., 245
Satcher, David, 8
Schwandt, T., 195n1
science, American sexual inequality repro-
    duced by, 10–12
Scott, Robert, 50
Segal, Lynne, 152, 167
self-efficacy, 120n3
sex education. *See* sexuality education
Sex Information and Education Council
    of the United States (SIECUS), 4, 9
sexism: challenging, in sexuality education
    classroom, 79, 82; as form of struc-
    tural violence, 3
sexual abuse. *See* childhood sexual abuse
sexual access, for people with disabilities,

176, 177, 178–80, 194, 196n6, 197nn7,
    8, 199n20
sexual agency: as mechanism of sexual
    inequality, 6; of Mexican immigrant
    women, religion and, 161–66, 168,
    171n3; of people with disabilities, 188,
    189; struggle for, 23–24
sexual conservatives, structural sexual
    violence promoted by, 9, 15
sexual culture: origin of concept of,
    16; and sexual behavior and HIV
    prevention in Mexico, 110, 114–19;
    surrender of self to, 22; U.S., 7
*Sexual Ecology* (Rotello), 135
sexual education. *See* sexuality education
sexual enslavement. *See* comfort women
sexual equality, HIV prevention work and,
    109, 113–14
sexual harassment, of girls in sexuality
    education classes, 79
sexual health, WHO's definition of, 9–10
sexual identities, research on gender and,
    176, 196n4
sexual inequality: challenging culture of,
    21–25; defined, 1, 3; effects of, in U.S.
    vs. other countries, 5–6; factors repro-
    ducing, 10–16; history of addressing,
    4–5; overview of, in U.S., 7–10; para-
    digm shift in analysis of, 1–2, 177–78;
    positionality as influencing analysis
    of, 7, 25n2; sexual prejudice as
    approach to, 3; social movements'
    influence on academy's thinking
    about, 12, 13–14
sexual initiation, Latino gay man's account
    of, 43–44. *See also* childhood sexual
    abuse
sexual innatism, sexual inequality repro-
    duced by, 10–11
sexuality: adolescents' expanded view of,
    233–34; avoidance of scientific study
    of, 11–12; change in academy's view
    of, 14–15; change in public attitudes
    toward, 9–10, 15–16; as human right,
    4–5, 12; including social inequality in
    studies of, 177–78; linked to positive
    sexual health, 9–10. *See also* disability
    and sexuality
sexuality education: controversy over,
    8–9; defined, 9; emphasizing dangers
    and risks of sexuality, 66–67, 68;

information on female sexual pleasure in, 66, 67; public opinion on, 9; suggested reform of, 82

sexuality education (North Carolina), 66–83; attitudes and behaviors of students in, 75–77; debate over sexual knowledge imparted in, 77–82; methodology for researching, 70–73; setting for research on, 68–70; sexual knowledge taught in, 73–75; Teach Abstinence until Marriage (TAUM) legislation on, 66, 68

sexuality research: scientist in, as agent of change, 21–25; spurred by AIDS crisis, 15

sexual knowledge: attitudes and behaviors of students being taught, 67, 75–77; debate on, presented in sexuality education, 77–82; for girls in sexuality education classes, 82–83; taught in middle-school sexuality education class, 73–75

sexual liberalization, safe sex promoted by, 109, 112, 119

sexually transmitted diseases (STDs), 66, 83n1, 91–92, 102n7

sexually transmitted infections (STIs), 66, 83n1

sexual pleasure: American society's attitude toward, 10; information on female, in sexuality education, 66, 67, 81; sexual expectations and desires and, in Mexico, 114–19; traumatic childhood sexual encounters as confusing, 46

Sexual Politics of Disability (Shakespeare, Gillespie-Sells, and Davies), 196n2

sexual prejudice, defined, 3

sexual rights movement, including people with disabilities in, 178, 192–94, 199nn18–19

sexual risk behavior: by young gay/bisexual men, 51; childhood sexual abuse and, 39–40, 46, 47; intention-behavior incongruence in, 53–54

sexual roles, HIV prevention work in Mexico and, 115–19

sexual violence: Matthew Shepard case of, 2, 7–8, 236, 249; as violation of human rights, 4

Shakespeare, Tom, 196n2

Shepard, Matthew, 2, 7–8, 236, 249

Shildrick, Margrit, 199n7

Shuttleworth, Russell, 23, 70–71

SIECUS (Sex Information and Education Council of the United States), 4, 9

Signorile, Michael, 135, 136

silence: about sexuality among Mexican immigrant women, 150; about sexuality in Mexico, 110, 112; anthropological, about ethnographers' sexual experiences in field, 184, 198n13; interventions targeting, about childhood sexual abuse, 48; sexual, among Latino gay men, 41–43, 45, 46

Smith, Barbara, 82

Smith, Dorothy, 152, 168, 169

social movements, and academic view of sexual inequality, 12, 13–14

social oppression: experienced by Latino gay men, 53–54, 55, 61; HIV stigmatization as internalized, 54–55, 64; new paradigm of sexuality-based, 1–2; structural violence as causing, 2–3

social policy, as concern of academy, 18–21

social science: as mechanism of social change, 21–25; positionality of scholars in, working in sexuality, 16; sexual inequality reproduced by, 10–12

Social Science Research Council Program in Sexuality Research Fellowships, 20–21

sodomy laws, 6, 25n1

Soh, C. S., 100

spectacular subculture, the Circuit as, 126–27

Stoller, R. J., 13

Stonewall Community Foundation, 129

structural violence: forms of, 3; HIV/AIDS as linked to, 6; positionality as tool in studying, 16, 18; social oppression caused by, 2–3. See also sexual inequality

subculture, the Circuit as, 126–27

subjectivity, of research subject vs. researcher, 22, 23

Sullivan, Andrew, 135, 136

Surgeon General's Call to Action to Promote Sexual Health and Responsible Sexual Behavior, 5, 8–9

Surgeon General's Report on Comprehensive Sexuality Education, 10
survival sex, 3
Swallow, J., 216
symbolic interactionism, 73
Szalaha, L., 235

Tanaka, Yuki, 88
Teach Abstinence until Marriage (TAUM) legislation, 66, 68
Teunis, Niels, 7
*Texas, Lawrence v.*, 6
Thornton, Sarah, 127
Travis, C. B., 151
*True stories of the Korean comfort women* (Howard), 90

United Nations Educational, Scientific, and Cultural Organization (UNESCO), 11
United States: change in public attitudes toward sexuality in, 15–16; reproduction of sexual inequality in, 10–16; risk of HIV among Latino gay men in, 36–37; sexual inequality in, 5–6, 7–10
unsafe sex: at Circuit events, 125, 136, 137; Latino gay men in U.S. engaging in, 37
U.S. government, abstinence-only policy of, 5, 8–9

Vaid, Urvashi, 19
Valdiserri, R. O., 51–52

Vienna conference (1993), 4
Violence, antigay, 2, 7–8, 236, 249. *See also* structural violence

Warner, Michael, 8
Waxman, Barbara, 196n2
Weeks, Jeffrey, 175
Weinstock, J. S., 217, 219, 221, 229
Welfare Reform Act, 9
Westheimer, K., 235
Weston, K., 217, 221
*When the drama club is not enough* (Perrotti and Westheimer), 236
White, J. W., 151
White Party (Palm Springs), 123–24, 129–30, 140–41
Whitford, G. S., 215
women. *See* girls; lesbians; Mexican immigrant women
women's health movement, influence on academy, 13
World Conference on Human Rights (Vienna, 1993), 4
World Health Organization (WHO), 9–10, 15
Wright, P. J., 214

Yi Kwang-ja, 98–99
Yi Ok-sŏn, 91, 92
Yi Sun-ok, 86
youth empowerment, GSAs as element of, 235, 237–40, 249–50
Yun Tu-ri, 96–97

| | |
|---:|:---|
| Text: | 10/13 Galliard |
| Display: | Galliard |
| Compositor: | Integrated Composition Systems |
| Indexer: | Jean Mann |
| Printer and binder: | Sheridan Books, Inc. |